Trans-global readings

MANCHESTER
UNIVERSITY PRESS

theory•practice
•performance•

The series offers a space for those people who practise theatre to have a dialogue with those who think and write about it.

The series has a flexible format that refocuses the analysis and documentation of performance. It provides, presents and represents material which is written by those who make or create performance history, and offers access to theatre documents, different methodologies and approaches to the art of making theatre.

The books in the series are aimed at students, scholars, practitioners, and theatre-visiting readers. They encourage reassessments of periods, companies, and figures in twentieth-century and twenty-first-century theatre history, and provoke and take up discussions of cultural strategies and legacies that recognise the heterogeneity of performance studies.

The series editors, with the advisory board, aim to publish innovative challenging and exploratory texts from practitioners, theorists and critics.

also available

The Paris Jigsaw: Internationalism and the city's stages
David Bradby and Maria M. Delgado (eds)

Theatre in crisis? Performance manifestos for a new century
Maria M. Delgado and Caridad Svich (eds)

'Love me or kill me': Sarah Kane and the theatre of extremes
Graham Saunders

Negotiating cultures: Eugenio Barba and the intercultural debate
Ian Watson (ed.)

Trans-global readings

Crossing theatrical boundaries

edited by **CARIDAD SVICH**

Manchester University Press
Manchester and New York

distributed exclusively in the USA by Palgrave

Published by Manchester University Press
Oxford Road, Manchester M13 9NR, UK
and Room 400, 175 Fifth Avenue, New York, NY 10010, USA
www.manchesteruniversitypress.co.uk

Distributed exclusively in the USA by
Palgrave, 175 Fifth Avenue, New York, NY 10010, USA

Distributed exclusively in Canada by
UBC Press, University of British Columbia, 2029 West Mall, Vancouver, BC, Canada V6T 1Z2

British Library Cataloguing-in-Publication Data
A catalogue record for this book is available from the British Library

Library of Congress Cataloging-in-Publication Data applied for

ISBN 0 7190 6324 8 *hardback*
　　0 7190 6325 6 *paperback*

First published in 2003
11 10 09 08 07 06 05 04 03　　10 9 8 7 6 5 4 3 2 1

Typeset in Minion and Futura by
Northern Phototypesetting Co. Ltd, Bolton
Printed in Great Britain by
Bell & Bain Ltd, Glasgow

Dedicated to my parents for giving me the courage
to cross . . . with love

CONTENTS

IV Crossing bodies

LIST OF ILLUSTRATIONS

ACKNOWLEDGEMENTS

This book would not be possible without the artists who contributed of their time in speaking to my colleagues and myself. Ohio State University Department of Theatre, New Dramatists in New York, and Harvard University's Radcliffe Institute for Advanced Study provided practical support during editing. Thanks are due to Lesley Ferris, Chair of OSU Department of Theatre, Todd London, Artistic Director at New Dramatists, Jim O'Quinn at TCG, Greg Bossler at The Dramatists' Guild, Daniel Mufson, Thom Heyer, and Jennifer Flores Sternad, my research assistant at Harvard University. The interviewers are credited at the end of the volume, but their spirit of collaboration must be acknowledged. Likewise to the photographers who provided their photos. With gratitude to Frederic Amat, Anne Bogart and Shawn Sides. Special thanks to Todd Cerveris and Sarah Wright, who were instrumental in making this quixotic venture a reality, and to Peter Lichtenfels and Maria Delgado who kept me on track. As always, my work would not be possible without the love and support of Emilio and Aracely Svich.

The dynamics of fractals: legacies for a new tomorrow
Caridad Svich

One of the inheritances we have been granted by the fecund creative experience of the last century has been without a doubt the possibility of artists to work in different mediums, especially in the visual arts. That is how I understand my own work: as an archipelago of different kinds of expression, between which I travel, trying to make sense of one to the other. It would not be at all absurd to say that I paint films and film paintings. My experience as an artist is like that of a kaleidoscope that configures one image and then another, some unforeseen and unexpected. The same eye and sensibility create these multiple images.[1]

Split the seam on a new century. The preoccupations of artists remain rooted in how to represent nature, humanity, time, memory and space, how to live in the world, and keep up with its pace, and how to simply be. The globalised marketplace unites cultures, and fragments them economically and artistically. Technology offers possibility and access, yet what to make of it over time? The past and future are eternally bound in the ever-changing present. An artist who crosses boundaries prescribed by society, culture, or the very form of the art they make is poised always on the brink. One discipline merges with another, as the visual arts, music, dance, theatre and opera create new forms out of the old, and old forms out of the new.

The artists in this volume work across a wide spectrum. They seek out the edges of language and media, myth and reality. They cross cultures and the limits of space. They are the media generation and its post-media

---

1 From unpublished e-mail interview conducted September 2001 by Caridad Svich with Frederic Amat, visual artist/filmmaker based in Barcelona, Spain.

children addicted to motion, travel and the pleasures and spiritual rewards that the nomadic spirit offers. Unbound by formal restriction and sometimes working under threat of censorship, the practitioners in this volume are ardent warriors of civilisation, and passionate artisans exalted by the necessity of creative expression. Constantly wrestling with what it is that makes them do what they do, and how what they do can impact their immediate community and society as a whole, they express the conflicts and passions that are an essential part of being an artist in the twenty-first century: an artist faced with the greatest media influx, largest decentralised virtual audience base, and politically fractioned global terrain in quite some time.

The fact that the global village and the globalisation of knowledge has changed the way artists identify their 'village' comes up again and again between these pages. For some artists, especially those working in music theatre or new music forms, the globalisation of knowledge, which has progressed throughout the twentieth century and is now seen as simply a by-product of electronic culture, has allowed them to weave and mix indigenous sounds with non-indigenous ones, and has made cross-cultural collaboration and exchange more possible through new technologies. The community for them is continually expanding and their audience could live anywhere. For other artists, the importance of staying connected to a regional sensibility, to an absolutely specific physical community of citizens with whom they can speak to directly has affected their use of technology, and the web of information which circles twenty-first-century lives. In the end, the common ground here, despite many differences, is a belief in making work, and the vitality of such making for the artist as citizen.

Crossing media

I'm a product of my culture, so I think by making the kinds of plays that I would want to go to we are speaking to that culture. I don't think we can transcend it. I don't know how that would be possible. But we can ignore the traditions that have become obsolete (or transform them) and exploit the ones that still resonate.[2]

This book began in the summer of 2000 while I was about to go into rehearsal for a workshop of my play *Iphigenia Crash Land Falls on the Neon Shell That Was Once her Heart (a rave fable)* with Actors Touring

---

2 From unpublished e-mail interview conducted September 2001 by Caridad Svich with Shawn Sides, artistic director of Rude Mechanicals theatre company based in Austin, Texas.

Company of London at the Euripides Festival in Monodendri, Greece. Director Nick Philippou, who is interviewed here, and I spent a great deal of time discussing the nature of the mediated self in a media-saturated culture, and how to engage with the past, with ancient forms and traditions, and to learn from and rediscover new ways of seeing. The body in time was one of the first topics of our discussions: how does a body respond to time, to its culturally inherited memory, and how does it see itself in the cultural mirror, past and present?

Time is both finite and elastic. It stretches over centuries and counts the seconds in which we live day to day. Theatre is about time: the essential nature of time passing. Like other forms of live performance, it demands the audience's attention, and the stories are constructed with the knowledge of time as their measure. Meter, tempo, rhythm and silence are all elements of theatrical constructions of text and space.

The performing body is bound by the time it takes to execute and complete a motion or a gesture. Within this time that is shared between performer and spectator there exists also the notion of suspended time, which is connected to memory and how we imagine or remember events, feelings and sensations even while we are engaged in a concrete activity, be it passive or active. When an artist crosses media in performance, multiple time-frames exist in space. The body is not only the live body but also the mediated one on film and video, or it is disembodied as only a voice pre-recorded, and therefore severed from its origin, yet somehow still signalling its liveness in theatrical space. Territories for the transformation of the body are laid out and marked in the space. Confluences of time converge during a performance as present, pre-recorded, and the many layers of suspended time inhabited by memory, sentiment and spirit play themselves out. In addition, if music is involved, then the added element of precise musical time becomes part of the performing body's and the audience's body of action, reflection and remembrance. In examining how bodies relate to space, memory, territory and territorial boundaries, we can better understand how it is that we live as beings in history, and how our stories are indebted to a notion of time which is both quantifiable and yet also out of reach. How artists cross media, using both low-tech and high-tech methods, to tell stories, and especially how they work with music to create new emotional and physical sites of performance, served as the launching point for the first section of this volume.

The initial discussions around a dinner table in London with director Philippou, that then carried over into our work in the practice hall in Greece, resulted in e-mail, live and phone conversations with other artists, performers, directors and composers dedicated to the act of performance as their primary means of communication and creative expression. These conversations, the majority of which have been documented in this volume, reflect a joyously intersecting polyphonic discourse of artists who are necessarily and unequivocally of their time. These artists speak formally and informally about how they stay connected to the work, their vital engagement with their own and other cultures, and the strength and courage it takes to focus on process instead of exclusively on product in a world that more and more celebrates the end result above all.

Working at the intersection between forms (between theatre and film, pop and classical music, CD-ROMS and installation) the practitioners in the first section of this book share a desire to honour their impulses and a tradition of making work that has come before them. The influence of Robert Wilson, Pina Bausch, The Wooster Group, Mabou Mines and Robert Lepage (all artists who exemplify cross-disciplinary work in one way or another) is cited again and again. Not exclusively bound to the media generation,[3] the artists interviewed also cite Shakespeare, Euripides, Chekhov, Brecht and Beckett as major influences. Challenged by the experiments of the past, they are aware of the crossroads at which they stand in each of their primary disciplines in order to forge a new path for the future. It is not surprising, then, that most of them practise their craft in the realm of music-theatre or performance, where boundaries are constantly broken by the fluid demands of the form itself, and where some of the most hybrid and uncategorisable work is being created today.

Reclaiming opera in the Wagnerian epic sense and also in the more chamber-like manner of Debussy has fuelled many of the new music-theatre artists that grace the world's new concert stages and performance venues. Opera, however, is not only restricted to the musical stage, but has also served as a model for not-primarily-musical though sonically inventive pieces for theatre and performance created by mixed media artists who have understood that one of the ways to meditate upon and respond to the confounding and epic nature of contemporary life is to explore the operatic scale and ambition offered by the traditional models of classic music literature and performance.

Whether working in rock music or world music, solo performance or nonlinear, yet text-based narrative modes, artists Peter Gabriel, Rinde Eckert and Mikel Rouse are exploring the limits of sound, the potentiality for the different ways in which music can be heard and experienced, and the time-based structural components that affect lyrical and musical composition. Experimenting with media, interactive software, live film

---

3   See RoseLee Goldberg, *Performance Art: From Futurism to the Present,* rev. edn
    (London: Thames & Hudson, 1988).

scoring and historically driven character pieces, they represent in their own unique ways, the range of possibility inherent in new music theatre recording and performance.

At the other end of the operatic spectrum, so to speak, stand the artists who cross media and mix media to create contemplative, raucous, free-wheeling, or minutely detailed works on an epic or intimate scale about the human, socio-political, spiritual condition. Clearly influenced by new music and sound technologies, artists Marianne Weems, John Jesurun, Tim Etchells and Richard Foreman are representative of makers of the kind of visually rich and complex works that have been at the heart of avant-garde theatre for some time. Whether working in collaboration or individually, they are time-travellers of the performance space. They create work that shifts and radicalises audience perspective, disrupts expected notions of linearity and time continuum and layers the theatrical experience with personally iconographic material alongside recognisable elements from the classical repertoire and popular culture.

Poised between the commercial world of the Broadway musical and the classical music world is composer Maury Yeston, who stands both inside and outside the academy to reinvigorate traditional forms with the knowledge, expertise and skill of a contemporary master. Deeply involved in the creation of new opera for the musical theatre, his radicalisation of media has to do with the very fact of his observance and strong link to past forms, old forms, highbrow and lowbrow forms that weave in and out of his compositions. A child of the television and radio age, Yeston serves as the link between old and new media, and his work reflects the sometimes uneasy, sometimes harmonious balance that can be struck by musically collecting the strands of past and present history together. History, in fact, is what draws many of these cross-media artists to make work and to acknowledge or bear witness to the passage of time.

For composer-performer Rinde Eckert the pull of history stirs his work. Eckert 'unearths artefacts shaped in such a way as to act as lenses' (p. 28) for him to see where he has come from and where he is now. In a sense, Eckert navigates through time to realise what the present can be. A traveller at heart (and this is a repeated motif throughout the volume), Eckert finds his place in the world through contact with the past, with world literature, and a wide range of musical cultures he can bring to bear when composing. Video artist-poet John Jesurun does not see his function as an artist as archaeological but as someone who through a sense of motion can have a greater appreciation for stillness. His focus on the still and moving image in relationship to live text and time (as opposed to pre-recorded time) radicalises an audience's perception of 'what is "live" or not'.[4] Although he tends to work within the established theatrical establishment, as represented by experimental spaces such as New York City's The Kitchen and Performing Garage, Jesurun remains a radical artist, resistant to the dominant culture's modes of performative expression.[5]

Like the other artists in this volume, Jesurun is someone who has created his own mechanism for survival and support within the critically ratified and recognised avant-garde, and continues to discover different ways of working despite the defining 'aesthetic of the moment'. Creating video designs and making plays with film, Jesurun sees technology as a 'symptom of spirituality and the search for it' (p. 45) in the contemporary world. Through his sophisticated and far-reaching use of technology, Jesurun creates ancient-seeming texts for a new global village. His desire, in the end, is to connect and communicate in a pre-postmodernist manner, while he uses the gadgets and devices of the postmodern age.

Composer-performer Mikel Rouse, a frequent collaborator of Jesurun's, combines structure and emotion in his multimedia works to expand the idea of music generated film/performance. Taking on the ubiquitous talk-show format for his 1996 opera *Dennis Cleveland*[6] Rouse subverts audience's expectations of what an opera can be, not unlike how filmmaker Baz Luhrmann challenged an audience to look differently at the structures of the traditional musical in *Moulin Rouge* (2000). Formal play is evident throughout the work of the artists in this volume. It is one of the primary elements that distinguishes them as practitioners who not only cross boundaries of form, but also who in seeking forms from other cultures (not their own) and merging their sensibilities and practical strategies with them find another way to express their vision and shape a dramatic or musical world.

Director Marianne Weems, for example, 'looks back at theatrical forms that preceded much of what is now called multimedia performance' (p. 55) to examine how the live and mediated coexist in Western society's collective imagination; Richard Foreman opens up his notebooks on his website to encourage artists to make something new from what he has made. Composer Maury Yeston bridges the past and the present as he moves between the fields of classical music and commercial theatre, cognisant of the times which have shaped his sensibility, and have

---

4   See Philip Auslander, *Liveness: Performance in a Mediatised Culture* (London and New York: Routledge, 1999).

5   See Baz Kershaw, *The Radical in Performance: Between Brecht and Baudrillard* (London and New York: Routledge, 1999).

6   Rouse's *Dennis Cleveland* is the first successful contemporary opera to use the talk-show as its subject and format. It precedes the Richard Thomas and Stewart Lee *Jerry Springer – The Opera* developed by Julian Crouch which made its debut to great acclaim at the Edinburgh Fringe Festival in August 2002.

allowed for the circularity of music to have happened, thus making his options as an artist greater. Some, like musician Peter Gabriel and multi-media theatre artist Tim Etchells, work from their respective strengths as practitioners but also continually venture outside their niches and inter-sect with the worlds of science and technology.[7] Almost all admit, how-ever, to the luxury of time necessary to explore material, to realise how it lives in space, and to understand the way a piece is never fixed, but always evolving. Evolution is crucial to creation, and so is its place within a broader scheme of society and history, between what has been deemed over time either 'high' or 'low' art.

The intersections between high and low art is a dominant motif in this volume. Many of the cross-disciplinary, cross-media, cross-cultural, intercultural, and cross-linguistic artists herein are creating plays, pieces, music, librettos, theatre actions, myths, improvs, spectacles and living art events that are situated right at the crux between the many definitions of what is sublime or vulgar (i.e. common, popular). They are changing the definitions of what a piece of theatre or performance can be, and are thus emblematic examples of artists energised by social rebellion and recon-struction. Scholar Michael Cerveris's eloquent essay (which follows this introduction) foregrounds many of the ideas that will re-occur in the ensuing conversations: how art has been stratified by cultural desires and mores, how 'old forms' such as vaudeville and music hall are being rein-vestigated and reconfigured for a new audience, and how a democratic exposure to varied artistic work, has resulted in artists who are actively engaged in the rupture of rigid structures for their work, and the breaking down of societal and artistic barriers.

Crossing culture

I think strictly linear, psychologically-driven plays speak less successfully to our culture. Maybe that's arrogant since all I really know is that they don't speak successfully to me. I just get really bored watching them. I keep wish-ing, when I'm watching those plays, that some character would do just one thing that is seemingly unmotivated or that like a hundred feral cats would run through the space or something.[8]

The reaction against realism has been a strong guiding force, albeit prin-ciple, of much of the work of the avant-garde in the twentieth and twenty-first century. Even artists who are not ostensibly avant-garde in

---

7 See Tim Etchells, *Certain Fragments: Texts and Writings on Performance* (London and New York: Routledge, 1999).
8 From unpublished e-mail interview conducted by author with Shawn Sides, September 2001.

their sensibility or approach or aesthetic to material have been exploring the different ways stories can be told, and moreover, how memory culturally and scientifically restructures perception of a tale, and its effect on the body in culture. The claiming of identity, just like the reclaiming of the operatic form, is at the still-nascent heart of cross-cultural text construction, especially in the discipline of playwriting, where artists of colour have been making their voices heard comparatively recently when you think about the long arm of history that has silenced so many non-economically dominant voices. Economics, discrimination and prejudice have affected the way in which artists of colour are understood or received in Western culture. Yet the need to be heard and to re-tell, and re-author their cultural life-scripts has played a significant part in the new work being written and devised by intercultural and cross-cultural artists. Retrieving linguistic and emotional memory and displaying the effects of retrieval over time through and across mediated and non-mediated landscapes is central to the work of the practitioners in this section.

Living in one culture while being raised in another, or being a product of several cultures at once affects the practice of playwrights Migdalia Cruz and Chiori Miyagawa. Both writers discuss how memory – familial, personal and historical – has altered the way they see the world and their work. Miyagawa is 'fascinated by how people remember events; [how] there is no absolute truth in history, personal or global' (pp. 207–8). The interplay of the invented and the real offers Miyagawa a way to reconstruct events theatrically and change more traditional dramatic relationships between space and time. Cruz 'tells and re-tells family history which serves to educate the family to come' (p. 72). Her mission as an artist is to tell the truth and to debunk history, even while she is nurtured by memory.

Dah Teatar's Dijana Milošević and Kathy Randels are interested in how one culture, by being exposed to another, can be enriched, while preserving the 'beauty and uniqueness' of each culture (p. 75). Milosevic and Randels show how through the making of their work, even in the most perilous of times, harmony can be achieved. Their connection to memory and culture comes from folk rituals and songs. These rituals become the place of contact and connection when they work across cultures within the ensemble, and when presenting the work as they travel the globe. Technology for Dah is less of an issue than the concrete, non-virtual act of performance for an audience in a given site at a given time.

Fighting for inclusion or caught in a seemingly unending racialised discourse in society serves as fuel and seed for rebellion for artists Ricardo Bracho, Jorge Ignacio Cortiñas, Tanika Gupta and Guillermo Gomez-Peña. In a discussion with critic Jose Esteban Muñoz, Bracho and Cortiñas talk about the determinative socio-cultural force immigration has had on US society, and how hybrid histories complicate the reading of texts by trans-local artists: artists committed to the particular within the universal, artists who 'stretch global histories [to] include some meaning for their local concerns' (p. 70). Gupta advocates change in the mission and management of theatres so that work by artists of colour is naturally included in a season-to-season line-up so that audiences of colour do not feel theatre is a 'bastion of the privileged' (p. 102). In a frank discussion with scholar/dramaturge Lisa Wolford, seminal performance artist Guillermo Gomez-Peña notes the importance of not shying away from cultural and methodological differences. The cultural body exists to be examined and dissected. Where you come from, how you came to where you are, which border (physical, sexual or metaphorical) you had to cross to get there are all facts ripe for truly un-riddling body and culture, and the body within culture.

Crossing language

If you don't feel some ownership, if you don't feel like your ideas and vision matter deeply to the whole, then there's no reason to stick around.[9]

The language we learn as children, the one we develop as adults, and the common cultural language to which we have access and are a part of, lives in our bodies over time. From poets e.e. cummings to Edith Sitwell to T.S. Eliot to Gertrude Stein, language has served as the ripe field for rich play, investigation and discovery. Committed to un-earthing the structures we have learned and taken for granted as speakers and writers of a language, these poets and others have encouraged readers and audiences to examine how it is they speak, and why, and how words can be in and of themselves objects of fascination and study. Language is a science, and its laboratory is found in the work of artists who are primarily concerned with breaking down, and restructuring its elements for a new audience.

Moving a step beyond those who are examining the essential components of a language from a specifically ethno-cultural perspective (and one where the claiming of a social-cultural identity is a part) are practitioners who are dedicated to language itself, to semiotics and structure, and to language's connection to mythology, and cultural origin. Artists as diverse as Joanna Laurens and Susan Yankowitz view language as geography. Their work is topographical in feeling. Through sound, image, text and the moving body they create a layout from which audiences can see an invented, imagined world that inevitably reflects our own. Poets of the theatre, these language artists take a strong cue from the musicians, librettists

9 *Ibid.*

and mixed-media practitioners from the first section of this volume. In fact, they too see the making of text as musical composition, and ask audiences to not only think of story and narrative, but also (and sometimes, instead of) think of motion, space, tempo, rhythm and time as its own narrative strategy. Archaeological in impulse, these artists scavenge, dig, exhibit, recall and reclaim forgotten words, histories, mythologies and places in the imagination in order to liberate dramatic texts from the constraints of theatrical tradition.

The limits of language, its spatial energy and gravitational pull are thus the subject of this section, which looks at a range of practitioners who cross boundaries of light, mythology and the remains of history. Seeing language as their site, their place of play, artists like Joanna Laurens and Erik Ehn reshape the landscape to fit their imaginative needs. Unburdened by Freudian psychology and its naturalistic limitations, they are intoxicated by the very function of living. Honouring the pleasure of creation, they seek to reconfigure the way we view life, hear words or re-learn what we thought we knew. Laurens, a playwright who is deeply influenced by music and its structures when writing, defies categories while at the same time adhering to the demands of a narrative. Playwright Ehn reacts to the noise of culture by embracing myth language. For Ehn and Laurens, myth shapes construction of stories. Origin is unlocked by digging into the past, and into the curves and edges of language, which they reuse and remake.

Susan Yankowitz discusses how encountering the work of Joseph Chaikin and working with the Open Theatre in the 1960s galvanised her to throw open her assumptions of chronology, character and narrative. In an effort to show how the past, present and future coexist in life, the map Yankowitz makes as a writer and librettist is one of movement and image, out of heightened fragments of experience. Her sense of geography is expansive and inclusive rather than rigid and exclusive. Playwright Hilary Bell describes her connection to landscape as the site for understanding or making sense of work 'Where is vision formed?' she asks. 'Its landscape is in your blood, its sounds and smells' (p. 111). Reflecting on what happens to a geographically transposed playwright when she must 'interface with new elements', Bell relates a conversation she had with playwright Naomi Wallace, another writer who writes from a place of transposition. Dislocated and displaced, Bell and Wallace root themselves in language, in the theatrical worlds they create, and in the experience they bring to bear upon those worlds and words themselves.

Designer Jim Clayburgh in an e-mail correspondence with play-wright-director Matthew Maguire questions the authenticity of vision from the perspective of someone who is in the profession of shaping light, and therefore affecting space and how it is perceived. 'Can there be honest architectural lighting?' he asks (p. 119). The landscape is a shifting one for Clayburgh as the correspondence between him and Maguire moves through cyberspace from fixed points where both of them find themselves, most often affected and effected by their immediate surroundings.

Giving voice to unvoiced passions and political issues through the use of a formal stage language, both visual and verbal, the artists in this section move within the rapidly fluid territories of word, action, and image to up-end the English-language alphabet and make a new geographical site for their borderless linguistic play. Inverting, subverting and cataloguing new ways of seeing, hearing and feeling text and light in space over time (like their fellow colleagues who cross media and culture) these practitioners illuminate history with their language-dense, language-opaque, language-transparent work, and make us re-remember who we once were in time, who we might be, and thus realign the points on the bone-structurally remembered cultural map.

Crossing bodies

> I knew these were people who wanted to mess around with form and structure as well as content, and were willing to be pretty brave about that. I also knew these were people who weren't going to bag when it got boring. And that's how we've survived – we confide in each other and fight a lot and support each other and clean up after each other's burn out.[10]

The bones are inside the body; they make the body, and the animated skeleton is the ever corporeal non-phantom presence on stage, in society and in the practice hall. At some point contact is sought and needed. Human contact is the root of creative expression. Theatre is made in contact between performer and audience, performer and performer, and collaborator to collaborator in the practice hall. The body is liberated in the space between the contact points, and the audience can witness the full effect of a body being moved, moving and fixed in one place, in one situation, in one moment at a given time. Mediated or non-mediated, unbound or restricted by spoken text, living midst many cultures, the body in space is the cultural sign that is constantly being deciphered in performance, whether it be through sound, historical revision, costume, light, or the ecology of a site.

The many rites of passage involved in collaboration, and thus, how indeed collaborating bodies behave and function is the heart of the final section of this volume. While the constancy of process and practice has

10 *Ibid.*

been the source of examination throughout the interviews that have preceded this section, now the focus is on how process is enabled by directors and designers and others in the rooms, halls, fields, offices and
tundras of the rehearsal process (a process which can sometimes begin
before performers walk into a practice hall). Negotiating differences and
exchanging methodologies, artists work to create and present a shared
vision on stage. Getting there is half the battle, and reading the body's
signs, making contact with each other and the gods ultimately shapes
what the audience will witness in performance.

Opening with a correspondence between artist-scholar Stephen J.
Bottoms and performance artist Julie Laffin, this section brings the spirit
of play front and centre. Working in different cities as they collaborate on
a piece entitled *Junior*, Bottoms and Laffin literalise the word through
their performing bodies. 'Walking becomes speaking and writing' (p. 149).
Space is the negotiating zone for bodies to enact their stories.

Artists as diverse as Phelim McDermott and David Greig call upon
the importance of listening and reacting to the body, to its messages, and
how they are sent through society in order to shape and construct new
work with their respective companies, Improbable Theatre and Suspect
Culture. Nick Philippou recognises that 'actors carry culture in their
bodies' (p. 171). This recognition affects his relationship not only with
performance, but also with text and how it too is a body that carries culture and is meant to be read and understood.

Peter Sellars brings out the hidden worlds that exist in the collaborative process as he speaks about his long-term relationships with designers
George Tsypin, Adrienne Lobel and Dunya Ramicova. The surface bodies
of sets can be seductive or dangerous. The costumed bodies of the actors
tell a story before a single word is spoken or note is sung. The democracy
of a design for the theatre or opera can make its own political statement
about equality and a fair society. Peter DuBois finds in the unforgiving
landscape of Alaska a template for American society and its ongoing socio-
historical concerns. DuBois's sense of place connects him to community
and changes the way he stages the body in space. Through distance and
isolation, he finds cohesion and intimacy. Juxtaposing mythic spaces next
to prosaic ones informs how he can as a director show audiences the
blurred lines of identity and the multiplicity of positions we all live in.

Sound designer Darron L. West concludes the section with a meditation on his working relationship with director Anne Bogart and SITI
Company. His conceptual approach to sound as a living body in the playing space allows him to have a dialogue with the text, movement and actors
as well as the audience. His subtle processing of sound cues sensibility
and emotion and creates memory links for an audience. His ongoing

exploration of space with regard to all its sonic possibilities, and to a dynamic exchange in the practice hall is emblematic of the democratic spirit exemplified by the artists in this volume.

Excited by and delighting in the power of the human body within the space, the practitioners in this section admit to their complex relationship with new technologies. David Greig is suspect of the lure of high-tech, while West acknowledges how technology has made some of his work easier. Both believe, however, in the primacy of the individual, and the artist's intuitive intelligence and intellectual acumen to devise original solutions for artistic problems during the process. The grammar of the computer and the web is only an interface for the real work at hand, and at best, a tool to enliven how artists can think about and structure material. In the afterword, eminent theorist Patrice Pavis offers his contemplative take on new technologies and dramatic form through his discussion of Robert Lepage's multimedia collaboration with Peter Gabriel *Zulu Time* (1999) alongside the work of contemporary French dramatists Minyana and Durif, among others. Sceptical and invigorated by what he sees, he calls into question where we go from here. Where is the future now that we have taken a step into the past?

> The moment, the now in which we live, has not invented new muses. What do we have now? The muse of making money? The muse of speed?[11]

While consumerism and celebrity increasingly dominate Western culture, the artists who have generously given of their time to share their views for this volume are either seeking an alternative path to new consumerism, or are actively engaged in critiquing culture's obsession with celebrity and materiality. Some of these artists struggle to make their voices heard amid the fast din of slick smiles, tabloid sheets and the latest word on what's hot at the box office. Others have found themselves working within the mainstream quite by chance, and thus have chosen to remain cognisant of the delicate balance they must strike between experimentation and 'staying alive' in a very fickle and demanding marketplace. The unexpected success of Cultural Industry's *Shockheaded Peter* (1998) is certainly not lost on its co-creator/director Phelim McDermott. Thus, his remarks on the importance of seeing beyond such popular success offer a lesson in grace. Peter Gabriel admits that he must meet an audience and the record industry's demand, but tries to cultivate time and space to experiment, and support the work of other artists around the world. Peter DuBois lives within the question mark of the struggle

---

11 From unpublished e-mail interview conducted by author with Frederic Amat, September 2001.

between staging popular, commercial work and material which is more adventurous than his audience might desire. It is the question mark and its mystery that enlivens these practitioners. With humour and passion, they are aware that their artistic choices are determined more by what moves them simply by being awake to stimulus in the world than a quest for fame or celebrity. Rather than submit to the culture of expectation, these practitioners are alive to the culture of curiosity.

> The truth about the theatre is that it contains myriad textures and colors between intimacy and spectacle. It can be so *many* different kinds of experience and so many different sizes. Theatre offers a vast range of possibilities.[12]

Two years and many travels since that summer in 2000 sitting at Nick Philippou's dinner table in London in pre-rehearsal discussions, I am now aware that another destination point along my writer's journey soon awaits me: Cambridge, Massachusetts. The passage of time is marked in these pages, as are my concerns about the necessity to make work, advocate for change, and seek understanding for new work that cuts across border lines, be they artistic, cultural, national, sexual, or economic. After 11 September 2001, I interviewed playwright Chiori Miyagawa in New York for this book. It was the last full interview I conducted for the volume, and I remember how difficult it was for each of us to talk about our work, as we were both hurt in diverse ways by the physical and emotional chaos surrounding us. Yet as we spoke, the pleasure of making a connection, of sharing our sincere joy in writing, and in how we both were indebted to the memory of so many who had come before us eased the initial shock waves with which we had begun our conversation. The responsibility we felt toward speaking something meaningful at a time when much seemed meaningless gave way to what simply carries us from day to day: the belief in making, in creating, in trying to see the new, and in not holding back.

Moving like fractals in the complex, chaotic design of our world, artists are changing the topography in which we live by calling attention to the strange attractors in our midst. What engages the heart, the mind and the soul is the pivot point upon which other interests turn. A sound loop, a slant of light, or simply a body in space illuminated by both visible and invisible signs are what we return to again and again in the search for meaning, which is at the root of what drives art, even art that is devoted to the absence of conventionally received and/or understood meaning. Riding form and content with equal parts bravery and passion,

---

12 From unpublished e-mail interview conducted by author with Anne Bogart, artistic director of SITI Company, June 2002.

the double route to chaos is paved here with ambition, beauty, and a dedication to craft and its investigation as something worth doing at the end of a long day. The conversations that follow are a provocative reminder of why the creative act continues to stir our essential humanity.

Intersection, crossover and convergence: fluidity in contemporary arts (a perspective from the US)
Michael Cerveris

Michael Cerveris is Chair of the Creative Arts Division and Director of the D'Angelo School of Music at Mercyhurst College in Erie, Pennsylvania. He is a pianist, chamber performer, conductor and director, and a specialist in interdisciplinary works, performance and music-theatre. He was Founding Chair of the Interdisciplinary Arts and Performance Department at Arizona State University West, and former Director of the Institute of the Arts at Duke University in North Carolina.

Duke Ellington had a favourite phrase he used to describe his music, or more precisely, the concept he used to describe his work as an artist: 'beyond categories'. Many critics today deplore the term 'crossover', which refers to icons of pop culture participating in the forms and venues of high art. The term also applies when classical artists broaden their perspective to include performing or creating works that have a broad audience attraction. This appeal is based on communicating via a more accessible artistic language and venue. The misanthropic among us see such efforts merely as a means of survival for classical artists or a means of ego satisfaction for pop artists. But 'beyond categories' carries with it a much more encompassing view. It implies a future that will bring a new aesthetic that doesn't distinguish between classical, jazz, country, new age, decorative, minimalist, commercial, etc. Where, in fact, the kind of appropriation implied would preclude defining itself in terms of a blend of pre-existing styles. In time, it will indeed prove we will have evolved a sea change from the traditional twentieth century Western concept of art and non-art to something more likely to define nothing short of a new aesthetic for the twenty-first century.

At the present time, we may be going through the final phases preliminary to this sea change. The practical mechanics of technology, commodification, multiculturalism, post-modernism, gender identification, feminism, globalisation, and all such forms of inclusion, continued to evolve during the last half of the twentieth century and provided a fertile context for the current genre blending in the arts.

Consider the following statement by Lawrence Levine that as long as democracy is confined to politics, 'culture is left free to select its groups and proclaim its hierarchies', but once you extend the I-am-as-good-as-you-are-formula beyond politics, 'culture, with its eternal decision-making, will naturally die . . . for culture induces a mighty scorn of those who do not know enough to be humble before Masters'.[1] If anything can be sure about those who participate in twenty-first-century US culture, it is not likely they will ever be humble. Culture will obviously survive; it may change, shift its centre, and be unrecognisable to those of previous generations, but something will be in place to answer the need for an aesthetic dimension to existence. At the same time, it cannot be denied that these are perilous times for the arts in the US. Funding for high art is receding. Many elite institutions have disappeared. Audiences are greying and attempts to encourage younger audiences to take responsibility for participating in the traditional arts have not been entirely successful.

The terms high art and low art and the critique of mass culture that often accompanies these terms have been around for two hundred years. Currently, and perhaps more than ever, their confluence has become more apparent and more frequent. And although these terms may seem narrow and used pejoratively by some, they are commonly accepted concepts, and for purposes of clarity, will be useful here for their generally accepted meanings describing two ends of a continuum. Standard English dictionaries explain intersection as a figure formed by two lines. The standard auto driver's licence manual gives explicit instructions that govern the rules of behaviour for motorists when entering a traffic intersection. Unfortunately, we have no such rules of the road for the forces that meet in an aesthetic intersection. Where high art and low art meet each other, as evidence shows they are doing in our present-day cultural climate, the public, the artists and the presenters are seeking new 'rules of the road' for the aesthetic experience. In the world of traffic control, opposing forces are protected from merging 'contamination' by rules of the road. In the world of artistic merging, cross-influences and mutual affects and interaction are inevitable and can be quite desirable.

A look at the early nineteenth century finds US audiences presented with a generous fusion of what we would now call high art and low art,

---

1 Lawrence Levine, *Highbrow/Lowbrow: The Emergence of Cultural Hierarchy in America* (Cambridge, Mass.: Harvard University Press, 1988) p. 219.

often within the same performance event. To audiences of that time, it would seem there was very little need to categorise experiences that would portray a hierarchy of values in the way we have come to think of high art and popular entertainment today. On the same programme, for example, symphony orchestras offered traditional European repertoire as well as more popular works; minstrel shows presented dramatic readings and elaborate musical numbers as well as folk songs and skits. Vaudeville shows had opera and ballet stars on the same bill with jugglers and comedians. Around the mid-century mark, a process characterised by some as 'sacralisation' appeared, as America prospered in a period of industrialisation. High art attained venerated status and became a shrine for Western European art traditions transplanted to the New World for the benefit of the wealthy upper classes. The result was a gradual polarising of high art and popular culture that separated the cultured, educated class from the rest of society.

In today's world, with the technological advances of the twenty-first century, the pluralism of our society, the rise in literacy, of feminism, multiculturalism and the dominance of the middle class, we note the gradual marking again of a period merging high art/low art that has a resemblance to the conditions as they existed at the end of the nineteenth century. But this time around, with a difference. Whereas, the reasons for intersection between high and low art at the end of the nineteenth century had more to do with the demographics of the audiences, the move now seems to come more from the perspectives of individual artists and presenters reacting to changes in society and economic realities. For a good deal of the twentieth century, many creative and performing artists remained identified with one genre or the other. Now some artists are looking at the intersection of dominant and subdominant culture as a context for creating new works not necessarily identified with a specific genre and new audiences to present them to. While there are likely economic reasons that this is occurring, there are, at the same time, artistic and intellectual reasons as well.

Emerging from adolescence onto the world scene, the energies of turn of the nineteenth century US were involved with the modernisation of political and economic structures willing to absorb immigrants at a tremendous rate and provide them with jobs and support. All this provided a setting that was more socially egalitarian than later generations would come to be. Audiences for entertainments had not yet separated themselves into highbrow, middlebrow and lowbrow as defined by Richard Chase.[2] In discussing the meeting ground between classes before the turn

2 Richard Chase, *The American Novel and its Tradition* (New York: 1978).

of the nineteenth century, Lawrence Levine writes not only of the frequent legitimate productions of Shakespeare but of burlesques and parodies of the Bard as well. His thesis holds that in order to parody references to Shakespeare's plays, the audience, no matter what their social status, would have had to know the original reference.

Opera was also much performed and appreciated by mixed audiences. Companies such as the Pyne and Harrison English Opera Company frequently toured the US doing foreign language operas but translated into English to have as broad an audience appeal as possible. Often the more violent scenes from famous operas were promoted to bring in broader audiences. From coast to coast, many popular tunes of the day were derived from operas. The popular song 'Away with the Melancholy' was derived from an aria from Mozart's *The Magic Flute* (1791). Opera in America, like other art forms at the time, was not presented as a sacred text. Artists who felt free to embellish, add and subtract from the printed score performed it. Sometimes, performances included inserts of popular ballads sung in English; a practice that harkens back to the seventeenth century European tradition when comic opera scenes were interpolated between the acts of serious operas. Genres and mediums were mixed freely and to a degree that would have seemed quite improper to the more formal audiences of later generations. But this rather fluid cultural climate was not to continue very far into the new century.

In May 1849 at the Astor Place Opera House in New York City, an incident occurred showing that class distinctions were gradually becoming a part of the cultural scene. Two leading actors, William Charles Macready, an Englishman, and Edwin Forrest, an American, had become symbols of a growing stylistic difference: the English more cerebral acting style and the vigorous, more flamboyant style of the American actor set in opposition the wealthy gentry and the less sophisticated public. On 7 May, as luck would have it, both actors were appearing in productions of *Macbeth* (1606). Forrest's performance at the Broadway Theatre was a huge success, while Macready's was drowned out by boos and hisses. On the evening of 10 May, Macready, persuaded by the likes of Washington Irving and Herman Melville, appeared again on stage, while outside, ten thousand people lobbed paving stones at the theatre. A riot ensued and the militia was called in. In the end, twenty-two people were killed and many others injured. The New York correspondent of the *Philadelphia Public Ledger* lamented a few days after the riot: 'It leaves behind a feeling to which this community has hitherto been a stranger – an opposition of classes – the rich and poor . . . a feeling that there is now in our country, in New York

City, what every good patriot hitherto has considered it his duty to deny – a high and a low class.'[3]

Gradually, the context(s) for experiencing the arts was changing. Some writers have referred to this as a 'sacralisation' of the arts, which was transforming the face of American culture; art that was now exclusive, inviolate. The concept of the 'other', resistance to treating the arts holistically, and the legacy of suspicion and disdain that goes along with it, has extended through much of the twentieth century.

With the fruits of the Industrial Revolution and modernisation reaching these shores and the rise of professional specialisation, Fordism (essentially, assembly-line procedure and job specialisation) and trade unionism, the affect of fragmentation in American society was indisputable. It was clear to the emerging wealthy class in America that they would have to pay for the arts they wanted. The multiplicity of early America brought about by heavy immigration was counteracted by the elite class that developed enclaves of culture. Newly evolving cultural structures required wealthy directors mainly through participation on boards of sponsors and the like. In an age that spawned the development of dynasties such as the Mellons, the Carnegies and the Rockefellers, the notion of an elite class also developed and with it a special idea of artistic standards.

For many of the nobly-minded champions of high culture it was believed that art was the last bastion of moral good while other social forms were 'bending.' Many stressed the arts and culture as the only way to keep America from becoming totally corrupt, money grubbing and morally bankrupt. The prevailing attitude among spokesmen for culture at the beginning of the twentieth century, was that only by insisting on the highest standards of performance purity and an equally highly-informed audience, could this society preserve the values of its European traditions. In this way, the idea of highbrow, of orthodoxy in the arts, and a hierarchy of aesthetic values became the basis for what we think of as high art in the twentieth and twenty-first centuries. And this idea was used to criticise 'lesser' kinds of aesthetic experiences.

To be sure, we can appreciate the high standards of technical proficiency that resulted from such a focus. They clearly characterise today's professional artist as well as the standards of our modern arts conservatories as by-products of this early effort to 'purify' the arts from inferior performances. A corollary to the high performance standards demanded of artists, was the fact that it was de rigeur that the audience should be well informed about the art forms it attended; one should acquire a

3   *Ibid.*, 66.

knowledge of musical form and history, an appreciation of the nuances of theatre and dance, of the values in modern art. Gone were the earlier days of rowdy audiences who made their appreciation or disapproval clearly known. Elevated decorum was plainly proscribed. This segmentation pitted one type of experience against the other. Lines were clearly drawn. Audiences and artists were typed.

Well into the second half of the twentieth century and persisting in corners even today, some audiences and artists are divided along these same lines of high and low although the proportions certainly were not equal. Proponents of high art and artists have been eclipsed by the appeal to large masses of audiences from the entertainment industry; entertainment can make less intellectual demands on an audience and can absorb technological advances as quickly as they are developed. Whereas to stay alive, high art can essentially only appeal for support in the form of philanthropy and subsidy. Foundations and endowments were created to insure for future generations the survival of the arts and artists. During the middle part of the twentieth century, elite artists, relying on this support, began to leave their audiences behind.

In his introduction to *Dead Artists, Live Theories and Other Cultural Problems* (1993) cultural critic and theorist Stanley Aronowitz writes that there is little, if any, value in the distinction between high and low art, except socially, lending support to the hypothesis that high art is more of a cultural construct than part of an innate aesthetic hierarchy. Much of Aronowitz's discussion deals with choices made by audiences that have defined various styles of creative activity and periods of cultural change. Audiences have had a role in determining high art from low but it is the artists that have had a role in determining the intersection of both. From this, various questions arise:

1] Does a levelling or mixing of high art/low art result in diluting traditional values of proficiency, expertise, and adeptness of craft, technique and accomplishment?

2] Does creating greater suitability to a broader audience represent a 'dumbing down' aspect in the matter of intersection? If such is the case, what implications does this have for artists and the public in relation to artistic values and audience expectations?

3] Is public access to the aesthetic experience a consideration that should be part of the total picture?

4] Has the erosion of philanthropic support for the arts and the decline of public education in the arts combined to contribute to an impoverished audience with limited access to the arts with the crossover phenomenon serving a kind of audience development aspect for survival of the artist?

Sometimes referred to as 'crossover' but looking not unlike the fluid conditions in the late 1800s, one can look comparatively at the Next Wave festival programming at the Brooklyn Academy of Music. A view of the array of recent production includes works by John Adams, Frank Zappa, and baroque opera. Such programming is more than just a strategy to get more people in the auditorium, although that is a goal in itself. It reflects an eclecticism born of an intersection of high art and popular culture that not only has historical roots as we have seen, but also demonstrates the pluralism of the present-day culture and arts climate and the general level of literacy and communication of our society.

But the intersection of pop culture and 'classical' art goes beyond the designing of festival events. Established artists from both sides of the continuum are expanding their possibilities. Mabou Mines, a seminal avant-garde theatre group, opened a staged version of Peter Pan entitled *Peter and Wendy* (1996) which was extremely faithful to the original book rather than the various film versions. The premiere took place in a new theatre dedicated to works for children in the revitalised Times Square area. Cirque de Soleil has brought audiences a fusion of dance/ballet/whimsy and traditional circus skills into an altogether new art form. The 1996 Broadway revival of the Rodgers and Hammerstein musical *The King and I* was choreographed by Lar Lubovitch, whose main dance milieu has been the world of modern dance and classical ballet. Elton John has produced not only *The Lion King* (1997) in collaboration with Julie Taymor, but also *Aida* (2000), and Pete Townshend of The Who, together with Des McAnuff, created a traditional book musical of The Who's concept album *Tommy* (1992). In a cut called 'High 5 (Rock the Catskills)' from the album *Odelay* (1996) by the rock musician Beck, one finds an eclectic mixture of rap, rock, jazz, folk, etc. About a minute into the cut, and before a sequence of white noise, one is presented with the B minor theme from Schubert's 'Unfinished' Symphony (1822). Art keeps leaping over formal boundaries.

The energy for crossover has not been limited to performing artists. As with so many of the aesthetic 'isms' earlier in the twentieth century, where visual arts often took a leading role, in 1990, the Museum of Modern Art (MOMA) and its director Kirk Varnedoe together with Adam Gopnik, art critic for *The New Yorker*, mounted a daring exhibit called 'High & Low'. The exhibition set out to demonstrate the links between modern art and four areas of popular culture: graffiti, caricature, comics and advertising. The catalogue for the exhibition stated:

> Our goal is to examine the transformations through which modern painters and sculptors have made new poetic languages by re-imagining the possibilities in forms of popular culture; and, as a corollary, to acknowledge the way

those adaptations in modern art have often found their way back into the common currency of public visual prose.[4]

While the exhibition caused quite a stir in the art world at the time and among elite patrons of MOMA, it sent along a strong statement about contemporary art: 'Modern art's most salient and valued attributes have to do, not with absolutism and exclusivity, but with this heterogeneous inclusiveness and unprecedented open-endedness.'[5] Broadly taken, this statement applies very well to the range of creative artists unintimidated by traditional boundaries.

Howard Gardner of MIT, a leading authority on arts education and culture, once stated in a conference addressed at the Lincoln Center Institute, that Americans had no culture. What he meant was we do not have a common shared culture as people. He allowed that what we do have that possibly substitutes as a common culture is television; access to which is practically an entitlement and evidence of which is present everywhere. Sociologists might have much to say about Gardner's idea and specifically how different groups in our country process differently what they see collectively on television. Nevertheless, my interest lies more in extracting from this idea the notion that there is something like a common contextual experience in the US, and that it is from such a shared cultural context that we are seeing crossover emerge.

Musicologists often refer to music composition in the eighteenth century as music from the 'common practice' period. That is, a common understanding as to the style and procedures of the creative act. In that era, the practice of composing was far less a matter of discovering one's special artistic voice, and more in line with 'following the rules' for proper execution and procedure, hence, a universal style. Individuality, if at all, could come later after the rules were mastered. In the various arts and in various style periods throughout history, some kind of general context was a starting point for creative talents – a milieu that was shared as a source from which creative efforts emerged. Gardner indicates that our frame of reference is television, but really it goes beyond television to cover the vast area of media, technology and communication to which we are all continually exposed.

Consider the case, for instance, of Yale-trained contemporary composer Michael Dougherty whose résumé includes Broadway pit musician, circus organist, Las Vegas accompanist, and who also has written works for the New York Philharmonic, and the Tokyo Wind Ensemble. His release on Argo Records is a five-movement work based on the Superman

4 Adam Gopnik, *High & Low* (New York: Museum of Modern Art, 1990), p. 19.
5 *Ibid.*, 21.

hero, the 'Metropolis Symphony', and his opera *Jackie O* (1997) premiered at the Houston Grand Opera. With recitatives set to texts by Achille Lauro hijackers and Patty Hearst, Dougherty does what most common practice artists do; he makes art out of what he knows, out of his experience. And much of his experience has naturally been from television.

Frederic Jameson, renowned as a commentator on contemporary culture, speaks of commodification and postmodernism as

> The effacement of the older boundaries between high culture and mass culture, and the emergence of new kinds of texts filled with forms, categories and contents of that whole landscape of advertising and motels, of the late show and the paperback bestseller, in other words of that very Culture Industry so passionately repudiated by an older modernism.[6]

In other words, by appropriating and sharing the common experiences of the modernism of the 1950s, 1960s, and 1970s, many artists now find themselves comfortably engaged in a kind of artistic fluidity that allows them freedom to move comfortably along a broad continuum of high art and popular culture.

To fluidity among genres, fluidity among styles, among creative and performing artists the commercial and the recondite has also been added the convergence of cultures. Consider the implications of the production of *Tree* (2000) at BAM by Ralph Lemon, which involves the blending of cultures. In this work a recording of the blues singer Robert Johnson is heard while a folk musician from China improvises on the same tune. Meanwhile a cultural expert from Yunan appears in minstrel black face instead of Beijing Opera make-up. Or what of the development at Robert Wilson's workspace in Watermill, Long Island, where he has brought multi-cultural artists from all over the world together for the purpose of creating new works?

The inclusion of cross-cultural perspectives has become an almost automatic response in contemporary culture. Those in our present-day society with creative impulses have matured in a milieu of mediated sensory saturation where they were and are integrated with high art and popular culture, postmodern amalgamations, multi-culturalism, and 'isms' of every stripe on a daily basis. The ubiquity of this information and appropriation by the media of whatever is successful tends to erase or minimise the differences between high art and popular culture. It is not surprising, therefore, to find an ease and fluidity that allows artists with this kind of exposure in their formative years to shift from one to the other with aplomb. Within the vast majority of the population, leaving

---

6 Frederic Jameson, 'Postmodernism and Consumer Society', *Amerikastudien*, 29: 1 (1984), 55.

aside for the moment the very serious inequities of opportunities that still exist in the US, there has been, over the past one hundred years, an appreciable rise in literacy, communication and assimilation of user-friendly technology that has created an accessibility quotient to what the new artists have to say.

In the nineteenth century, an age of technical expansion and industrialisation, the cult of the individual was paramount. In the high arts, it is easy to understand how the image of the virtuoso became so identified with this age. Not only the machine itself, but also the extent to which humans could achieve machine-like perfection became a celebrated end in itself. Technical virtuousity and skill in the arts were appreciated and rewarded. For most of the twentieth century, a period of high specialisation, it is natural that high art would reflect this phenomenon and at times resemble a spectator sport with stars to be admired. In the trend toward intersection in the twenty-first century, it would be confounding if virtuosity and craft remained the exclusive realm of high art and broad public access defined the domain of low art.

We live in a period of egalitarianism, democratisation and decentralisation, one that questions authority, credentialisation and limited admission. Both artists and audiences share what might be termed a twenty-first century 'common practice perspective'. It is clear that artists, managers, presenters, organisers and entrepreneurs are seeking to broaden their audience base that will provide the necessary support for the arts and artists. With the erosion of support for the arts by the US government, the corporate sector and foundations, it seems that audiences are being relied upon more than ever before to foot the bill. Larger audiences are needed. The arts can no longer depend on the discernment of a chosen few, a highly specialised audience with a narrow aesthetic gambit. Just as clearly, a broader audience base will tolerate fewer specialised interests.

Diminished primary and secondary education in the arts has created a naive and inexperienced audience. On the other hand, mass media empowered this same audience to feel entitled to engage with just about anything. If Duke Ellington was right and 'beyond boundaries' is what the future holds for us, what is the future landscape going to be like and how will we relate to it? Are we at the threshold of a new common practice period that places a premium on fluidity, intent, integrity, accessibility, communication and universality as the dominant meaningfulness? Are we, in the early stages of the twenty-first century, facing a situation not unlike the state of affairs at the beginning of the twentieth century: a situation that can be reflected in the implications present at that defining moment of the twentieth century esthetic, namely the premiere of Stravinsky's *Le Sacre du Printemps* (1913)? On that occasion, a new world was being revealed to a startled public – a world away from charming Mozart piano concertos and hyper-emotional Mahler symphonies. Here was a rallying cry for the world of the 'Other', in this case, the primitive, the mass delirium of the mob.

Can we read anything prophetic into the resurgence of late of attention to Stravinsky's work in the many festivals and celebration of his works? Could this lingering fascination with a clarion musical language from the past, coming, as it does now, at a time when the classical world seems unsure of itself and the ubiquity of popular culture seems daunting if nothing else, be Stravinsky's legacy telling us yet again: the past is behind us, the future is before us?

Crossing media

The Kitchen's production of *Black Maria* written and directed by John Jesurun

Witness and witnessed
Rinde Eckert in conversation with Caridad Svich

Rinde Eckert is a singer, composer, movement artist, actor, writer and director. His stage work includes *And God Created Great Whales*, which premiered at The Foundry Theatre in New York in Autumn 2000 under David Schweizer's direction; the radio opera *Four Songs Lost in a Wall* (1995), and *Highway Ulysses*, which premiered at American Repertory Theatre under Robert Woodruff's direction in their 2002–03 season. Eckert's longstanding commitment to the creation of new music theatre and opera at a time when, while experimentation abounds, little of it is sufficiently funded in the US and therefore seen by an audience, bespeaks of his passionate stance for the furthering of the form, and the embracing of eclecticism. His rigorous, playful and profound librettos and scores delight in juxtaposing classical sources (literary and musical) next to contemporary Pop culture references. An original and daring artist, Eckert's handmade approach toward creation and execution even within a sophisticated technological framework places him, to paraphrase Henri Bergson in his 1896 piece *Matter and Memory* as someone with 'one foot in the past, and another in the future'.

This interview was conducted via e-mail between February and July 2001.

CARIDAD SVICH As a singer, writer, composer, actor and director, you are able to express your talents in so many ways. Has this ever been a conflict for you?

RINDE ECKERT Directing work I'm still in the process of writing is difficult. The director in me argues with the writer in me before the writer has had a chance to respond. Composing, acting and writing at the same time seem to be complementary processes. Acting and directing at once is almost impossible. Acting and co-directing can work for me though. Still, with enough time in process any of these combinations can work. The major conflict for me has been in the area of general perception. Because my talents and interests range across the borders of artistic disciplines I don't feel I'm afforded full membership in any of them. I think I'm considered a bit of a freak. Then again, perhaps I am. Sometimes I like it, other times I get lonely. I'm challenged by the demands of the various disciplines. As long as I'm still learning, all avenues will remain open.

CS It is the aspect of learning and wanting to learn more that fuels your investigation into different areas of your talent and testing the range of your skills. Working outside the box is freeing because you are following your impulse and the work is thus defined from where the impulse springs creatively, be it a score, play, or movement piece. How do you start a new work? Are there specific themes toward which you gravitate?

RE I seem to need to imagine myself within some new landscape or situation in response to my past or as a response to a piece of literature. I haven't been interested in straight confessions or adaptations. Redemption, ambition, control and love through science, art and religion keeps coming up. These are large worlds the ends of which I cannot see. I should be digging here for the rest of my life, unearthing artefacts (stories) shaped in such a way as to act as lenses. The performance then is both the form of investigation and its published results. And I expect to be changed by it.

As far as process goes, I have to trust my instinct for fertile ground (the basic story) then plant myself. So, I'll be looking one way for a long time thinking the sun is about to come up only to find I have to turn around. *And God Created Great Whales* started out as an investigation of the desire for perfection blasted by ungovernable nature. I had this vision of a piano tuner struggling with some grand idea; he was this obsessed Ahab-like figure. At first I thought he was just struggling to tune his piano perfectly, an impossible thing that would drive him to despair. I soon realised 'tuning' was too abstract an affair to offer much in the way of dramatic analogues. When I made him a would-be opera composer working on an opera based on Melville's 1851 masterpiece *Moby Dick* everything fell into place. It turned into a meditation on memory and desire for wholeness (among other things). I love my protagonists, however odd or derailed they are. My performance within their situations changes me. I like to think it makes me smarter, stronger, more courageous and more alert. The work should be the confirmation of the integrity of the dig.

CS Are there artists who inspired you early on, and continue to inspire you today?

RE My vocal work with Phyllis Curtin was crucial not only to the evolution of my technique but to the evolution of my intelligence. Phyllis has the kind of alertness, analytical acumen, eloquence and generosity of spirit to which I aspire. I've learned from all my collaborators through the years but especially from my San Francisco collaborators Paul Dresher, Margaret Jenkins, Ellie Kopp and Michael Palmer. I made some crucial discoveries in collaboration with George Coates. My work with Terry Allen and Robert Woodruff was also seminal. I took early theatrical inspiration from work by Robert Wilson, John O'Keefe, Peter Brook, Giorgio Strehler, Stan Laurel, Buster Keaton, Charlie Chaplin, Ingmar Bergman and Tadeuz Kantor.

I find it useful to remind myself that Art with a capital 'A' (along with philosophy and much of science) is of little importance to the vast majority for whom life is complicated enough without the consideration of complex ironies. It wasn't that long ago that artists were being burned at the stake for heresy or thrown into prison for political satire. Galileo was killed for maintaining that the earth might just be travelling around the sun.

Most of the people of the world are not very well educated, worldly or intelligent. Of the few well-educated people only a handful are interested in art; of that handful only a fraction are interested in new art. So one is advised to assume marginality and get back to the work. One has to ask oneself: Do I have something to say? Have I found the means to say it? I have been asking myself those questions for years now. The longer I am able to continue the practice the better my example, I suppose.

cs Has technology helped better your practice in any way?

RE Advances in technology have made it possible to quickly and more graphically model design ideas, but the two-dimensional is the two-dimensional whether one draws on a scrap of paper or one uses Pho-toShop. Volume, weight, height, distance, smell, colour, and texture are what I find most interesting. Inasmuch as technology aids my appreciation of a moment on the actual stage I find it useful. When I got my first computer I tried writing on it. I found myself thinking too quickly. The words looked so finished on the screen, each word drawn with the same force and size. The lines were so straight, the sentence so clean, all inelegant mistakes erased, none of the palimpsest character of the messy mind evident in crossings and marginal corrections. I had to go back to writing in my notebook where I could see in my awkward hand some strength or weakness, some uncertainty or confidence, a subtle change of rhythm, an exaggerated word. Music technologies worked differently. Advances in processing and sequencing allow me to record otherwise ephemeral improvisations. I can review and improve. Technology in general is more interesting to me for the ironies of its social impact than it is as a facile agent of theatrical idea.

cs To expose how technology has affected the way we communicate, and sometimes distorts individual intentions behind the desire to communicate is one of the ironies you have mined so well and movingly in your work. How have you managed to find a way to express your very unique gifts as a performer-creator despite shifting tides of taste over the years?

RE Faith in one's work, it seems to me, is developed. Canetti says the artist becomes more impudent with age. I suppose so. I approach my work as a puzzle I am trying to solve. I've put several elements in play. Each element is like a point of pressure on a nebulous clay block. As one sculpts, the nature of pressure (its force and direction) changes. When one is satisfied that all the pressures are balancing each other, that all the ratios are satisfying, that there is nowhere to push that won't destroy some other critical aspect of the piece, then one is done. When I've done what I can do with the puzzle or the argument, I'm satisfied. As for seeking new challenges, I think it's the other way around: new challenges are seeking me. One has to work to avoid them. I welcome them.

I do think about the timeless, the grand idea or deeply human dilemma that might be relevant to any age. For this reason I have often written from the point of view of an isolato, who, although placed within a specific landscape or situation, is, in his *isolation*, free to express himself without reserve and dream large dreams. Myth, symbolism, allegory, the religious, the philosophical (including science) are at play here. I have heard an artist say, 'I can't stand metaphor.' Since metaphor is intrinsic to human thought this statement seems the disingenuous pose of a knee-jerk iconoclast. I understand the perceived need to be purely secular or 'pragmatic' to avoid pretentious symbolism or hyperbolic sentiment, but to extend this coolness into disdain for the simply emotional or grand bespeaks a lack of courage or insight to me.

I feel that, whatever idealistic gloss one puts on one's work won't save it from the flawed hermeneutics of a baroque human sensibility. We are messy, thoughtful creatures in a messy, thought-provoking world. There is bathos but there is also depth of feeling, there is the grossly sentimental but there is also the poignantly lyrical, there is torturously overt symbolism but there is also the mythological and sacred. Sometimes one needs to be cool, riding above the maelstrom of the reactive heart wryly or serenely remarking on it and sometimes one ought to struggle in the soup of feeling and be reminded of our compelling vulnerability, artlessness or vulgarity. Ultimately one is both witness and that which is witnessed. This, to me, is the great cosmic paradox. So, for me the sacred and profane, the high and low, the timeless and the timely are all yoked together. To privilege one of the pair over the other is to draw one's cart in too tight a circle, spinning in one direction alone.

Chasing ruins
Tim Etchells in conversation with Caridad Svich

Tim Etchells is the award-winning artistic director and writer behind Forced Entertainment, a group of Sheffield-based artists who have been working together since 1984 producing new works in theatre and performance as well as projects in digital media, video and installation. Forced Entertainment's active presence in the British performance scene as well as in the international one is unique in a country where such a strong script-based tradition exists, and is given more attention by the press. While alternative companies like Impact and Bloodgroup in England are no longer alive, Forced Entertainment continues to experiment and serve as postmodern provocateurs within their field, and thus have an impact on younger companies like Swansea's Frantic Assembly and Glasgow's Vanishing Point. This conversation begins with Etchells describing how Forced Entertainment has kept its commitment to working outside of non-traditional spaces, and touches on some of the company's working methods over the years.

This interview was conducted via e-mail in September 2001 while the company's project for middle-scale theatre *First Night* was about to open in Rotterdam.

CARIDAD SVICH When you create a piece with the company, do you determine the site for the piece first?

TIM ETCHELLS We don't often have preconceived themes but rather we let themes and ideas emerge from objects, spaces or events that happen in improvisation. So for *First Night* (2001) the first thing we started from was a line of the performers smiling (fixed rigid, game-show host grins) and from these grins came the costumes, and from this visual look we more or less derived the whole piece. Our making strategy is to trust whatever whimsical fascination we might have for certain things – pieces of music, costumes, spatial arrangements and so on – and to trust that structures and content will arise from them.

The process of making tends to be a combination of very 'free' improvisation and exploration next to, or alongside, a lot of talking, analysis and theorisation. We've often likened this to the nice cop/nasty cop of interrogation – that on the one hand we'll be spontaneous, even arbitrary about what happens, what gets used and how and on the other hand we'll be brutally analytic about the content and structures that are made in this way. We tend to reject considerable amounts of material in the process and most rehearsals are videotaped so that we can sit down together later and look at what happened. Tapes are often a source of reference later in the process too, as we check back on the content or mood or structure of sections as they originally appeared. In terms of spaces we tend to think about entering into a dialogue with the kind of expectations they engender. We try to use the resonances – we stage *Quizoola!* (1996), where possible, in cellars or basements because we like both the secret/hidden away quality of these spaces as well as the association with interrogation or incarceration. *First Night* has been made very much with middle-scale theatres in mind, and, as a kind of twisted vaudeville, it enters into a dialogue with the expectation of such traditional 'entertainment' theatres in the UK.

CS Working secretively in 'hidden' places affords you a tremendous amount of freedom. You are free enterprise artists! In basing the company in Sheffield instead of a major city centre like London, for example, did you ever feel, especially when you started, that you were so hidden, you would never be found?

TE I think the best decision we ever made was that we weren't interested in being a successful theatre company. It took us ten years to realise that fully – that the ladder one was meant or expected to climb in the UK at least – was of no interest to us. From that point on we were confident that expansion sideways into installation projects, new media, video and so on, were of more interest to us than trying to forge relations with the mainstream theatre venues or whatever. It's a very liberating moment when you admit that you aren't even tied to particular forms or strategies: that the next thing you do might be a publication, or a twenty-four hour performance or CD ROM or, indeed, a completely text-based performance, that you're tied to ideas, nothing more.

CS You are guided simply by your imagination and where it leads you, and thus you can pursue an idea in whatever shape or form it is best suited outside of labels or categories. Your book *The Dream Dictionary for the Modern Dreamer* (2001) is a playful examination of how it is we dream and take action or inaction on our dreams in contemporary life. Is there ever for you as an artist too much dreaming?

TE I'm interested in the way that our dreams (our imaginations) are shaped and formed by society, culture and landscape. I'm also inter-ested in the way that our dreams (desires) can only be realised through the technologies of culture, which (as literature, as speech, as film, as new media, as object making) always has limits, agendas and problems. All these restrictions, all these edges and boundaries are a key to the way we make and understand our world and things that people make in it. I'm especially suspicious of dreaming when it is linked to technology where the rhetoric about freedom and possi-bility tends to get extremely out of hand. I don't trust the promise of infinite possibilities and I'm politically sceptical about all that supposed 'freedom'. I'm as interested in what technology can't do as in what it can, and I'm attracted to the limits of technology and to using it in simple, economical ways. *Nightwalks* (1998 CD-ROM created in collaboration with Hugo Glendinning) and *Frozen Palaces* (1996 Digital Media) are these sumptuous worlds, navigable landscapes for which we very deliberately choose to exploit just one fairly simple new media form/device (Apple's QTVR panoramas) in what amounts to a minimalism. They're interactive, they're not linear-narrative in form but they are full of edges, decisions, impossibilities and restrictions.

cs The Situationists were dedicated to making of their lives art. It is not a completely foreign concept but in this moment in time, so much of Western culture is dedicated to the individual behaving as a consumer or passenger.

te We've largely made performances for theatres. You can consume these. You buy a ticket. It has a beginning, middle and an end. (As a joke we say it has a beginning, a muddle and an end.) I suppose what we have done very much in this context is try to make work that creates a problem in the act of consumption. We've done that in many different ways: chiefly, in the theatre work proper by making the pieces demanding or reflexive, by creating situations that challenge the public in some way, or where their role or expectations become a large part of the performance. We do this through making open structures, performances that really ask the public to join the dots, to make connections – pieces that demand they run contrary or contradictory scenarios in their heads as the performance unfolds etc. We also tend to employ a performer-presence in the pieces that is what we describe as 'workmanlike', everyday, banal, or best of all human scale. It's something that tries to exist under the rhetorical strategies of theatre (though we've had our interest in these too!). We've been interested to be either more or less than what theatre 'ought' to be. We've also been fond of turning the performances back around to face the audience and to get them to think about what they expect and what lies behind those expectations.

In addition to these ways of making a problem out of theatre we've spun outwards to make projects in lots of other areas/media including performance projects, which become in a certain sense unconsumable. So our durational performances which have lasted anything from six to twenty-four hours and for which the public are free to arrive, depart and return at any point abandon the framework structure and trajectory of beginning, middle and end which the audience are normally meant to experience together in unison in favour of letting people determine their own shape of start(s) and end(s). The twenty-four hour performance *Who Can Sing a Song to Unfrighten Me?* (1999) is something I often think about as a kind of unknowable (and hence unconsumable) object. Even the people who try to see all of it end up falling asleep in the auditorium, letting the show mix with their dreams. I like that . . . that you can't see the performance . . . that it resists that.

The Situationist understanding of the spectacle, which in their description relentlessly appropriates all that it does not yet possess, remains pretty valid. Perhaps what's more doubtful by now is the possibility to even imagine a space or life outside of this process. Perhaps that idea of theirs was always a provocative fantasy rather than an achievable reality. But for us, the chances (in art and in life) seem to lie more in the idea of hollowing out spaces inside the spectacle itself, in its ruins, in its own neglected areas. There's no pure space left. We can regret this. We can be angry about it. But we have to live in the result.

cs How do you keep the element of play alive in the work?

TE We often work with the idea of levels – a baseline of performers-as-performers and above that levels of pretences, assumptions of character or whatever. We like the effect of a kind of slipping between these layers or levels. The rehearsal process is very playful, the performers switching in and out of role, on and off the script, deliberately sabotaging each other, letting fictions occur and then breaking them.

When it comes to creating completed performances we have two strategies. The first is the obsessive 'let's fix everything and recreate the videotape exactly' mode in which we improvise and then recreate the successful sections or moments. The second is a deliberate attempt to leave space for improv. So, in the theatre version of *Speak Bitterness* (1995) only about 70 per cent of the lines are fixed; the rest can be made up or chosen anew in any given live performance. And in something like *Disco Relax* the central performers (Cathy Naden and Sue Marshall) are free to invent new stuff within the parameters we've already established. In these works the improv stuff sits inside a framework that is absolutely fixed and which itself is often drawn from many hours of improv eventually hardened into a script.

cs When making a piece when/how you decide what to embrace technologically?

TE Technology tends to get used as it is kicking around in the studio. Hence a rash of shows with a record player, or a bunch of shows with video. We haven't used anything much more fancy than that in the theatre work because we don't like clever or supposedly sophisticated things. You could say that these days (around here at least!) record players and video stuff are basic aspects of human life. I like that these things are common technologies, which are overwritten with years of everyday use, that they become banal. With the computer stuff we've done, or mixed media installation, once again, there's no particular desire to be at the 'cutting edge' of technological development. Our process – rambling, trial and error, mitigates against using anything too complex. We'd probably spend six months building a complicated technological set/device and then decide after five minutes' work in the rehearsal studio that we didn't like it.

Each space demands its own strategies. But they're all equally places that demand that the self (or whatever) be staged, deployed, constructed, built. At a certain point that was a revelation to me – that writing is a kind of acting. But as soon as my essay work had started to employ fiction . . . and the theatre work had started to employ fact . . . well from then on, the boundaries were very much in question.

A singular vision of hope
Richard Foreman in conversation with Caridad Svich

Richard Foreman is the artistic director of Ontological-Hysteric Theatre in New York City, founded in 1968. Part of a media generation of artists which include Laurie Anderson, Karen Finley and The Wooster Group, Foreman's work as a director of theatre and opera continues to be wholly original and daring, despite the vagaries of time and theatrical trends. This interview was conducted on the telephone on 16 January 2001, as Svich was in Columbus, Ohio on a Thurber House fellowship at Ohio State University and Foreman was preparing to open his new play *Now that Communism is Dead, My Life Feels Empty* in New York.

CARIDAD SVICH Does it surprise you that you are still making theatre?
RICHARD FOREMAN I am ambivalent about it, because for many years I tried to do something else. I am no lover of the theatre. I don't like the theatre very much. I never go to the theatre any more. When I was young, I used to see everything, of course. I can't say I am surprised I am still making it, but on some level I am a little disappointed.

The world is such that I feel very negative about plays, who goes to the theatre, to whom I am really speaking in the audience. I can't complain too much about my audience. I think I have a better audience than most people in the theatre, but it doesn't seem a particularly relevant form to me at this point. I try to make it relevant. And I try to operate in a slightly non-normal theatrical way, but I have great ambivalences about it.

I feel the world, and certainly in this country, but I also think all around the world, the social and political situation is getting more and more oppressive and awful. When I talk about the frustration of making theatre, I feel I am preaching to a converted audience. I don't think any more that I am going to change the world with what I am doing. So, when I try to think of something else to do, I'm trying to think what else could I possibly do which might be a little more effective in changing the world, because I think the world is terrible. I used to feel I was participating in a tradition of Western art that was still relevant, so I would put on rose-coloured glasses and believe 'Oh, I am making theatre for Artaud or Lacan . . . ' I think that tradition is nearing the end of the line. I no longer have much faith that that tradition is going to be sustained in the new world we're moving into, and that makes it more problematic as well.

CS   Yet, there is the possibility of the net, cyberspace . . .

RF   It's the only hope. It may not be a viable hope, but I'm certainly interested. I use a computer. I go online. I think obviously many people go through the process of when they get old the world changes and it doesn't seem to be their world, so they think, 'Things are going to hell.' Now the only hope is something to do with this changing, global, networking brain. I see many problems with it, but it's the only place to look. There's no going back. So, I'm observing. I'm interested. I'm exploring it, not convinced that it may not be an evil force, but maybe something good will grow out of it.

CS   Have you any interest in creating work specifically for the net?

RF   We do have this Ontological website, which was sort of a stab in that direction. When I work, I write a page or so a day and they are disconnected. So, I end up with a huge stack of pages, and then I sort of collage plays out of those pages, which have no indication of who is speaking or what is happening. I have made the last twenty years of all of my notebooks available on my website. There are about 700 pages of raw dialogue. I invite anybody to go in and collage their own plays out of the material, just as I do. So, in a sense, that's an attempt to use the web in a creative way to provoke something or other.

CS   The web if used with imagination and intelligence is a splendid site for creative provocation. I have conceived, curated and participated in three online collaborations with artists that created texts neither one of us would have written alone in the same manner or experienced in quite the same way. The web is a curious, strange, virtual communal place of isolation, intimacy and bravery. Writers wrote in voices they never even knew they had as a result of our collaborations! It was extraordinary and unnerving, but the promise and future promise of the web continues to be there. Would you speak to your collaborations with other artists such as The Wooster Group and the late Kathy Acker?

RF I have always tried to make a theatre that was all mine. I deal with other people, but I think anybody will tell you I control all of the elements much more than any other director they have worked with. I try to exploit the colour and the particular energy of the different performers, but still it is like having different tubes of paint, and I am painting the picture. I'm obsessed with trying to figure out something for myself in my own work.

With The Wooster Group, and Kathy, I was still totally in control of everything. One of the two projects that I did with Kathy Acker's texts was this notorious opera *Birth of the Poet* (1985). And that was pretty interesting, not because of Kathy – who was terribly under-appreciated, and I think still a very important writer – but because of the painter David Salle. He did the scenery. And our agreement was we would do whatever we wanted. It wouldn't be the normal director–designer relationship where you talk about what you're trying to achieve and so forth. So, he gave me elaborate sets for this show, which were so off the wall. Some of which I could never figure out how to use in any relevant way, but others which were still off the wall, but opened up all kinds of vistas I would have never experienced had he not given me these very strange sets. So, that was the most intense and creative experience I have ever had in any kind of collaboration.

I have collaborated a lot. I did a whole series of musicals with composer Stanley Silverman, but in those instances, we each did our own thing. But the experience with David was very exciting. And there was another collaboration I did in the autumn of 2000 at CalArts, which was also exciting. Sophie Haviland, who has been my administrator for many years, and I collaborated on a piece called *Bad Behaviour*. I chose to do this and asked her to do this specifically because I wanted to break out of habits. We had a theme. We both wrote text relevant to this theme, and then we put our texts together, and folded them into each other. In the rehearsal process I would rehearse for three hours, and then she would take over for three hours. It was maddening because each of us would see each other changing things we thought were good. It was maddening but instructive and very liberating. It's not something I would ever want to do again, but it was a radical collaboration in a sense. We attempted to shake each other up.

cs Has your process changed very much over the years?

RF I think like any serious artist I am mining the same vein. I think that's
    what all artists do, with the possible exception of Picasso. One is hard
    pressed to think of an artist who does not essentially make a discovery
    and then explores all the implications of that discovery for the next
    thirty years of his creative life. When I make art, it is to feed me, to
    give me air. As the years go by, it gets worse, because there are too
    many options I have already taken and maybe I don't want to take
    those options. I'm older and slower. I used to pride myself on the fact
    that I could see five or six things going on at the same time, and keep
    control of all of them on stage. Now, it's down to three or two. It takes
    me longer.

cs What do you tell young artists?

RF The only advice is courage. And I can't imagine how people could do
    what I have done because the situation is so difficult. It's easy to say
    'Courage. Do what you want to do. Be true to your own vision.' But
    so many things are going to make it difficult for you to do that. We
    are living in a lousy society in so many ways. Yet, the people that are
    going to do that will do it and I think they have a fair chance at suc-
    ceeding. I'm always amazed. For people who stick at it long enough,
    somehow it happens for them, it seems to me.

A synesthetic response

Peter Gabriel in conversation with Michael Cerveris

Peter Gabriel has earned a worldwide reputation for his work in music and video.
He co-founded the band Genesis, which he left in 1975, and he has released
eleven solo albums. In 1993, he established Real World Multimedia to develop,
produce and publish innovative CD-ROMs and to push new technology to its
limits. *Zulu Time*, a 'techno-cabaret' theatrical piece was initially created in 1999
by director Robert LePage and his ensemble Ex Machina in collaboration with
Gabriel and his production company Real World. As one of the most influential
popular musicians of his generation, Gabriel's perspective on how an artist listens
to work, and makes new material allows us to witness in practical terms how an
artist can be at the nexus point of creative intersection, and how the divisions
between high and low culture, pop and classical music have become less significant than in previous centuries, and changed the way not only an artist but also an
audience listens to new music.

This interview was initially conducted on the telephone in November 1996, as
Cerveris was in New York, and Gabriel was in London in midst of various projects.
It reflects Gabriel's ongoing interest in artistic hybridity.

MICHAEL CERVERIS In the late nineteenth century, there was much more fluidity among the different styles of music than there was in most of the twentieth century, especially in the US. It wasn't until the emergence of a rather monied class, like the Rockefellers and the Mellons and so on, that this sort of elite culture developed. It was a cultural construct that had nothing to do with the music. But the question persists: is there a hierarchy in terms of artistic expression or is it just good or bad?

PETER GABRIEL There is some hierarchy . . . between musicians, I mean. It's in the classical musician's training to get to the top of his field as a dedication of practice to the instrument. Now, a rock musician would probably have put in the same number of hours, but not necessarily on the instrument. Maybe in record making. Maybe in all the stuff around it. The perception always used to be that the rock musician was the sort of lazy alternative. But most of the people I know who have done well in their field work extremely hard. There's a distinction in that most classical performers are interpreting other people's work. Most rock performers are composers, so they may have skills in writing and other areas, though not necessarily in technique.

MC In earlier periods in the classical tradition, the composers were the performers, too. Later, there did come a long period in which a high level of technical skill separated the performer from the composer. I think this is breaking down a bit. I could point to a performance of pianist Chick Corea. He played the Mozart A major Concerto with Bobby McFerrin conducting. I suppose there would be some who would not make favourable comparisons to other artists in terms of proficiency or adherence to style, but the performance had another kind of energy that seems to me to overcome that possible criticism. The performance went beyond that proficiency element.

PG It's an interesting phenomenon. Consider the film *Shine* (1996) and David Helfgott's own performance, which is being badly reviewed. But he's obviously really touching people and I think the film is obviously an emotional film where you see a man, the soul of a man, struggle to express himself against all odds. However much of that is truth or fiction, I think people very much want to subscribe to that as an idea. And I think if they see a committed performance from Helfgott, and if he's really engaged in the present, and I think he is, then the ritual is complete without necessarily requiring the technical skills that the best performers may bring to that.

MC It brings to the fore the question, what is the essence of a performer?

PG Surely it's partly to get the listener in touch with themselves, from their own soul, and perhaps through that story of the film, he's better able to do that.

MC If we do accept the fact that there is a shift in perception, however, do you have any opinion about what would be the root cause: is it economic, artistic?

PG It lies to some degree on a range of distinctions and boundaries and differences. Part of the whole counter-culture of the 1960s questioned those divisions and said: which of these actually do have meaning and are worth something, and which are just irrelevant abstractions? That process has happened in all parts of Western society and is beginning to happen in the arts as well. Particularly since the 1960s, it has happened in the arts. People have opened their ears a little more and tried to trust what they hear and more importantly what they feel; more than what they feel they should hear and feel. If you have openness, you try to allow people in, with whatever strength and weaknesses they may have. I think it was Duke Ellington who said something like, 'There's just good music and bad music.' And I think that's quite right. In a sense there was a perception that the rock musicians were just a sort of teenage rebellion for profit and that there were the pure artists on the classical side. I think all those barriers have been eroded.

MC Do you feel this enters in as a factor in your work?

PG I've done little bits of things with Nigel Kennedy, for instance, who's a string player. But it's more than just working with string players. We have in the World Music arena a lot more crossovers. For the last twenty years now, we have been trying to consciously make different things happen between musicians from different backgrounds and cultures.

MC You're dealing with media and visual images in your work to a greater degree than other artists are in your field. What contributed to your interest in media?

PG I don't know if it's a little dyslexic or something, but I've always responded well to visual information and I had a choice between music or film school. In a way, I have tried to ride a path between the two a little bit. In some ways, video and multimedia are natural extensions of the work that I do. Some people just listen to music and have pure, unadulterated thoughts, or perhaps let their minds create the pictures, which is fine. I choose that for myself very often. But I love the mixture, the 'synesthesia' between the visual and the musical, and so, when it works really well, as it does in the hands of a great film director, that is something to aspire to. It's also something that turns me on personally, so I try to work with it as a musician.

MC Do you become involved in the technical part in terms of the actual manipulation?

PG More in the conception and a little bit in the manipulation. That is one of the great empowering things about the computer. Around the set is the stuff that used to be very much the province of experts but is now open to lay people. That's another general trend that is having an impact on what you're talking about.

MC Taking the pressure off the skill factor through the use of applied technology has suddenly opened up a lot more possibilities. Maybe we won't have to slave in the studio for hours and hours practising skills.

PG I was looking at an instrument today, which has some hexagonal honeycomb layout about it, but it is an interface for a keyboard, and it means that you could hit sort of three hexagons, and you get a major chord, and you get a sort of triangle pointing to the right. And if you get a triangle pointing to the left, you get a minor chord. And if you go up vertically, you get fifths, and if you go up diagonally you get augmented. But it's just a different way of thinking about composition and chords, and I think it will be a great aid. With a lot of technology, there's so much empowerment to do artistic things. Seventy to 90 per cent of it can be done inexpensively on a computer now. Then you just pay a lot of money to do the last 15 to 5 per cent of it. Soon you will get artists using multimedia language that is well developed, which will involve music, visual image and subtext and highlights from their life which hit their heart button and get recorded.

MC If you were to do something like that, would you give consideration to the audience you were targetting?

PG You have some people who are in the more ivory tower department and know that their experiments aren't going to reach a larger audience. There are others who, while they may be interested in experimentation, act in accordance to their own taste, which is in tune with where popular culture is, and where it is heading. Then there are those who just chase the goddess of popular culture and big income and success. I am probably in the second category. But I find I don't think too much about how other people will see my stuff when I write things. When I go out and perform them I am reminded of that very swiftly.

MC In terms of the classical artist, there are so many struggling to stay alive, to exist. When that type of artist makes a stretch, do they run the risk of losing a livelihood altogether and, in fact, have no context for their work?

PG They could lose a great deal.

MC They could be accused of debasing something noble. One thinks of the 'three tenors' phenomenon. Well, maybe that's not the best analogy, but there's commercialism to that.

PG But I think that's still beneficial to music as a whole because they are introducing a lot of people to opera who would never even consider wanting to hear any opera.

MC When an artist has international stature like that, that is one way they can really communicate to a larger audience. I have been talking to some people in the classical music record business and they speak about the demise of classical music altogether and the death of orchestras. Classical records are not selling, so record companies are resorting to all kinds of gimmicks to try to bring audiences in. Perhaps that can backfire.

PG I think it's a lot like love. If you chase the person you want, they will almost inevitably run away.

A natural force
John Jesurun in conversation with Caridad Svich

Since 1982 John Jesurun has written, directed and designed over twenty works including multimedia pieces *Deep Sleep*, which won an Obie in 1986, *White Water* (1986), *Everything That Rises Must Converge* (1990), as well as fifty-two episodes of his serial play *Chang in a Void Moon* (1982–97). He has received the National Endowment for the Arts, Rockefeller and MacArthur fellowships. Jesurun's innovative work in the use of film, video and live performance distinguish him as an artist who has always sought to explore powerful ways of expression in order to tell a story, specifically to an audience who grew up with television and film as its primary source of visual communication. Investigating the role of the mediated body in the age when the rise of the associative, non-linear, visual text would alter ways of seeing and comprehending information for the MTV and post-MTV generation, Jesurun is a true pioneer in his field. As an artist of Latino origin, he has also within his own cultural community made inroads to create an alternative model of Latino expression, one that runs counter to both the boulevard comedy tradition favoured by many US theatres devoted to presenting the works of Latino artists, and the 'crisis of identity' plays written by more conventional US Latino dramatists.

This interview was conducted via e-mail from May to June 2001.

CARIDAD SVICH You trained as a sculptor, and then studied film as well. What drew you to theatre and performance?

JOHN JESURUN I was drawn to theatre/performance because it was one approach that could contain all the aesthetic ideas that interested me simultaneously. My dimensional search went through painting, sculpture, film and video in rapid succession. Each of these disciplines dealt with time and space in a different way. My urge was to put all these forms of perception together. What triggered the jump was practicality. Having made short films for a few years I was frustrated at the financial restraints it imposed. I had all the elements except the film and camera, so I decided to make a film without filming it. The audience would be the camera and the film. I wasn't interested in theatre or theatricality – just a space to make a presentation which could include all these things happening live in real time. It's the difference between 'I saw it' and 'I was there.' The most mysterious attraction to this conglomeration of elements was the use of spoken language.

cs The Kitchen in New York has been a strong artistic home for you. How essential has its support been for you in your continuing development as an artist?

jj From 1986 to 1997 I did four major pieces there as well as seven episodes of *Chang in a Void Moon*. The Kitchen co-produced *White Water* and *Everything That Rises Must Converge*. This was a very important time in my development and the Kitchen really came through with financial and moral support. I was lucky to be at the Kitchen while Bobbi Tsumigari and Scott Macaulay were working there. The atmosphere they helped create was particularly helpful to many others and me. They were genuinely interested in the work they brought there and there was a mutual respect between artists and management. Since then the Kitchen has been through various administrations, and artistic continuity has not been encouraged in the same way. I have to say that La Mama has been just as if not more of an artistic home for me in NY. I did my first three plays there in 1984. La Mama has always been open to me for any project I want to do regardless of its form. As a result I was encouraged to do some of my most risky pieces there with no interference in the form or content. This is rare these days.

cs Rare indeed because of the way funding operates, and the way the political climate has shifted since Ronald Reagan's presidency. These days interference is almost to be expected, even if it is subterranean, and content, while not monitored in terms of censorship necessarily, is still questioned, especially since the infamous 'NEA Four' case and the Mapplethorpe scandal in Cincinnati. The US has changed as any country in evolution does, but the climate is tougher for artists experimenting with form. There are fewer venues available for presentation, and subsequently less funding domestically. Do you feel connected and/or sustained by a theatre/performance community here in the US?

jj Since most of my real support comes from outside the United States I feel part of a larger artistic community which includes the US. There has been a lot more international movement of artists in the last fifteen years. Interest and financial support from other countries is only part of the story. Now artists are more willing to travel, explore and develop projects with each other independent of institutional involvement. There is much more of a worldview in the community now. Artists feel less tied to their country, culture and language.

cs And this is true partly because technology especially in the field of communication has made access through the internet, for instance, more possible than before. Collaborations can spring up more readily now between artists in different countries. Would you speak as to what the collaborative process offers you as an artist?

JJ I don't collaborate a lot but collaborating with artists such as Christian Marclay, Molissa Fenley, Mikel Rouse, Martin Acosta and Neil Greenberg has been very rewarding. These are artists that have such a high degree of conviction in their own work that there was never a question as to how we would collaborate. These were situations in which everyone was confident about what they were doing and why they were doing it. I found the sharing of aesthetic space an exciting process. For me it's usually a calming experience in which I can look at my work from another point of view. It's a willingness to let something completely different happen to your work so it's a liberating element rather than a restraint. It's also a chance to contemplate someone else's work at a close range. It expands your understanding of their work and sheds light on your own. You learn something different from every artist you work with.

cs Although you were born in Michigan, your parents are from Puerto Rico. You also grew up rather nomadically. How have you negotiated your relationship to bilingualism and/or biculturalism as an artist?

JJ I became accustomed to travelling at a young age and so it is a natural thing for me to move around so much. Early on I got a sense of the world as a constantly moving, changing place where everything is happening simultaneously. It became a practical fact for me that for the world to work organically, a certain amount of people have to be moving at any given moment. I feel lucky to be one of the moving pieces. I do consider New York my home but for me it's sometimes necessary to have multiple homes. It's not realistic for me to live in New York all the time. To be able to live there I have to give up living there a certain amount of time each year. And I do like the sense of motion. It also gives me a greater appreciation for stillness. All this movement in my early life has affected my work. These ideas of motion and change can be found everywhere in my work from the structure to the content to the writing.

I grew up speaking Spanish in the house but we were usually in a place where no one else spoke it so that's where it stayed till later. So it was a separate experience as was the food we ate and where our relatives came from. And it does become part of your personal identity. It reminds you that you have a personal identity at all. Growing up as an army brat it didn't seem to be an issue; there were so many mixtures all around you. You were one of many, you were part of it and it was part of you. And it was fun going from one reality to the other: having the choice.

As a child, being bilingual gave me an insight into language and all the wonderful things you can do with it. It also gave me a second reality in which to experience the world. Language wasn't just a way to communicate; it was an idea and a fluid process. With two languages you could apply the rules of one to the other with amazing results. You could play with structures, sounds, rhythm and multi-layered meanings. I began to think of speaking itself as an experience. I wondered then if people speaking Spanish enjoyed themselves much more while they were speaking than those who spoke English. If that was so, were they communicating on a higher and more intimate level? Being bilingual/bicultural constantly brought questions like these to my mind. In any case my writing was deeply influenced by the mixture of emotional, philosophical, conceptual and social questions that my situation served up. All this began to develop in a very natural way long before I became an artist. Also it gave me an opportunity to work in Spanish in Spain and Mexico. My work has been performed more in Spanish than in English. Also, speaking of 'home' – I probably feel most at home when I hear my work in Spanish even if I'm thousands of miles away.

CS *White Water* was such a groundbreaking piece. Its exploration/critique of the media landscape was incredibly sophisticated and yet it also spoke to something very ancient, an almost impossible yearning, longing …

JJ It's true that in *White Water* as well as other works there is a primal element that connects with the technology used. There is a fear that technology destroys spirituality but I actually see it as a symptom of spirituality and the search for it. It's the result of a very long line of irresistible human attempts to bring the inside to the outside, break free from physicality without having to pay the penalty of death. I include it as a natural element. Because film and video can be manipulated and manipulate at the same time I have to treat them with some respect. Film and video have their own physical presence beyond the visual images they may represent. There is tension there between a live and mediated performer but this is also natural. I want that tension to also exist in a real way in the presentation. When live and mediated images communicate verbally a third reality comes into place as a result. I don't wish to theatricalise or shortcut the mediated atmosphere for the purposes of making the show easier to watch. In these pieces the aim among other things is to put into place an actual situation with its inherent live, not imitated tension. Sometimes images on the screen are better left alone to say what they will in their own way. Because film and video by their nature tend to be very demanding, they are subject to common-sense decisions like every other element in the piece. In particularly difficult technical situations there is definitely a tension between the humans and the machinery that always begins to lay bare something deeper. It's a kind of inarticulateness that reveals intangible things through its clumsiness: the 'longing' you identified in *White Water*. This struggle is always part of the process. It's one of the necessary elements of the work.

cs   Do you think the climate for experimentation is better or worse these days? And how do you stay committed to your fiercely interdisciplinary logic?

jj   The climate for experimentation has not been great for a while now. It doesn't seem to be the time for it. The prevailing taste doesn't see any logic in it. The last ten years have been a time of retrenchment. I see a pattern of conformity here as well as abroad. Experimentation is generally not encouraged or seen as a worthwhile pursuit. Presenters and producers of high and low art have gone for the middle of the road to fill seats and have been very successful at it. I think they were correct in reading their audiences as well as their artists. People want to see the conventional things that people are making. They want to be part of something they recognise. It's not my taste but at least people are going to theatres. It's a necessary part of the cycle. It's changing, and artists and audiences are beginning to challenge each other again. Television, music and science have been much more innovative and experimental but it's the time for that. Theatre will have to be dragged kicking and screaming into the twenty-first century.

   As far as staying focused on my way of working, I have never seen it as interdisciplinary. I was shocked early on when it was described that way although it is a way to help describe it. I don't really see the boundaries between one and the other. It seems natural to me that they should work together. They seem to be part of one another. Creatively they are all interconnected.

Between technology and emotion

Mikel Rouse in conversation with Caridad Svich

Mikel Rouse moved to New York City in 1979, where he formed his contemporary chamber ensemble Mikel Rouse Broken Consort. His opera *Failing Kansas* premiered at The Kitchen in New York in 1995, as did his second opera *Dennis Cleveland* (1996), which has set and video design by John Jesurun. His work has been seen at BAM, Lincoln Center, and international venues devoted to the presentation of new music theatre, opera and interdisciplinary forms. Rouse's work as a composer, performer, filmmaker and musician are distinguished in the crowded and competitive field of new music by its sense of ambition and risk as well as its singular vision. This conversation offers a glimpse into the workings of one of the most engaging, and complex musical minds in contemporary performance.

This interview was conducted via e-mail in November 2000, while Rouse was on tour with *Dennis Cleveland*, his talk-show format opera.

CARIDAD SVICH Where does the process of creating an opera begin for you?

MIKEL ROUSE I'm interested in combining all the possible elements into a unique whole. It doesn't have to make common sense but it does have to make sense. Much like a well-crafted piece of music has its own reality, I try to bring that same sense of neutral reality with all aspects of the production. It's also important for me that it is of this generation. So, there's the rub: how do you make it currently believable while still holding historical interest (in my case, a kind of non-narrative presentation). Well, it starts first and foremost with the music but I suppose I'm lucky that I've always been interested in the craft of lyric writing as well. This offers an advantage in that I'm never trying to set some unwieldy text by a writer who may very well be a good novelist but doesn't know beans about meter or lyric phrasing. And this wedding between music and words is at the core of why the thing will ultimately work. On top of that, you've got all that technology at your disposal and a thirty to fifty-year history of how it has been used (both commercially and conceptually) and you can reference those uses but it's not very interesting unless you come up with ways to make them your own. I use the example of *Dennis Cleveland* in discussions of this sort because while it draws from historical sources of non-narrative music, theatre and opera; it raises the bar for a new generation that has come to understand connecting the dots in a new way. The setting of the TV talk show, with its inherent thrust into the audience, composes a piece characterised by unrelated images and sounds at the same time placing the audience in what appears to be a familiar setting. This allows memory and expectation to merge, thereby updating the model.

CS *Dennis Cleveland's* use of the talk-shot format is radical for opera. The talk show has become the most ubiquitous form of popular performance art in US culture and while it is always ripe for parody, you manage to show us the form from the inside out formally and musically in your piece.

MR The musical and lyric structure of *Dennis Cleveland* is pretty complex, but I use the built-in non-narrative approach inherent in talk shows to full advantage. This format allows me to link disparate texts and combine them with various rhythmic permutations that transform the meaning of the words through the musical structure. The talk-show staging also helped provide a solution to performance presentation that I felt was outmoded: the opera/music-theatre spectacle of performers bursting into song. Since so many of the talk shows were venturing into what could only be called 'performance art', there was now a new possibility of introducing structured elements into the mix, but in a way that seemed real or believable to an audience. Is it a radically new way to stage opera or music theatre or is it an incredibly surreal talk show?

CS *Dennis Cleveland* is part of a trilogy of pieces that explore different kinds of media presentation, and how lyrics can be set to music. The pieces also touch to greater and lesser thematic degrees on aspects of the American psyche. What was the genesis of your trilogy *Failing Kansas*, *Dennis Cleveland* and *The End of Cinematics?*

MR The complete trilogy, especially with regard to structure and stage concept, was conceived in 1988. I knew I wanted to explore this vocal writing technique I called Counterpoetry (put simply: unpitched voices in strict metric counterpoint). The vocal idea first came to me in trying to set court transcripts from the Holcomb murder case, the same case that inspired Truman Capote's true crime novel *In Cold Blood* (1966). I'd done a number of sketches (what would become the 1994 CD *Living Inside Design* and a 1994 chamber work for strings, percussion and voices, *Autorequiem*), and wanted to expand the possibilities by doing larger scale works and adding live performers to the equation.

In addition, I'd been working with video artist Cliff Baldwin on a number of music/film/video projects and wanted to expand the idea of a music generated film/performance. After we decided on cutting a 75-minute film to the structure of the music composition, I started thinking about the film aspect of staging a live performance that would be presented as a film (the potential staging for *The End of Cinematics*, which premieres in 2002). Now we're up to about 1993 or 1994 and the vocal and staging ideas are pretty straightforward. It wasn't until after the 1995 premiere of *Failing Kansas* that I came up with the expanded talk-show presentation. I'd been working on sketches for *Cinematics* and *Dennis Cleveland* for a year or two. I thought *Cinematics* would probably follow *Failing Kansas* until the staging idea (live talk-show format with cameras capturing both performers and audience and displaying those images as part of the multimedia environment) for *Cleveland* hit me and I went full steam ahead with that instead.

CS   Your constant experimentation with form and with instrumentation led you to write *Quorum* in 1984, the first piece of its kind written for sequencer. How did it come to be?

MR   I wanted to explore this new (and at the time very crude) technology in a way that the pop market was not even thinking about. I knew it was an historic piece, but no one would touch it (remember, this was a good ten to twelve years before techno). Judith Jamison had got wind of it and used it for a piece with the Houston Ballet. From her, Ulysses Dove asked to use it (something, I'm told, that never happens among choreographers) and created *Vespers*. I was knocked out by the combination of structure and emotion, something I was working towards which also signalled a departure from the previous genera-tion. I think Philip Glass made the distinction between inventing language and packaging language. Pop culture always gets hold of the machines first but I've never been intimidated by this. My concerns are usually so different that there aren't any conflicts.

CS   The climate for arts funding in the US has certainly become more and more erratic in its energy and focus.

MR   I have never been a fan of grant-driven art. I have produced every work of mine so far with my credit cards; and then slowly I have paid them off. I've been building my own media studio and am proficient in all aspects of recording music, shooting, editing and posting video, etc. I think the bar has been raised and the old models won't work any more. You have to be self sufficient, especially regarding knowing how to perform all aspects of the work technically. Of course, one gets dis-couraged or lonely but no one put a gun to my head to do this. Was it Jasper Johns that said the only reason to do this is that you simply have no other choice? I certainly wouldn't consider what I've pursued as a 'career choice'.

CS   If anything, it's a life choice. How do you see yourself further mixing media?

MR I've really liked the collaboration process, but I've been looking
forward to returning to film and other media outlets that weren't
heretofore affordable. I've been producing my own records in my
studio for about ten years and now I've recently developed a full
media studio. I just finished the feature film *Funding* (2001), which is
a stand-alone film but includes a modular element for live actors and
chamber musicians. I'm interested in incorporating all these elements
together around a solid structure, in my case a musical one. At the end
of the day, I think these theatrical presentations have worked so well
because of the underlying music structure. Yes, the staging ideas are
good and novel, but it's the underlying structure that prevents the
ideas from devolving into parody or worse. The structure takes a good
idea and lets it live.

CS The combination of structure and emotion, which you've been
working towards, is something that speaks to so much of what is
happening now in the arts in reaction against work that is purely
ironic, or more appropriately, cool and clever.

MR I just know it is a conscious effort to bypass those tried and true sign-
posts of 'progressive' work. It's like anything else: life is ironic
enough, that will come through anyway.

Weaving the 'live' and mediated
Marianne Weems in conversation with Caridad Svich

Marianne Weems is artistic director of The Builders Association, an ensemble that
creates large-scale theatre projects exploring the interface between live performance
and media. Since 1994, the company which includes Jeff Webster, performer;
Dan Dobson, sound designer; Jennifer Tipton, lighting designer; Chris Kondek and
Peter Norrman, video designers; and John Cleater architect/set designer, has collaborated on seven large-scale theatre projects, including *Xtravaganza* (2002), *Jet
Lag* (1998) and *Jump Cut (Faust)* (1998). Weems has also worked as an assistant
director and/or dramaturg with Susan Sontag, Richard Foreman, The Wooster
Group and others.

This interview was conducted via e-mail from March to June 2001.

CARIDAD SVICH When and how did you become interested in cross-
media performance?

MARIANNE WEEMS In the 1980s I worked with Art Matters, an arts foundation which funded a lot of 'cutting edge' work, and so for seven or

eight years I had the opportunity so see a great deal of what was happening in performance and the visual arts in New York. At that time, there was an emerging aesthetic which drew from Nam June Paik and Laurie Anderson, but took media into higher and lower places, often using more critical or political content, and staging the work in smaller galleries where more flexible experiments could be enacted. I was influenced by the early video installations of Judith Barry, Gretchen Bender, Graham Weinbren, the visual art of Jenny Holzer, Peter Nagy, Barbara Kruger, and the combinations in performance of Robert Ashley, Robert Whitman, Richard Foreman and The Wooster Group, among others.

The Wooster Group's *LSD . . . Just The High Points* (1984) was a watershed for cross-media work. The actual media in the performance was pretty low tech, but the aesthetic was built on a sophisticated electronic sensibility, for example, 'rewinding' and 'fast forwarding' through enormous sections of text, or staging some performers on monitors, and some live. The thing that distinguished this work from performance art's mandatory-television-on-stage aesthetic was that the inclusion of the technology was pragmatic, content-driven. For instance, it was necessary to put Michael Kirby on tape because he couldn't be at the show that night, and it was necessary to rewrite, speed through, and 'blur' the text because the Group had been threatened by a lawsuit from Arthur Miller (for their adaptation of his 1953 play *The Crucible*).

I went to work with the Group as a dramaturg and assistant director in 1987 and among other things I worked with director Elizabeth LeCompte on developing a set of guidelines for the inclusion of video in live performance.[1] These experiences, along with projects I undertook with Ron Vawter, Susan Sontag and many others, sparked me to begin my own company, The Builders Association, in 1994 with a group of collaborators and friends. While we draw on some of the orthodoxies of earlier experimental theatre, this company is emerging at a time when our culture has been saturated by the presence of digital information, and our work centres around the growing issues of dealing with this in a 'live' format. Our projects explore the interface between media and live performance in a culture, which is irrevocably mediatised, not a culture that still privileges 'liveness'.

cs Would you speak about the creation of your piece *Jet Lag* and collaborating with Diller + Scofidio, and how that process was different

---

1 Marianne Weems, 'Brace Up! Notes on Form', *Felix, A Journal of Media Arts and Communication*, 1, No. 4 (Autumn 1993).

than the creation of your collaboration with John Jesurun in *Jump Cut (Faust)*?

MW In 1996 The Builders Association was commissioned by the Theatre Neumarkt in Zurich to create a performance; we settled on Goethe's *Faust* (1808 and 1832) as a central text, something the Swiss producers encouraged us to undertake because of its canonical status in Germany and Switzerland.

We commissioned the American playwright and director John Jesurun to write a contemporary version of Faust; this decision was based largely on his adaptation of another classical play, *Philoktetes*, an idiosyncratic and brilliant piece that he wrote for Ron Vawter in 1992. Jesurun wrote the text with the understanding that I planned to weave it through several other versions of Faust, including selections from Goethe's *Faust* (Part One); the transcripts of the trial of Susanna Margaretha Brandt (1772); eighteenth-century German and English puppet shows of Faust; Mountford's English farce (1652), Marlowe's *Faust* (1588) and the film versions of F.W. Murnau (1921) and Gustave Grundgens (1963). By the way, the actress who originally played Gretchen in the Grundgens film reprised the role of Gretchen in our production.

The performance space included references to the Elizabethan stages where Faust was first performed, the lower stage housed the mechanics for producing stage effects and the gallery was where the effects would be revealed. In our version, the lower stage was surrounded by a track for moving cameras, and there were additional cameras planted throughout the set, so that each scene was set up both for the theatrical space below, and for the cinematic space above – the screens where the stage effects were revealed. The production resulted in a 'live film' of Faust in which the mechanics of the transformative aspects of media were revealed.

The video designers Chris Kondek and Ben Rubin, the sound designer Dan Dobson and the set designer/architect John Cleater created the substantial frame of the piece. Jesurun's text contributed a significant contemporary rereading of the original story, however text functions as just one level in these productions. There are other equally important threads of visual and audio information, which impact and propel the narrative.

It was during this period that we discovered that our interest in combining live presence with technology was shared by the architects and media artists Diller + Scofidio, who invited us to collaborate on *Jet Lag*. *Jet Lag* is based on two actual personalities in recent history. Paul Virilio, in his book *The Third Window* (1988), speaks of an American heroine Sarah Krassnoff, renamed Doris Akerman by playwright Jessica Chalmers, who kidnapped her 14-year-old grandson and travelled with him from New York to Amsterdam, then Amsterdam to New York, back and forth 167 times consecutively over a period of six months, all in an attempt to elude the boy's father. After six months of continuous air travel, the grandmother finally died of jet lag. Virilio calls her a 'contemporary heroine who lived in deferred time'.

The second true story is based on Donald Crowhurst who joined the 1969 Round The World sailing competition which was sponsored by the London *Sunday Times*. Driven by the guaranteed publicity of the event, Crowhurst attempted the difficult voyage without adequate preparation. Encountering severe difficulty, he aborted the race during the first leg. However, rather than returning home, Crowhurst sailed in circles off the coast of South America, producing a counterfeit log and sending home regular reports documenting a (fake) ten-month voyage around the world. The BBC had provided Crowhurst with a film camera and tape deck to record his journey, and these tapes became a key part of our research – in them you see him rehearsing and recording reports on his fictitious journey, and working to create and sustain the identity of a successful sailor. While circling at sea, Crowhurst also kept a haunting diary charting his real state of mental deterioration and increasingly delusional episodes. While in the apparent lead of the race, Crowhurst threw himself off his boat, and presumably drowned.

These two stories clearly touch on many contemporary cultural conditions; most notably, Crowhurst was an early example of the fabrication of a self-image created specifically for, and by, the media. Also both of these true stories feature the critical role which technology played – these two people's lives were enmeshed and changed by complications of time and space brought on by contemporary technologies.

We worked for almost a year with various collaborators, including playwright Jessica Chalmers, on shaping the stories and the concepts behind the piece. Then we did two video shoots, one at the Brussels International Airport and one on a sailboat off the North Fork of Long Island, and went into rehearsal. The only real-time technology used in the show is live editing between prerecorded and live video material, which was ingenuously constructed by Chris Kondek and Peter Norrman, with additional computer graphics by James Gibbs, and the sound score created by Dan Dobson. *Jet Lag*'s use of technology is actually quite modest, for instance, Jeff Webster, as the sailor, performs the entire 40-minute piece to one camera (recording his logs or rehearsing and recording, rewinding, and rerecording footage for the media), and talking through lags and delay effects on his microphone to the other performers, whom he never sees. He is isolated and framed by these simple devices that structure his 'life at sea' onstage. The largest frame around the piece is the obvious presence of the technicians working to create the spectacle. Through this weave of live and mediated material technology became both the content and the form of the project.

On and off we toured *Jet Lag* for almost two years, passing through innumerable airports. Each trip became increasingly surreal as we suffered from the kinds of pathologies which arise from constant travel (sleep deprivation, aural hallucinations, the compression of time and space, the erasure of a sense of 'journey', etc.). We also drew extensively from the actual space of the airport – the announcements and ambient sounds, the transport devices, the way bodies adapt to waiting areas and aeroplane cabins, the small details in architecture, maintenance and cuisine which are intended to distinguish one airport from another – these all bled into the project. So our experience of performing the piece deepened as our exposure to 'jet lag' went on.

The chaotic context of globalism informs all of our work, and I personally thrive on this multi-location. Of course our status as artists from the first world protects us from many of the material dilemmas of contemporary life. Our next project, *Allahdeen*, is a collaboration with Moti Roti, a group of London-based South Asian artists and will look, I hope, at how cultural differences are both blurred and enforced in global culture. Both companies approach this project with a desire to rethink conventional 'multicultural' collaborations, and the basic terminology that has grown up around them. Rather than expressing India, Britain and America as monocultures, we will draw from our lived experiences as citizens of the hybridised urban landscapes of New York, London and Mumbai. The interaction of ethnicity and cultures within these sprawling metropolises blurs the line between identities, and reflects how cultures borrow, steal and reinterpret each other's signs and stories. In *Allahdeen*, the ongoing exchange between Hollywood and Bollywood, the various historical cultural interpretations, and the overlays of translators' voices all contribute to make this legend a model for contemporary, global/cultural interaction. Over a period of centuries, these narratives were elaborated and transmitted though oral traditions that followed historical trade routes. *Allahdeen* will attempt to retrace the ancient Silk Route using contemporary technologies to retell this archetypal 'rags-to-riches' story.

CS   There is a hunger for the past, for old genres, especially American ones in a lot of new work. I think of the fascination with burlesque, vaudeville, etc., which speaks to trying to understand where the US performative tradition comes from.

MW Our latest project, *Xtravaganza*, speaks entirely to these issues. This piece was created somewhat as a reaction to *Jet Lag*, and to the fact that many European critics called it 'the future of theatre', which displays a kind of cultural amnesia about theatre's past which I wanted to explore.

Xtravaganza looks back at theatrical forms that preceded much of what is now called multimedia performance. Extravaganzas of the mid-nineteenth and early-twentieth centuries were large-scale presentations which mixed live performance, music, dance and, later, film, in a variety show which was based on the visually spectacular nature of each 'act'. So multimedia is not something which emerged in the experiments of the 1960s or even with the advent of the television, but with the epic pageants staged by Steele MacKaye, the technical wizardry of 'The Electricity Fairy' Loie Fuller, the lavish stage-scapes of Florenz Ziegfeld, and the spectacularisation of the camera which accompanied Busby Berkeley's move from stage to screen. By the way, dramaturg Norman Frisch was instrumental in helping the company put this material together.

Coincidentally, three of these theatrical pioneers had their beginnings with William F. Cody, or 'Buffalo Bill', as he was popularly known. Buffalo Bill's Wild West Shows were the original American extravaganzas – outdoor spectacles featuring hundreds of 'authentic' Indians and cowboys, as well as horses, cattle and buffalo. Buffalo Bill's company travelled to Europe and extensively across America, restaging historic events with the actual creators of those events (including his star attraction, Chief Sitting Bull). Steele MacKaye staged the first of Buffalo Bill's shows in an indoor arena – New York's Madison Square Garden – while Florenz Ziegfeld and Loie Fuller both appeared in the Wild West Show during their youth. Forty years later, Ziegfeld would train Busby Berkeley to carry on in this spectacular tradition, collaborating together on the film *Whoopee* (1930), a musical fantasia based on life in the American West (complete with iconic showgirls in Indian headdresses!). *Xtravaganza* also borrows from contemporary VJ and DJ styles, using club idiom as the latest manifestation of multimedia entertainment. *Xtravaganza* moves from analogue to digital in the course of the piece, as acts are introduced acoustically and remixed electronically.

From 1900 to 1915, early performance technologies were significantly developed, both on the stage, and through the brief competition waged between cinema and theatre. The emergence of film, then television, and its indubitable status as the dominant means of cultural expression have of course eclipsed the status of theatre, but the stage remains an ideal laboratory to pursue this investigation of what live performance currently means in a digital age. At the same time, while we are attempting to reanimate theatre for a contemporary audience, we are simply using current tools to interpret old forms. *Xtravaganza* embraces that very issue of past forms … However, we are not technophiles, and the demonstration of technologies is not the point of the work. Our use of technology is always dictated by the content of the material we are exploring. Given these parameters, we will continue to articulate our aesthetic utilising technological tools.

You could propose a genealogy in which Schechner's generation of experimental theatre was created in opposition to mass media, The Wooster Group as a kind of transitional model where media is incorporated on stage but the live performer is still the centre of attention, and The Builders Association (among others) is emerging as a fully-mediatised theatre where the media is the real protagonist of these productions, and mass media is the acknowledged and unavoidable context in which this work is created. In the rehearsal process we sort through material using the shorthand performance, video and sound styles we have developed. Sketching and resketching through the pieces, we refine the content and the visual and sonic language of the performances. 'Cut it' is the phrase most often heard in our rehearsal process – what survives rises to the top.

Inside and outside of the academy
Maury Yeston in conversation with Michael Cerveris

Maury Yeston has had a long and distinguished career in American musical theatre. He won the Tony Award for Best Score for *Titanic* (1997), and the Tony Award and two Drama Desk Awards for *Nine* (1982). His music and lyrics cover a variety of styles. He has written classical music on commission from Carnegie Hall for its centennial celebration, and his score to *Phantom* (1991), with a book by Arthur Kopit, has received national and international acclaim. As a composer working primarily in the commercial theatre and music world as well as the classical one, Yeston's commentary on how music has shaped his life and evolved over time, and how the Broadway song has matured and 'crossed over' in its incorporation of different folk and classical styles serves as an informative guide to a specific and culturally significant form, especially in Western culture, and Yeston's distinct position within it.

This interview was initially conducted in New York City on 3 August 1997, and completed on 28 July 2001.

MAURY YESTON When De Tocqueville defined democracy, he obviously implied an extraordinary democracy of the arts as well. The greatness of American culture and certainly American musical culture has been that the aristocracy hasn't dominated it, and it hasn't been dominated by the Academy. It's simply been a combination of influences from Europe plus the barbaric yawp.

MICHAEL CERVERIS As the sophisticated, monied people in dominant American culture began to formulate institutions, hierarchy in art became a cultural construct more than anything else. The individuals you wrote about in the musical *Titanic*, for example: weren't they clearly committed to a hierarchy of social status?

MY Yes. But I'm talking about the slave music of the sixteenth and seventeenth century that we now know is an important precursor of twentieth century blues and popular music. That too was American music. Legitimate music has been defined by the academy and clearly that term has been forced on us by earlier generations of musicologists and historians. It's no different from the country club that's excluded blacks. The concert hall excluded Scott Joplin in the same way. But you can't slap at water; it just flows around you. Popular music is the lifeblood of our culture.

I think America has given the world two revolutionary new musical art forms. One of them is American jazz, with all of its attendant and related forms (rhythm and blues, boogie-woogie, rap, etc.). The music of African Americans, so often a thinly veiled protest music and thus always somehow political, filtered European harmonic structures through revolutionised rhythmic forms. It became disseminated through a process of minstrelsy – white imitators popularising black musical forms. Ultimately jazz has become not only an American but also an internationally practised art form.

The second great musical gift America has given the world is its musical theatre, which is a related form to jazz and, interestingly (though a different kind of mix), it is nonetheless profoundly influenced by European operetta, opera and the music hall, combined with the musical styles and entertainment styles of Black America. It's really the early minstrel shows, particularly the cakewalks, the reels and the folk dances, which catalysed the creation of the form. There was a fantastic comedic potential when those influences were combined with elements of slapstick and/or tap dancing – the rhythmic outgrowth of American pop jazz choreography. That then gets fused with storytelling, Germanic song and syncopated melody – and it becomes musical theatre. This too is now an internationally practised form.

There has been a consistent pattern of evolution and dissemination to all this. Black America creates an intrinsic and visceral musical, or musical/dance, or music/theatrical form, which is powerful in the extreme but deemed artistically impolite by sectors of the white community in its pure form. What generally happens is that we get a 'white minstrelsy' – a kind of sanitised white imitation of the black form which first becomes accepted. But in the final analysis the original form is rediscovered.

This sort of imitation, or minstrelsy (white people dressing up in black music), seems to be a leitmotif of American musical history. First, Meade Lux Lewis plays the boogie-woogie, then somebody else plays the boogie-woogie, and the next thing you know The Andrews Sisters are singing a boogie-woogie and it becomes acceptable and enters the mainstream. The same with Elvis, who was the first great black-voice minstrel.

Over the long run, it all gets homogenised. But issues of authorship and credit, ownership and money are one thing. Historical issues of what might be called 'patterns of acculturation' and their meaning are quite another. There are deep cultural differences between European and African tribal musical forms. To be on a European concert stage is to cleave to a 'proper' way of performing for the sake of the artwork. We admire artistry and virtuosity and human sensitivity. On the other hand, African American music inherits from its cultural ancestry an additional social function that in some cases unifies, in some cases spiritualises but in all cases has an anthropological component. In its historical roots its elements may have served as a sacrament or had a function for birth, marriage, death or indeed for everyday life. It has roots in experience.

Hence the work song which, in a tribal belief system, is a magical incantation that in itself does part of the work. The magical component is 'word magic'. So 'abracadabra' I sing this song and the work gets done. Later, the American musical descendant of the work song unites the workers who sing it in the very musical Africanisms that characterise its intervals, rhythms and cadences. And, later still, it lightens the hours for schoolchildren who sing 'I've Been Workin' on the Railroad' on a yellow bus. In each case, the use or purpose of the song (magic, political identity, ritualised play) is constitutive of the performance.

American children are raised in an extraordinary musical environment. Take a look at the phenomenology of music as the lived experience of a person growing up in the late 1940s and 1950s. I grew up at that time, and it was a golden age for American music because the invention of the LP made everything available. Everything existed at once, and was obtainable, and thus everything influenced everything else. Jazz, classical, rock, Broadway, folk music. It was an explosion.

MC There suddenly was a common denominator, as it were. All kinds of music were available to everyone, as opposed to the elitism and exclusion which had preceded this social explosion. How was your musical training affected by this?

MY I started playing piano when I was five. My mother gave me my first lessons at six. In the first years, one becomes imbued with Bach. By seven and a half, though, my favourite composer was Beethoven (and remains Beethoven). Mozart was perfect but unreachable – he could not be approached or duplicated. Bach was breathtaking and over-whelming in structure. But Beethoven's music was the only music I felt was *about* something. There was a story in it. The composer's struggle to create it was somehow within the music.

By the time I was ten I was bored with piano lessons. I was listening to the Everly Brothers and Jerry Lee Lewis on the radio and I wanted to do that. And I was writing music. My parents found a new teacher. In those days you could take lessons in what was called 'popular' piano. The teacher's name was Nat Glatt, and he played club dates. Nat gave me a notebook and said, 'Okay, here's lesson number one, this is the circle of fifths. Don't ask me how it works, it works. Here's how you do it.' He brought me a thing that was illegal at the time. It was called a 'fake book'. And suddenly I learned what seemed like a thousand songs – every great popular song ever written in American history, from Berlin and Kern to Loesser. And then, by the time I turned thirteen, two additional explosions hit American music. One was folk music; the other was Elvis. So I started to play the guitar.

MC Was there still room for Beethoven and Mozart?

MY I was listening to everything. I never saw any real divisions. Music was music. You could turn on the radio and switch stations, rapidly hearing different styles, and it was all equally wonderful. But then one day The Modern Jazz Quartet brought baroque counterpoint into jazz and began mixing disparate things together. And Miles Davis and Gil Evans were doing their own syntheses. It was clear to me that Gil Evans and Bartók used similar sonorities. It was simply a question of how you got to those chords.

One's musical personality comes from so many happy accidents. When I was old enough, I could take the train from my hometown of Jersey City to New York's Greenwich Village. Every week I could buy a new LP – Schoenberg one week, Miriam Makeba the next. Then I'd play it all by ear on the piano. Summers we'd visit my father's relatives in French Canada. There, in the early 1950s, it seemed the radio played only Piaf. That became a part of me. As a kid, I saw *My Fair Lady* (1956), and loved it. I wanted to write like that. My father, who was raised in London, sang English music hall songs endlessly. And my mother's father was a part-time cantor in the synagogue who could, without inhibition, sing the most affecting hyper-expressive music replete with twists and turns and vocalisms that hearkened back to early Byzantine music in the Middle East. And, to me, this was all just a part of ordinary life.

By 1958 or so, look what's been poured into this vessel: Jewish can-tillation, the Everly Brothers, classic jazz, Piaf, English music hall, Beethoven, Schoenberg and Elvis. I absorbed it all – a great wave of post-World World II music, including the post-Webern school of American composers, as well as Copland and Bernstein, Schoenberg, Hindemith, Stravinsky, Bartók and Kurt Weill. And, soon after, came the modern folk music movement, Bob Dylan, and a musical world with an obvious political element in it.

MC Art is never totally apolitical.

MY And then the Vietnam War hit, along with the Beatles – and here I was in college, just beginning to confront those who saw a distinction between music and so-called serious music, which was a very false distinction because all music is serious. And I saw the beginnings of the great academic turnaround in American thinking about music.

My first composition teacher at Yale was Donald Martino. Martino is (a) a clarinetist, (b) probably the greatest proponent of twelve-tone music, and also (c) a jazzer. He played with Bill Evans. He used to show us this great fugal arrangement of the song 'Lover Come Back' in which he made a counter subject out of the bridge. With Don Martino I wrote tone-rows, and pointillistic music, and studied Elliot Carter and became interested in what was then the birth of electronic music. Mel Powell (Benny Goodman's former piano player) taught at Yale and he was putting together one of the first electronic music studios in the country. We were there, watching him do it – saw-tooth wave generators, square wave generators. This was the new world.

But then *Fiddler on the Roof* opened on Broadway in 1964. At the end of Senior Year I really didn't know what was going to happen to me in my life. If I had gone on to graduate school I may have become exclu-sively a new-music composer – but there was everything else that I wanted to write. I got a lucky break. I won a fellowship that sent me to Cambridge in England for two years. I joined 'Footlights' (the theatri-cal club that spawned Monty Python and Beyond the Fringe). I also came to the realisation in England that it is as noble an enterprise to devote yourself to the creation of a melody that can last a thousand years as it is to write something for eighty instruments that can last maybe a thousand days.

When I got back to the States I immersed myself in musical theatre while pursuing a PhD in music theory. I joined the BMI Workshop, taught by the dean of Broadway conductors – Lehman Engel. He was a friend of all the legitimate composers of the American school (Virgil Thompson to Copland) and he also knew and worked with Cole Porter and Richard Rodgers. Lehman established the workshop to teach young writers the craft of music and lyric writing for the musical theatre. The workshop was free. You played some things and if he liked you, you were let in. Again, everyone saw divisions in musical worlds where I saw none. I was the pop guy in the academy, where I worked on the PhD. And I was the academic guy in the pop world, where I worked on musicals. I was always in the other place. But, of course, there was only one me and only one place – an America of increasingly democratised musical experience.

Ultimately, a number of trends contributed to a levelling-out of things. American students and composers generally got tired of working so hard on twelve-tone rows. They got tired of the aleotoric world. Along came Steve Reich and the advent and the lure of minimalism; and the thin wall between the two worlds began to disintegrate. Once you create an orchestral epiphany on a pop record and once you play a C chord for ten minutes in the world of new music, the boundaries break down and finally the worlds seem to be talking to and informing each other. Finally when everyone stopped taking themselves so seriously . . . they could truly start taking everyone else seriously. In the absence of self-importance, that which isn't oneself becomes more important.

MC Do you feel that this meeting of worlds is happening in all the other art forms as well?

MY In film. In architecture. The international style, first fostered in Europe and spread by Mies and his proponents, is long a thing of the past. There are pop elements in architecture now (think of American hotel architecture) and a mixture and variety of materials used that are as improvisational as jazz. In poetry it's an old story. We've watched the vernacular intrude from T.S. Eliot to cummings. You can make a case for rap as poetry, and watch the minstrelsy in action. A few years from now there is going to be a Pulitzer Prize-winning lily-white poet somewhere and the work is going to be influenced by rap and it's going to be okay. It won't be gangsta rap. It'll be legitimised and sanitised; but that's the way American culture often seems to work.

MC This brings us to another point: public support for the arts. If we look at the absolute capriciousness of the government support for the arts and even foundations, artists are finding there's not much they can count on. As a result, artists are beginning to realise they have to please the public more.

MY I've spent half my life in the academy, and half my life away from it. I've survived in the commercial world, where you have to make it on your own, and I've observed the other world of what might be called 'subsidised art'. This is what I've learned from sitting on committees like the NEA (National Endowment for the Arts) in Washington DC, and various other foundational boards. There are people who, for want of a better term, have a fantastic gift for grantsmanship and while grantsmanship can be very wonderful, it is also dangerous. Grantsmanship is simply the ability of certain personalities (through a combination of acumen and ambition) to find the right words to say to get the grant. They've got the jargon down. They're on to the trend. They know when flash (or absence of flash) is what impresses. I'm not saying untalented people get grants. But too often the really talented ones don't, because they lack the talent for presentation (or the bravery to put themselves forward). Count Waldstein has been replaced by the Guggenheim Foundation, but there are modern Schuberts who, like that extraordinary composer, fall between the cracks and starve. So arts grants are given to people who are good at getting them. And people who impose their own agendas give them. Think: if we are going to have operas in America, they're going to have to be subsidised, and if we're going to have *new* operas they're going to have to be subsidised. But of course, what's *Rent* (1996)? Is that a new opera? What's *Titanic*? Is that a new opera?

The musical theatre runs along its own track but, like opera, it undergoes constant reform. I think both forms attempt an impossible trick – to make people think we are speaking when we are in fact singing, so that the reality of the drama will shine through. From the moment opera was invented in 1601 it immediately began an endless period of reform – it seems every 40 or 50 years or so. Rameau, Gluck, Mozart, Verdi, Wagner . . .

Since the late 1940s American musical theatre too has gone through similar reforms. The music of *West Side Story* (1957) has held up, but some of the 1950s slang seems a bit hokey. *Fiddler on the Roof* was a thrilling show but *Hair* (1968) felt more like the way we talked and sang. Soon, though, *Hair* seemed locked in its decade while *Company* (1970) and *A Little Night Music* (1973) offered a believability and grit through Sondheim's genius lyrics and music, that made us believe again. After a while, 'Sondheim-ism' had its own aesthetic and its own artificiality, and audiences responded to the demotic plain-spoken-ness of *A Chorus Line* (1976). The actors told their real stories right across the footlights. We keep trying to keep what is sung seem less artificial. In *Titanic* there are moments on the bridge of the ship when sung lines alternate with spoken ones. This is simply my attempt to get you to relax and accept the speech and the recitative as being equivalent.

MC There are no rules. It just flows.

MY Perhaps, ultimately, all this effort may well inspire a counter-ideal. We'll throw up our hands and say, 'Why hide it? We're singing. Let's celebrate it.' Or a couple of years from now somebody's going to figure out another way to be real. This is the mark of a living organism evolving in the hands of its practitioners. It is constantly being reformed. In many ways, I hate musicals, which is why I keep trying to write one I can sit through.

   Writing a musical is a very arcane discipline. It's the lyrics that make musicals different from everything in the whole world, because the lyrics are as important as the music. That's not true in opera. In musical theatre the pre-eminence of the lyrics requires that the music be often shaped the way it is. The kind of melody I write for musical theatre is, I suppose, out of date. I feel like I'm a dinosaur, but I'm a happy dinosaur. The reason I like to work on subjects with a historical setting is that it gives me permission to write old-fashioned melodies.

MC Young people are looking more at broader issues, and are interested in the humanities and liberal arts, etc. There's a sense that they don't know exactly what the end product is going to be but are interested in what they are going to do. There's even a kind of faith in the future.

MY Yes, I think in fact they do have faith. But where are their examples? One of the things I find depressing is that, with the death of Aaron Copland, we lost the last of the generation of true symphonists connected to the great eighteenth and nineteenth century symphonic rhetoric. Hindemith, Stravinsky, Bartók, Copland . . . they are gone. There was a time when the world believed in the symphony and anticipated new ones the way we anticipated the Beatles' next album. I mourn the passing of that age. It makes me feel I want to write a symphony.

MC Do you think you would run a professional risk if you did that?

MY I don't care. I want to write a ballet based on Mark Twain's *The Adventures of Tom Sawyer* (1876), which will be stylistically as transparent as Prokofiev's *Peter and the Wolf* (1934). To write it, I must subsidise myself with what I earn from commercially successful things I've done. Or, I could teach and write it in moments of stolen time. One must write from where the best ideas come, and not for money. But money can be a great lure. I imagine the most successful artists have at some point risked hackdom but somehow avoided it.

MC I applaud the idea of subsidising artists, but you can lead people into a false sense of complacency with the subsidy mentality.

MY That's the problem when people base their whole careers on their grantsmanship. When that's taken away, there's no where else to go. Parenthetically, when I first got the idea for writing the ballet it was in 1990, after *Grand Hotel* opened and closed. I applied for a Guggenheim grant to write it, and I was denied. I had the usual letters of recommendation from folks like Milton Babbitt and so on. I had one Tony Award and had just been nominated for another, but the Guggenheim group wasn't interested in helping me write a ballet. Maybe they thought I had a lot of dough. Or maybe I came from the wrong side of the musical tracks. Or they weren't crazy about my work. In the end, they did the right thing. If I were to write a ballet it would be best to be solicited by a dance company that values my work and believes we can collaborate to make something wonderful. Making something wonderful – that's the point. All the rest is just noise.

II

Crossing culture

Travelers by Dah Teatar

Towards translocalism: Latino theatre in the new United States

Ricardo Bracho and Jorge Ignacio Cortiñas in conversation with Jose Esteban Muñoz

Ricardo A. Bracho was born in Mexico City and raised in Culver City, California. His plays include *The Sweetest Hangover (and other stds)* (1997) and *Fed Up: A Cannibal's Own Story* (1999).

Jorge Ignacio Cortiñas is a Cuban-American playwright and fiction writer. His plays include *Maleta Mulata* (1998) and *Sleepwalkers* (1999).

INTRODUCTION BY JOSE ESTEBAN MUÑOZ Lately I have heard colleagues in academia stumble on the word *maquiladora*. It's a word I grew up with since several of my aunts and female cousins worked in sweatshops when I was growing up. They would come home from the factory and mock the floor-lady's walk or complain about the impossible quotas imposed on them by the management. I had not heard the word for a while. Some members of my family found employment elsewhere while others even became the once derided floor-lady. Eventually these *tias* took off as well and found some other employment. Their positions were taken up by more recent waves of immigrants from Cuba as well as from Haiti and Central America. The notion of the *maquiladora* receded in my memory. It was now a story about my youth, about growing up a first-generation immigrant in an ethnic hub, and the strivings of the recently arrived. So, it was more than a little odd to hear the word '*maquiladora*' bandied about in this place that my migrant upward mobility has led me to. The '*maquiladora*' is perhaps the example par excellence that colleagues use when making an argument for trans-national, cultural or feminist critique. The example of exploited women working the '*maquiladoras*' the other side of the border is often used as evidence that implicates the evils of globalisation as it reveals the vicissitudes of trans-national capital. This is not a project that I simply wish to debunk. Indeed, I am quite sympathetic to it. But I also want to turn to this word *maquiladora* that awkwardly tumbles out of the mouths of critics who seem to always be interested in the sweatshop on the other side of the border. Trans-nationalism as a paradigm is meant to underscore the linkages between over here and over there, but more often than not the critique gets caught up in the analysis of the other place and it is often the case that the meagre and impoverished conditions of possibility that local people of colour negotiate within the quotidian sphere are ignored.

In the interview that follows, my colleagues and I rehearse our scepticism about the transnational paradigm. While we are aware of recent attempts to rehabilitate the concept of cosmopolitanism, we are not convinced that this particular concept of worldliness should be reinvented. If the object of this new cosmopolitanism is to abandon the nation, we would naturally be opposed to such an undertaking, since the writers who converse here share an interest in re-imaging cultural nationalism. From a feminist and queer vantage point, we are interested in reconsidering the project of cultural nationalism. As the interview displays, the notion of transnationalism that most interests us is the idea of collational linkages between different modalities of cultural and political nationalism. To this end we pursue the idea of translocalism as a way of rejecting the cosmopolitan worldliness that we see shadowing some transnational enquiries. The translocal is meant to talk about the political particularities of different groups and the potential identifications and collaboration between these different groups, both inside and out of the nation's and/or state's boundaries. Again, we do not reject the importance of understanding the exploitation of the *maquiladora* worker in El Salvador, but we insist on also considering the case of women working in sweatshops in Hialeah, Florida. I am currently writing a book on affect and ethnicity, and the work of Ricardo Bracho and Jorge Ignacio Cortiñas both figure significantly in that writing project. Through their work I see other ways to talk about particularity and connection. The characters that occupy the playwrights' worlds perform a modality of affective difference too complicated to be reduced to any notion of identity. Such complex particularity is linked to the ways in which collectivity is problematised and re-imagined in plays like *The Sweetest Hangover (and other stds)* and *Sleepwalkers*. These plays tell complex stories about the ways in which characters affiliate, connect and forge a sense of group belonging that again surpasses the limits of identity as a category. The work of these playwrights informs my attempts to theorise the local in relation to a larger political and historical sphere that resists the urge to displace the particular. Bracho and Cortiñas's work performs a sense of the particular that works against fake universalism and instead insists on the dense and essential materialism of particularity. This interview, conducted at New York University on 21 February 2001, is one manifestation of an ongoing dialogue of which I am fortunate to be a part.

JOSE ESTEBAN MUÑOZ So often transnational is about who gets to be transnational or who has access to transnational capital.

JORGE IGNACIO CORTIÑAS As an artist I am much more interested in the historic fact of immigration in this last century, and the determinative force that has had culturally and socially. Huge population shifts have occurred that so much cultural production and critical thinking manages to not have engaged itself with. And the three of us have also been marked as subjects through immigration. One question I always have for the international tourist: not only where are you going, but also what are you running from? And why is it that the darkie you have to go to take a jumbo jet to visit is always more interesting to you than the one you have to share a subway car with?

JM For you another kind of transnational model means the migrant.

JC Not just the migrant, but certainly including the migrant.

JM Immigration marks us and is a condition of possibility for our practice and our work in a kind of transnationalism that is intimately connected to capital.

RICARDO BRACHO In that intimacy there is the possibility of both seduction and its refusal. But that rarely leads the transnational artist to a critique of capital because they, the artist of and for the colonial metropolis, who now lo and behold can even be 'coloured', need those nations that they're hopping between and borrowing costumes and languages from. I don't know if that necessarily is about that person being a migrant. Maybe it's about them being a displaced indigenous person.

JM That gets into the problem of discourses we organise under and that's much more the story of displaced nativism, about California and Chicanos, than about migrants from the Caribbean basin, living on the East Coast.

RB Not necessarily given the history of the Puerto Rican community here and their recent experiences of displacement from gentrifying Manhattan.

JM How long do you have to be here to be indigenous to Manhattan?

JC There's nothing more native to New York than a Nuyorican. My map of the Caribbean includes the island of Manhattan.

RB But does that make Nuyoricans or even the three of us at this table 'Latino'? Here we are: two Cuban-Americans and a Chicano and just how did that happen? Because it wasn't supposed to, given the distinct politics of our respective communities or our initial dispersions in this nation state. Within the rubric of 'Latino', lots of folks have very different and interesting interactions, but for the most part the politics I see happening between these different national groups do not include articulated discussions of our differences or our potentialities.

JM But 'Latino' is a necessary makeshift shelter that we're keeping over us in the storm. I think of your first play *The Sweetest Hangover (and other stds)* because it's about Latinos operating off of and interacting with or being in tension with other racialised subjectivities, and not the typical way Latino is often dramatised, which is in some bizarre state of anthropological isolationism. You know, let's just focus on the kitchen, let's just make it a little microcosm of the world. The play is as much about Latino as a spatial demarcation as it is about an ethnic demarcation.

RB It's the criminal, localist transnationalism that is organised by urban gay men of colour who are into each other and underground house clubs. But it's not where a Chelsea or Castro queen can pick up some colour for the night. If you're a certain kind of white club or theatre-goer, going to the Latino club/play is like going to the bazaar, you're always picking up trinkets. It's crossing the tracks for the night, being on the bad side of town. I think the price of admission to another kind of Latino theatre, the one we are all trying to make, doesn't allow for the same sort of quick consumption. In the same way that your play *Sleepwalkers* was difficult for some people to digest in Miami. It was too grounded, too beholden, to present-day Havana, and not the myth of Cuba that is ideologically operational in Miami.

JC And there are good reasons why there would be that cognitive dissonance for audiences, why they should experience as so unfamiliar something they take for granted that they know. Particularly in the context of North American stages and movie screens, representations of things Cuban, often, it is worth pointing out, by Cuban or Cuban-American writers, seem to have coalesced around three different strategies: they'll deal only with pre-1959 Cuba; or they'll present this polemical, I think one-dimensional, condemnation of the current regime and socialism in general; or they'll engage with the Cuba of today but always through these highly folkloric flourishes, you know, lots of references to café and rumba dancing. Not surprising then that Miamians of my parents' generation who saw *Sleepwalkers*, a play that eschews those tactics, would respond by saying, 'That's not Cuba.' While more recent Cuban arrivals to Miami, those who had arrived since Mariel or the *balsero* crisis almost always responded by saying, 'How did you manage to portray conditions and the mood there so accurately?' And this in the context of a non-realistic play.

JM It makes you want to ask: what and who is Latino theatre for?

RB That's the big question and one we need to keep on questioning and fighting over. We should beware of any answer that isn't provisional, partial, local and conceptual. But when folks do answer it definitively they usually take either an assimilationist stance, or a preservationist position that can't hide its patriarchal, Catholic and colonial roots. But for me it's about a certain kind of lyrical indictment of whatever we come across: the state, our families and our dates. Theatre is for me unearthing the violence of daily life.

JC *The Sweetest Hangover* also troubled some audience members in many of the same ways. I think it was the multinational mix of the characters and the foregrounding of hybrid histories that made it difficult for a particular kind of identity-based critic to be able to read and to understand it.

JM Which sets up a sort of conundrum of problems with identity. Of identity's severe disabling limitations but also of an ability to abandon identity and to think about a work that fights for identity and fights within identity as a category. As opposed to trying to insulate that I am a universal artist, you know that sort of 'I am not a Latino artist, I am a playwright first.'

JC And that's a difficult quip to counter at this historic moment when the Left has been so thoroughly trounced. People react to my scepticism at their universalist aspirations as provincial on my part or hopelessly sectarian. What I love about Ricardo's play is that a lack of historical amnesia doesn't make the challenges facing his characters any easier. More difficult in many ways, as they try and stretch those global histories into including some meaning for their local concerns. The characters try to intervene in a global order that marginalises them, even as that global order is mirrored by local forms of social control. And the characters achieve agency through recourse to the histories, languages and improvisational skills of the post-colonial communities that now constitute the numeric majority in the major North American cities. Check out the census data. This country has shifted right under our feet.

Honouring mystery

Migdalia Cruz in conversation with Caridad Svich

Migdalia Cruz is the author of many plays, musicals and operas, produced in the US and abroad in venues as diverse as Playwrights Horizons in New York City, the Old Red Lion in London and Houston Grand Opera. An alumna of New Dramatists, she was born and raised in the Bronx.

This interview was conducted via e-mail between October 2000 and May 2001.

CARIDAD SVICH How do you see yourself as a writer reconstructing Latina myths?

MIGDALIA CRUZ What are the Latina myths? Would they be the 'woman as virgin/whore' kind of myth or do you mean the real myths, like the story of La Llorona? The Latinas who inhabit my plays are survivors, who have used their minds and bodies to determine their place in the world. They are human and so they sometimes fail to overcome the restraints of society or family or Church or men in order to fully realise their potentials. And their goals are varied. In one play *Lucy Loves Me* (1991), a daughter finds the courage to leave the physical confines of her apartment and the spiritual confines of her mother. In another play *Lolita de Lares* (1995), a docudrama about Lolita Lebron – arguably our greatest *Boriqua independentista* heroine – challenges with armed resistance the colonisation of her country by the United States government. Is this a reconstruction of myth or the attempt to give voice to a human being who is mainly silenced because of her darker hue or her Latino heritage? Has the act of giving voice to these women become the creation of a myth for the future? I try to find what is noble and beautiful in my characters – from whatever ground they walk on – sometimes it's mud and other times it's marble – but always they have stories that I think need to be told and through my work I honour them.

CS What role, if any, does cultural nostalgia play in your work?

MC If by cultural nostalgia you mean do I long for home in my work, I would have to say yes. I think the fact that I am a Puerto Rican born in the US with a cultural and spiritual tie to an island which is a de facto colony of the United States – makes it impossible not to long for a home, a country, a true and respected identity. When I was travelling in Mexico someone asked me how it felt not to have a real country. I told him that Puerto Ricans carry their country inside them. So does my work. Sometimes in my work I try to pay homage to my ancestors. In my most recent play *Yellow Eyes* (2000), I was inspired by the stories of my own great-grandfather who was a slave in Puerto Rico. I tell stories I need to tell and of course those stories often bring me to my history, *mi gente*. To me this is not nostalgia – which to me implies an impotent longing for good times past – it is a telling and retelling of family history which serves to educate the family to come. And these stories are both light and dark – they try to tell the truth. I don't long for history; I explore it, deconstruct it, relive it.

CS   Would you speak to some of your collaborations in music-theatre, or site-specific work?

MC   One of the most difficult writing tasks to undertake in the theatre – or in life in general – is collaboration. It requires that one dream the same dream with another, who may have been chosen for you, rather than be a partner of your choice. Collaborations can be assigned by producers or arise after the inception of an idea, so one has to work at the behest of someone else's inspiration. A music-theatre piece about Frida Kahlo, *Frida* (1991), which I co-wrote with a director and composer, was this kind of collaboration. I felt tortured from beginning to end, but in retrospect find that may have been a good mental state from which to write about Frida. The composer did not want to compose to the word 'blood', the director did not want me to give the play a point of view, and the producers insisted on toning down her lesbian lifestyle and minimising the Spanish. Without blood, lesbians and Spanish, how was I to write a play about an artist who literally bled most of her adult life – in person and on the canvas – who spent her last twenty years exclusively in relationships with women and who was Mexican and, of course, sang, cried and breathed in Spanish? I felt distrusted most of the time and certainly under-appreciated and yet I remained with the project. I did that because I respected all the artists I was working with, the cast and also the visual artists who created the set and the incredible puppetry, and also because I felt deeply connected to Frida. It seems that she has become an iconographic cliché of the tortured artist who women gravitate to like a goddess, but for me she became a part of my everyday life for five stressful years. And in the end, how reward-ing to have tried to give her a life on stage and to fight for her human and Latina integrity. I didn't win every battle, but I think it was a better project for my having been there to duke it out for her. I am sure it was difficult for the director and composer as well. How, indeed, were three such different artists supposed to have the same dream and create a unified vision of Frida?

cs How do you nurture and sustain your vision?

mc I feel that I have more of a calling. And that is from the people I have known and the place where I come from, to keep a record, as honest as I can make it, of their existence. In doing this, I try to show their beauty and pay them homage – even in the darkest of circumstance. So my memories and my people nurture me. The many artists with whom I have collaborated nurture my work: directors, actors, and designers – even dramaturgs – who help me define the world of each play. And small theatre companies, Latino and others sustain it, with guts and heart. And those places seem to dwindle each year. So, soon I will write an erotic novel and an action film. And maybe a gentle book about a carnivore and a herbivore who are having a baby: will it be dinner or diapers? I must write this for my daughter, Antonia. Maybe she will have a vision.

Light in midst of darkness
Dah Teatar's Dijana Milošević and Kathy Randels in conversation with Lisa D'Amour

Dijana Milošević is artistic director of Dah Teatar in Belgrade, Serbia. Kathy Randels is artistic associate of the company in New Orleans, Louisiana. Dah Teatar was formed in 1992 and was the first theatre group in Belgrade to create public performances in protest of the nationalist policies of Slobodan Milošević, the former President of Yugoslavia and Serbia. In the ten years the company has been together they have continually explored the tensions between personal and historic memory, and the boundaries of time and geography.

Interviewer Lisa D'Amour has an ongoing relationship with Dah as both collaborating artist and witness to their work. The following conversation focuses on Dah's piece *Travelers* (1999) since it is emblematic of their work, and speaks to the difficult and sometimes dangerous boundaries the making and presenting of such work can cross.

This interview was conducted in Ms Randels's apartment in New Orleans in February 2001 during rehearsals for *Nita and Zita: Undeveloped Negatives/Snapshots Never Taken*, a collaboration between Kathy Randels and Lisa D'Amour.

LISA D'AMOUR US performer/director Kathy Randels first saw Dah's work at the 1996 RAT conference in Austin, Texas. RAT is a loose federation of passionate theatre and performance artists who are committed to staging new work. RAT stands for 'radical alternative theatre', or 'regional alternative theatre' depending on who you ask within this cyber-federation. What is true of RAT is that it is one of the few meeting grounds and forums for alternative theatre artists in the US. Founder Erik Ehn, in addition, has stressed consistently RAT's connection to the world theatre scene, and Dah's participation in the RAT Conference in Austin was an example of RAT's interest in global exchange and in fostering an international dialogue with artists who believe in 'big, cheap theatre: theatre which is big on imagination but not necessarily well-funded financially. Kathy Randels, an actor and activist based in New Orleans received a grant from the Louisiana Arts Council to observe Dah's process of developing material in Belgrade. While in Belgrade, the *Travelers* project came to be. This project brought together actors from different cultures, and explored the very act of encountering someone from another culture, and what kind of spiritual, emotional and physical exchange results from such an encounter.

DIJANA MILOŠEVIĆ Yes, with *Travelers* we had actor Allister O'Loughlin, who was half British and half Irish, and then Sanja Ksmanovic-Tasic and Vladan Avramovic from Serbia, and Kathy from the US, and I thought this would be a great exchange or meeting of cultures. The idea was to explore the theme 'Why do people travel?' or 'Why do people leave their countries?' At the time we were in the middle of many years of civil war in Yugoslavia, and many people had left our country, among them some of the best people of the young generation, the most educated ones, many friends and relatives of mine. I realised that this was a crime, among many crimes that our government committed; it was like taking the future out of our country. On the other hand, I had these strong examples of Kathy and Allister, who came into this poor country that was under different tracts of war and bombing, and risked their well-being and safety and decided to work with us out of a love for the theatre. I wanted to explore this. We were all travellers.

LD Kathy, what do you remember about the process?

KATHY RANDELS Definitely the songs were the most concrete things that we brought from our culture. One of the songs we used was 'Row Row Row Your Boat'. A universal Buddhist song, actually. Sanja said every time she saw the sea when she was a little girl she would sing a song from the Croatian/Dalmatian coast. It was a very sad song about a woman singing to her lover, whom the sea has swallowed. But we put the two together: 'Row Row Row Your Boat' with 'Oh Mori Mori' (Oh Sea, Oh Sea). It definitely had this strange tension to it, both melodically and rhythmically. The songs were kind of competing against each other. But somehow that disharmony created a great harmony.

DM This is the beauty of this work because somehow it ripens our own culture in a way, and reflects the other, and both cultures are seen in their beauty and uniqueness, by being exposed to another culture.

LD And more than a simple appreciation of another culture takes place. An understanding occurs which affects how you view life and your own rituals and beliefs. This understanding can be profound, and perhaps even effect change. You began to work on the project during the war?

KR We began working on the piece in early October 1998. That was during the first bomb threat from NATO to Belgrade. We had gone into the rehearsal space and then suddenly we were in a situation where we might all have to leave the country. It was probably a month later that Dijana asked us to write down some images from that time period. There was very great fear for all of us, and for different reasons. For Allister and I, we had this fear of maybe never leaving that country, and never seeing our people again. And for those who lived there, for the Serbs, it was, 'What will happen to our city? What will happen to the people that we love here? How will we continue?'

DM In addition, we felt a great responsibility of having two foreigners in the company, and the government was warning them that they had to leave the country. So, Allister decided to leave, and Kathy decided to stay. Then everything calmed down and the bombing did not happen that time. Allister returned, and then we really shared this very strong experience. I think it was one of the biggest influences on the project. It was the shadow.

LD Because already there had been a rupture, but out of it there was also strength to move on. And the piece premiered in Belgrade.

DM On Valentine's Day 1999. It was tense, but we didn't believe that the bombing would happen. We were, of course, so tense about what was going on in Kosovo. The premiere was very nice, but what stayed with me about the premiere was the party that happened afterwards. We had the opening at my friend's café in a very beautiful part of town. It is a very small place with a warm feeling. The colours were brown and blue – it looked a little bit like Greece – and we had great food and drink and music and we really danced and partied until almost morning. I am mentioning this not just because I love parties, but because for me it became a metaphor of the whole situation we were in. At that moment, we had a guest from Britain, a guest photographer who came to work with us for six months and we had another guest from Italy, a set designer and painter, and Allister and Kathy, and many of our friends and family, and it looked like an ideal situation. It was very crazy that in the middle of our country, in the middle of threats of bombing and the possibility of war, we created an island paradise. You really can create this kind of a light in the midst of a big darkness.

LD Do you feel the piece resonated with your audience in Belgrade?

DM The audience had a very strong response and one reason was because many people in the audience did not have the possibility of travel. And that was like a dream, especially for the younger generation. And they didn't have the opportunity to meet people from other cultures, and so it was a great thing. Another reason the piece was strong was that it asked a question that was important for many people in Yugoslavia at the time: should they leave the country or should they stay? We didn't give any answer. We just put that question on stage along with many other possibilities. We cannot change things on the global level, but we can, in our art, change ourselves and change our surroundings.

LD You happened to be in the state of Georgia, in the US, when the Parliament was stormed by resistance leaders in Belgrade. Now you will be going back to what we hope is a different country in many ways. Do you have hope for the future of your work in your country, or is it too early and uncertain to be able to tell what is going to happen?

DM First of all I feel for the first time in many years hope about my country and about the new political situation we have. Everything is fragile, but I think some strong steps have been made. I think the best thing that happened was that the people finally understood that they have the power, and that they can influence things. About my work I never felt that I couldn't work in my country. My work has a reason to be in my country, a deep reason and sense, and so simply to stay there and to oppose all destruction is Dah. I will be very happy to explore different themes, other than political. I think we will have to wait for some years, though. Economically speaking, I think it will be a nightmare for the next few years to come, but I am really very excited to think that I will be returning to a new country. I didn't dream that could happen.

Navigating the minefields of utopia: a dialogue on artistic collaboration

Guillermo Gómez-Peña and Lisa Wolford in dialogue

Born in 1955 and raised in Mexico City, Guillermo Gómez-Peña came to the United States in 1978. His work, which includes performance art, video, audio, installations, poetry, journalism, critical writing and cultural theory, explores cross-cultural issues and North/South relations in the era of globalisation. His books include *Dangerous Border Crossers* (Routledge, 2000), *The New World Border* (City Lights, 2000) and *Warrior for Gringostroika* (Graywolf, 1994).

INTRODUCTION BY LISA WOLFORD This text is part of an ongoing series of conversations with members of Pocha Nostra, the performance company founded by Guillermo Gómez-Peña in collaboration with Roberto Sifuentes and other artists. The material for this interview was distilled from conversations that took place over a two-week period in late May and early June 1999, while Pocha Nostra was in residence at the Centre for Performance Research in Aberystwyth, Wales. In contrast to more formalised interview situations, Guillermo and I spoke in the midst of quotidian activities, as people smoked, drank coffee, exercised, and otherwise prepared for rehearsal and daily life. While I have tried, in the editing process, to smooth over fragmentation in the text, both the occasional discontinuities in the interview and the relatively charged nature of certain topics discussed can perhaps be attributed to the dynamic of informal conversation among artistic colleagues who know one another well. Since this conversation was recorded, various changes of personnel have occurred within Pocha Nostra, with certain collaborators becoming progressively more present in the work and others moving in directions that allow them to explore independent creative projects.

LISA WOLFORD For much of the course of your work, you've tended to collaborate for long periods of time with various ensemble companies – first Poyesis Genetica, then Border Arts Workshop [BAW], and more recently Pocha Nostra. What draws you to collaborative work, and what are some of the challenges, especially when artists work together in ways that push them to negotiate various axes of difference – of gender, ethnicity, culture, or professional background, for example?

GUILLERMO GÓMEZ-PEÑA I was very influenced by the *grupos* in Mexico City in the 1970s, the interdisciplinary collectives of the generation prior to mine. Felipe Ehrenberg was one of my godfathers. Very much in the spirit of the times, his generation created interdisciplinary collectives and utilised the streets of Mexico City as laboratories of experimentation, as *galerias sin paredes* (galleries without walls). At the same time in the late 1970s when I moved to California, I was surprised to find that there were also many Chicano collectives, such as Asco and the Royal Chicano Airforce. It was the spirit of the times. I think that the spirit behind it was a kind of utopian impulse, believing that to share visions, resources and efforts could only multiply the impact of art in society. Also, the belief that collaboration is a form of citizen diplomacy, which later on became the original impetus behind BAW/TAF [Taller de Arte Fronterizo]. If a multicultural, multiracial, cross-generational collective can in fact function in the real world, then maybe it's possible on a larger scale to sort out our differences and cultural conflicts. BAW/TAF believed at the time that if Chicanos and Mexicans, men and women, people from different generations, could in fact sit at the same table, then this would send a strong signal to the larger society that it was in fact possible to communicate across borders, to engage in cross-cultural dialogue. This kind of utopian impulse that has led me to work in a collaborative manner.

LW   What have you found to be some of the challenges of collaborative work?

GP   You are asking me to walk on a minefield . . . But it's important stuff to deal with, and I'll do it. This very utopian impulse I'm talking about carries its own seed of destruction, the fact that no matter how hip and progressive we think we are, we inevitably end up reproducing autocratic, separatist behaviour . . . It's basic human nature. If you work within a collective devoted to cross-cultural or cross-gender dialogue in an effort to create a more enlightened model of racial and gender relations, trying to deal with these issues directly, in this very quest it's possible to end up hyperintensifying the problem, and being devoured by one's own utopian dreams. Sadly, with BAW/TAF, it was precisely our inability to cross these microborders in our interpersonal relations that led to the destruction of the original group. In other words, BAW/TAF was not able to erase the borders among ourselves, the very same borders we were attempting to erase in the larger society, so we succumbed to our own sexism, racism, cultural prejudice and fears. Chicanos and Mexicans within the group were unable to overcome their mutual resentments so as to understand one another and develop a new mode of relationship. The men's attempt to be more egalitarian with our women colleagues failed. What we wanted to be a stage to confront and solve these matters, turned into a battleground. Again, our own chimeras and grandiose ideas devoured us. And as you know, this has happened to so many collectives . . .

LW That's certainly true, and often within groups that had fewer overt axes of difference to negotiate than BAW/TAF, fewer obvious tensions and possibilities for rupture. Yet you're not willing to give up this utopian quest you describe, because since BAW/TAF you have had other very close collaborative relationships. I know that your collaboration with Roberto [Sifuentes] is very special and has been your primary creative partnership for the past several years, but also you continue to work with other artists, people from different cultural backgrounds and different milieux. Is there a difference between the collaborative relationship you have with the artists of Pocha Nostra and that in the earlier groups with which you were involved, and if so how would you describe that difference?

GP There's many differences, huge differences. I remember one of the main ongoing discussions in BAW/TAF was between [Chicano visual artist] David Avalos and me. At the time, David was very much a Chicano nationalist and I was a post-Mexican anti-nationalist in the process of Chicano-isation. We were willing to sit at the same table, but we had very different opinions about cultural dialogue as well as about artistic collaboration. David comes from an activist political background, and I come mainly from an arts and literary background, encountering activism later. David believed that collaboration ought to be an unemotional strategy. He believed that it was better to collaborate with people who were good tacticians regardless of whether he liked them or not. For him, collaboration was first and foremost a political strategy, and this came out of his experience as a member of the committee on Chicano civil rights. I believe, on the contrary, that you first have to get along with your collaborators. Only then can you engage in any real collaborative process. This led to endless discussions about who should be a member of BAW/TAF, because the choice of membership for David was purely strategic – who could benefit the Workshop for whatever reason – and for me it was more sentimental. Who do you want to work with? One of the great lessons I brought away from the BAW/TAF years was that I decided I only wanted to work with people I got along with and respected, and for whom I felt true affection. For me, that was a clear decision in my life, never again to collaborate with people for whom I don't feel affection, compassion, and respect, just because we believe we are on the same side of an issue.

LW Some of the writing that Avalos has published that touches on this collaboration strikes me as extremely emotional. What are some of the other dynamics that led to the tensions between the two of you?

GP I can only speak from my own subjectivity, and certainly David would disagree with me, but I really believe that David, like many Chicanos of his generation, has a very big wound vis-à-vis Mexico. Growing up in ultra-conservative San Diego in the pre-civil rights era was probably very tough, and I remember innumerable times trying to persuade tough David to come with me to Tijuana and him being literally panicked by the idea of crossing the border into Mexico. I also remember one day when I jokingly told him I was going to give him a Cybervision Spanish course for a present, and he got really hurt. For him, as for many Chicanos in his generation, the relation to Spanish language was an infected wound. Mexicans used to make fun of the allegedly 'imperfect' Spanish of Chicanosâ. See, our relationship at the time was paradigmatic of Chicano/Mexicano relations. In a sense, David represented for me a kind of psychological access to the Chicano movement. He was in many ways the Chicano border guard of my Mexican identity, and vice versa. Being one of the most important Chicano intellectuals in San Diego, I think he symbolically represented the possibility of my entry into the Chicano movement. As a Mexicano, I perhaps represented his painful past, his other self, his lost Mexican-ness. So because of this, from both sides our relationship was a very dramatic one. Unfortunately, at the time we couldn't make sense out of these complexities, and our responses were merely visceral. I am still hoping that one day we can sit down together and try to work things out. Neither one of us can deny the fact that despite our differences, we were very good friends, and that hurts even more.

LW Are you willing to talk about the next step in your work after BAW/TAF?

GP My next major collaboration was with [Cuban-American writer] Coco Fusco. It was intellectually and artistically a very effective collaboration. It lasted for a little over three years [1990–93], and a couple of very important projects came out of it that were paradigmatic of the times, one being the legendary cage piece and the other Mexarcane International. Unlike Coco, I don't regret it, but the main problem with our collaboration was that we were also lovers, and this meant that political problems and cultural differences inevitably became personal ones and vice versa.

LW Such as?

GP To begin with, Coco was a Cuban-American raised in New York, and I was a Mexicano, born and raised in Mexico, who migrated to the US when I was 22 – very different experiences. Also, one of the main problems that Coco and I faced was that because of the sexism in the art world, critics and presenters were always emphasising my partici- pation in the projects. And although we tried to correct these *broncas* – and believe me, I did everything I could – it was difficult to counter the behaviour of the art world and also the cult of celebrity, and this inevitably created friction between us. We talked about it endlessly, and developed all kinds of strategies to deal with it, but it was never enough. The result was devastating. She ended up blaming me for complying with this sexism, and this turned the rehearsal room into hell. These frictions got intensified in the micro-universal stage of the collaborative process. The difficulties between Coco and me taught me another important lesson, which is that it's dangerous to collaborate artistically with a lover. You just can't win. It's an impossible situation, whether it's men and women together, or men working with men, women with women. Inevitably, it ends up as a complete mess. It's both very romantic and extremely combustible. Marina Abramovich and Ulay are the classic example. I've learned that it's dangerous to mix sex, love and art. What can I say? You learn from making mistakes. Of course there are always a few exceptions to the rule, couples who have managed to work together effectively, but they are really exceptions.

LW You mentioned earlier that you wanted to make peace with Coco. Would it be overstepping a boundary for me to ask you to talk about that?

GP I think that for two artists of colour concerned with similar struggles and engaged in parallel intellectual praxis to be fighting one another is frankly ludicrous. We are doing the job for the power elite, who love to see us fighting each other. I don't expect to ever collaborate with Coco again, but I certainly would like to at least complete the process we started in the early 1990s, to wrap things up so to speak, to shed resentments and to be able to treat each other respectfully. Maybe what we need is to engage in a public dialogue, or rather a cyber-dialogue that can eventually get published, some kind of ritual document in which we can sort out the real intellectual and aesthetic differences from the messy personal stuff. But there would have to be some basic ethical rules to the game – for example, no name-calling, no threats, no attacks.

LW Roberto Sifuentes has been your major collaborator for the past sev- eral years, ever since you stopped working with Coco. How did the two of you begin working together?

GP When Coco decided to edit *The Couple in the Cage* film (1993), she wanted to get away from performing. In the middle of a tour, Roberto, who was the technical director of the piece, offered to replace Coco in the performance of *The New World Border* (originally from 1996). In a week, Roberto memorised the lines and we changed the gender of the voice in the text, and at the next stop on the tour Roberto took over the role. It was a huge risk, but people loved his performance, and from that very moment Roberto became a dear collaborator. We've worked together for almost ten years.

LW I've noticed that no one in Pocha Nostra is involved with any other member of the group – not just within the core ensemble, but throughout the company. Everyone has committed relationships outside of the group, and that has to make a huge difference in terms of interpersonal dynamics.

GP We're militant about that. It's probably the only thing that we're militant about, and I'm convinced that's why we have survived for so many years. We are extremely close, but the first commandment of Pocha Nostra is to not get sexually intimate with one another for the well-being of the work. We respect each other's personal lives and decisions. We protect each other's backs.

LW And each other's privacy.

GP Precisely. We respect each other's spiritual eccentricities and the eccentricities of each person's sexual relationships outside of the group, but we keep them outside the rehearsal space. We no longer operate on the model of family, the clan, or the hippie collective, which is also very healthy. In prior collectives, it always seemed like the group really became the centre of everyone's lives, and this isn't at all the case in Pocha Nostra. Each member of the company has a full life, keeps other jobs, and takes separate vacations. Our public and social lives overlap, but we also have different milieux of friends. When we're not on the road, we are sometimes out of touch with each other for weeks at a time. None of us share living space, but when someone needs a place to live or somewhere to stay while working on a project, we all pitch in to help find them one. Having time away from each other is extremely healthy for us. Also, we work with an outer circle of collaborators who live in different parts of the US, Mexico and Canada. See, Juan [Ybarra] is living in Canada, Leticia [Nieto] in Seattle, Michele [Ceballos] in Phoenix, you're in Ohio, Violeta [Luna] and Yoshi [Maeshiro] are in Mexico City, and the rest of the *flota* is in San Francisco. We usually work intensely with these wonderful people for short duration on specific projects, then each person goes back to their own home and their own life. As a general notion of artistic community, this seems much healthier. We're like a global collective, in the best sense of the term global. It took us many years and lots of mistakes to discover this model.

LW I want to go back to the subject of BAW/TAF. The dissolution of the original group seems to have been a somewhat contentious process. When you published your 'Eulogy to Border Arts', this generated a lot of criticism from your prior collaborators. The text was very polemical, but I understood it to be a critique of institutional appropriation, not in any way meant as negative toward artists working on border issues, but instead examining the way that border art was being commodified by mainstream institutions. Did other people see this text differently?

GP These questions are certainly opening many wounds in my psyche, but I feel that they are pertinent, and I'm willing to answer them in the hope that others may learn from my mistakes. Besides, I don't see any other way to heal the wounds. The air at the border was really charged during the time the original BAW/TAF worked together [1985–90]. What in the beginning was a true grassroots movement slowly turned into an art expo. People who had jobs on the bandwagon of border hype and were benefiting directly from the festivalisation and exoticisation of border culture, people who were willingly embracing this new border chic, felt particularly implicated by my critique. Other collaborators felt that since my solo work was going well and I was being welcomed by the art world at that time as 'the border artist' and getting national prizes, that I didn't have the right to complain. So those were the two major criticisms. That short activist text stigmatised me for many years, more than any other piece I've ever written, even pieces that were just as controversial if not more so. People felt that I threw a bomb and left town, so to speak. It took a few years for me to be able to go back to the table with the border arts community and discuss these issues in friendly terms. Even then, not everybody was willing to reconcile with me. David Avalos and Victor Ochoa still see me as the border *chamuco* [devil], even after all these years. What really blew my mind was the fact that the text was not the product of a personal decision. The decision to write the text was a collective decision. Many artists were outraged by the creation of an elaborate machine of border arts and by the appropriation of the border paradigm by major institutions to obtain megabucks for binational *maquiladora* art projects that excluded or marginalised artists local to the region. Many of the very creators of the border arts movement sat with me on numerous occasions to plot this text. The creation of the text was consensual, but the repercussions weren't shared by all of the people involved.

LW And then when the bomb blew up, who was left in town?

GP   There were twelve or thirteen people involved in the discussion whose names I won't mention out of respect, but when the text got published no one realised what an impact it was going to have. No one foresaw that it was going to be an earthquake, and as soon as the earthquake happened everybody split and suddenly I was to blame. I insist: collective discussion informed the content of that text.

LW   So why was the choice made to mask collective authorship by putting it out in your name?

GP   We all felt that it would carry more weight and impact if I signed it, since I was supposedly the most visible one. Besides, since I was leaving town, I could afford the luxury of throwing the bomb. Some of the artists had more to lose. They were going to have to deal with the new powers that be, the new dynasty of border art, and the new chiefs and brokers of the *maquiladoras* of border culture. Many of the artists who stayed in San Diego were actually blacklisted, but I won't get into that. James Luna was able to survive the crisis because, being a performance artist like me he toured regularly and he wasn't dependent on the San Diego institutions, but many of the others were not able to survive the border cultural wars. The history of border art, just like the history of US/Mexico relations, is filled with blood. Even to remember those days makes me very sad. My only consolation is that I can say I was true to my convictions.

LW   I want to switch topics somewhat and also time periods. In Pocha Nostra, all of the people you're working with define their professional identities in terms of some aspect of performance – performance artists, dancer/choreographers, etc. You make a clear distinction between core collaborators and more peripheral or occasional contributors to the process, and also between members of the group and what you call 'involuntary performance artists' – people that you bring in for a specific project. It seems to me that all the people you work with now have strong, independent professional identities outside of the work you do together. How does this affect the collaborative process? I mean this both in terms of the advantages and disadvantages of working in a situation where everyone defines themselves largely in relation to outside projects, as well as the fact that everyone is bringing to the table what they do well and not running the risk of becoming a dilettante by crossing outside of their own milieu.

GP   The structure we have found that really works is very simple. You have three core collaborators, Roberto, Juan and I, who are involved in most of the performance projects. And Nola Mariano, of course, our beloved agent/manager and holy protector of our backs in the mean streets of the art world. It's like the first circle, the *flota*, so to speak. I still do some solo work, but it's really a small portion of the work we do. Most performance projects involve at least two core collaborators. Then we have this outer circle of people like Sara, Rona and Gustavo Vasquez, who are involved in about half of our projects, and who still have their own work outside. And then there is a third circle of people involved in specific projects, like dancer Michele Ceballos, actress Norma Medina and performance artist Carmel Kooros, who worked on the *Temple of Confessions* (1997), and Violeta Luna and Yoshi Maeshiro, who worked on *Mexterminator*, and so on and so forth. Then there's yet another, very ephemeral outer circle that involves local artists and eccentrics who join the process the week before opening night. It's only for the major projects that the whole community comes together, for the really large-scale versions of *Mexterminator*, *Borderscape 2000*, or the opera. The whole *flota* comes together as a huge community for the really big projects, and then once the project is over people go back to their own territories and I remain creating new projects, either alone or with Roberto and Juan, and at some point in the process we bring you into it to get your feedback on dramaturgy and staging. This model of collaboration works very well. I don't want to romanticise it, because there have in fact been some minor problems within the group and I'm willing to talk about them, but I would say it works marvellously. We all respect one another, and we never have major fights. We are very close friends, but we never get too involved emotionally. We have all managed to maintain our friendship for years, and to be both very close friends and respectful collaborators, so I think we are on to something. Still, there are incidents. Sometimes the temperature among the group involved in a project gets hot and the shit hits the fan. But through dialogue and performance strategies, we manage to work things out.

LW Earlier, when we were talking about the utopian impulse of collaboration across metier, across culture, across gender, you said that you believe this impulse carries the seeds of its own demise. Do you think that the seasonal, periodic nature of Pocha Nostra, the rhythm of the work with the core collaborators and the intermediate and outer circles, makes it easier to sustain this impulse over a longer period? People can work together for a month or two, but then they go away for six months, and then they come back. Is that part of what makes it easier to have these collaborative relationships, or are they still difficult? I'm looking at this from a more distant place, as someone who participates in maybe three or four projects a year, so I don't necessarily always see where the tensions are within the group.

GP There are some difficulties. Mainly because I carry on my shoulders the sole financial responsibility for Pocha Nostra, and that is a problem we haven't been able to solve, a sort of paternalistic structure which can become a drag. When the shit hits the fan in terms of money, understandably, no one is there to help. I have to face the IRS [Internal Revenue Service]. I have to go to the lawyers. I have to get out of debt. I have to go on the road as a solo performer for a couple of months to bring back money and pay our debts. But I assume full responsibility for not preventing this problem. Pocha is currently embarked on a process of reinvention in an attempt to decentralise this model after all these years.

LW How are you doing this?

GP By demanding that each and every collaborator assume more financial, creative and political responsibilities. That has been a sour point for some members, the fact that I become 'Dad' in many ways. And believe me, I hate that patriarchal position of being the primary financial provider for the whole operation. But we are figuring out ways to decentralise the operation successfully. Next year is going to be an entirely different ball game. That has been one problem. It's very hard to talk about it, because every time we talk about money, everyone gets very quiet and politely disappears from the room.

LW Are there other sorts of issues beyond the financial that you sometimes find difficult to negotiate?

GP Another problem I think has to do with cultural and methodological differences, which are potentially dangerous at times but which we don't shy away from. We have managed to survive these differences. For example, Roberto and I come from more activist backgrounds. Our work in the public sphere is completely connected to our work on stage. To do a benefit for La Galeria de la Raza or for a farmworker organisation is as important for us as to perform for the Walker Arts Center or the Corcoran Gallery, if not more so. To do a workshop with Latino youth at La Peña or at MICA [Montana Indian Contemporary Arts] for Native Americans is as important as to go to an international performance festival. Roberto understands this because he comes from a family of Chicano activists, and I understand it because I have been politically active for years. Sarita, however, doesn't share this history. Sara is a rebel choreographer, a dance outcast, so she doesn't know how important it is to go to community radio stations and advocate our ideas, to debate with activists in town meetings, to stage street interventions. All these things that we do regularly are not that important to Sara, so basically she feels awkward when these activities happen. When we tell her that she has to reconquer her place in the civic realm, it's a little scary for her because she doesn't come from that kind of tradition. Another occasional problem is the fact that our extremely irreverent working methodologies don't necessarily jive very well with people who come from highly trained backgrounds, especially actors and dancers. So a lot of wonderful collaborators go crazy when they are in the room with us. They want more discipline; they want more rehearsal time, and less blah blah. People like Juan and Sara, probably also Michele Ceballos – so many people of the people we work with are highly trained actors and dancers. They come into the rehearsal room and half the time Roberto and I are jiving, telling stories, discussing politics or philosophy or pop culture, and although they love us and are very patient with us, deep inside they don't think we're working on the performance, so they get a bit antsy. They want hands-on, disciplined work. But we end up pretty much resolving these potential tensions. You know, when conceptual artists that use performance as a strategy get together with trained performers, major negotiations have to take place. It's inevitable. We now allow for the coexistence of a multiplicity of methodologies and preparation methods in our performance. Before we go on stage, Roberto and I might be toasting with the crew in the dressing room and talking with friends, while Sarah and Juan are doing tai chi and stretching somewhere in the theatre. We are learning to make room for each other's ways of preparing. Also, after years of working with them, Roberto and I are becoming increasingly more conscious of the importance of training our bodies, while our colleagues are engaging more seriously with the philosophical, aesthetic and political dilemmas inherent in the work.

LW I understand what you're talking about in terms of feeling a little . . . off balance relating to Pocha's creative methods. It was very difficult at first for me to get used to the ethos of your rehearsals, and I've often joked that the biggest cross-cultural negotiation I've had to make in working with you has nothing to do with ethnic or national differences but rather with the expectations and conditioning that come from working in very different sorts of performance cultures. I would imagine that it's often a difficult adjustment for actors and dancers not to have a director in the conventional sense that tells them what to do.

GP It can drive actors crazy. But at the same time, what attracts a lot of actors and dancers, even opera singers to work with us is precisely the lack of hierarchy and authoritarian structures in the work, and that is exactly what they end up missing in the moment of truth. So many people have told us that. So many people have said that they came to us in the first place because it was such a relaxed and democratic process, a decentred process, a fun process, and then in the middle of the process they started getting nervous because they were not receiving clear commands and direction. I think it's a scary proposition to assume more political and aesthetic responsibility for your actions on stage. I see it as part of a democratic process. The thing is that Roberto and I are very good animateurs and coordinators, but very bad directors in the traditional sense. We can get things going. We can spark energy. We can mobilise people and engage them in exercises of radical imagination, help them develop their own material, but we cannot 'direct' and we don't want to. 'Directing' implies authority, and not necessarily moral authority, and that we don't like. Because we do interdisciplinary projects, our working methods are interdisciplinary as well. We are not just a performance troupe or an ensemble. We also make videos, radio pieces, organise political town meetings, write books, and so on and so forth. And each metier, language, genre and/or format demands a different set of strategies and methodologies. Besides, most of these territories overlap in our work, so we have to be able to combine, sample and pick from them all. But that is not necessarily the case for our collaborators working in particular realms, which demand more discipline-specific methodologies.

LW It seems to me that maybe another complication has to do with how small an organisation Pocha Nostra is. You and Roberto are performers, but you're also responsible for supervising the technical work. In *BORDERscape*, Juan and Sara are so skilled that they are able to arrive at a very high level of work with minimal structure, yet when I first started working with you all in the rehearsal room I could clearly sense that both of them were hungry for feedback. It's not that they wanted someone to say 'do this, do this, do this', but at some point they did want someone to say 'this is working, this is not', to give them very specific input about what they were doing. To what extent is the decision on your part not to provide that kind of specific direction or ideological choice not to impose your aesthetic on your collaborators, and to what extent is it connected to your various responsibilities within the project?

GP The bottom line is this. We have developed great performance exercises, true, but sadly, we don't get to use them ourselves as often as we would like because there is no time. Roberto and I spend 70 per cent of the time shaping the work of others, designing the overall project, talking to the media, and very rarely do we spend enough time developing our own actions and characters. We want that feedback as well, but the harsh realities of putting up large-scale projects often makes us diverge from our own discipline. It's a drag and we constantly have to fight ourselves for one more hour of rehearsal time, whereas our performance colleagues often have the whole day to focus only on performance matters. Sometimes I myself long for a director! Would you like to direct one of our projects?

LW I'm happier assistant directing! So far, I've been able to work with Pocha in such a way that I interface directly only with the actors and the text, and that's exactly how I like it! From what I've observed within Pocha's rehearsal process, though, you've worked out an effective way of using peer feedback to give each other the kind of input that people usually rely on a director for. The overall vision and structure of a piece is still primarily yours and Roberto's, but you've always been receptive to suggestions from other people involved in the process on how to fine tune an image, or ideas about how to expand on something you're doing, how to move from a striking tableau into developing a linked sequence of actions. But it's true that you and Roberto rarely seem to have as much time to work on your own actions as the other performers involved in a piece. It seems like whenever you're putting up a show in a new space, the two of you end up spending so much time dealing with lighting and sound . . .

GP The tech, production issues, and other peripheral things, the public relations, the video projections, as well as babysitting some people, etc. We are the only performers within our projects that don't have the privilege of rehearsing our material as much as we would wish. But we are getting a little better. Now, two weeks before the collaborative rehearsal project begins, I try to rehearse my own material in the solitude of my home, so by the time the battle begins, my weapons are sharpened, so to speak.

LW Moving back and forth among different professional realms as you do – working as a performer, an animateur, a cultural critic, a radio commentator, a journalist, an activist, etc., not to mention occasionally as a sound designer – definitely requires a particular and unusual combination of skills. How do you negotiate your different roles, and specifically how do you balance the aspects of performer and public intellectual?

GP After twenty years of crossing interdisciplinary borders, I have managed to get good at it, to somehow solve this crisis of professional identity. No matter what I do outside the realm of performance, whether it is recording a radio commentary for *All Things Considered*, teaching a theoretical class, or organising a town meeting, I try to do it from the positionality of a performance artist. Conceptually I always occupy a performative space, and my voice in that particular realm is an extension of my performance voices. As corny as it may sound, for me, everything I do is performance, of course with the exception of love – my love for Carolina, for my son, for my mother, for my friends, that's not performance . . .

LW   Not if you're thinking of performance in the sense of something fake. But even in your most intimate relationships, you bring people into a theatricalised realm. I'm thinking of photos of your mother and son in costume in different performance personae . . .

GP   Sure, but I understand that this is my *onda*, my trip, and not necessarily other people's, especially people who tend to operate in a more monodisciplinary mode and whose notions of the borders between performance and other realms are more fixed. In other words, I know that if I need to invite someone to speak to a specific political issue, I won't choose a pre-verbal dancer or vice versa. I would never invite Carlos Fuentes or Henry Giroux to be part of a performance piece strictly as performers and ask them to wear punk mariachi suits so as to be more effective as intellectuals, the same way I would never invite a *zapotec* shaman or a Chicano activist to participate strictly as performers in one of our pieces. Though there are always exceptions to the rule, I understand the clear differences and the contextual problems involved.

LW   Giroux is a good example of an intellectual who has a clear sense of how to present his ideas in a dynamic, performative way, a way that's compelling and captivating and doesn't leave people in the audience thinking, 'nice ideas, but I'd rather be reading this'. I can also think of a couple of occasions where you've included Baldemar Velasquez, who's a very important Chicano activist, in some of your pieces, in one instance as a musician as part of a spoken word performance in Toledo, and also in your performative town meetings, though there (if I understand correctly) it was basically the framing of the event that was performative rather than the way that the activists participated.

GP   Within the larger realm of the performance, we opened a space for political debate in which activists and scholars could perform their ideas, or better said, where they could be a bit more performative as speakers. After all, they needed to compete with skilled spoken word poets and performance artists, so they became acutely aware of presentational matters, of efficiency and timing, even of costuming. They all showed up dressed to kill. However, there is a difference between intellectuals and activists trying to present their ideas in a performative way, which is extremely desirable and which I think is the case with people like Giroux and Baldemar, versus aesthetic theoreticians who want to become performance artists overnight, which is not in itself a bad thing, but it rarely produces any interesting art, *que no*? Am I being clear?

LW Very clear. It can be very risky for people to work in a performative way if they don't have some degree of training or background, or at the very least a kind of innate aptitude that gives them a sense of whether or not what they're doing creates the effect they want.

GP It's inevitable that intellectuals in the performance art field want to perform their ideas, since one of the many paradoxes in the field is that traditionally people have been dealing with radical ideas in very conservative formats. So the question here is how can you reconcile the fact that radical theoreticians are presenting two-hour long boring papers dealing with radical ideas in the most traditional and authoritative way, standing behind a lectern under neon light in horrible rooms at nine in the morning? The field is hyper aware of this problem, and they want to jazz it up a little bit, to make it sexier and to find more radical formats to present innovative ideas. That is an extremely legitimate goal and I wholeheartedly encourage it, even if not all of their experiments are entirely successful. Most radical theorists have to figure out more performative ways to be compelling and innovative in how they present these radical ideas, otherwise there is an inherent contradiction. I don't want to sound so frivolous as to think that if an intellectual is not charismatic and performative and doesn't know how to deliver his or her ideas that we shouldn't pay attention to him or her. I understand that intelligence, in the era of spectacle, is also spectacle. To see intelligence at work can be extremely seductive and compelling. I just happen to believe that often radical intellectuals don't acknowledge the importance of context, costumes, props, etc., when presenting their ideas.

LW But even though intelligence is a spectacle, if someone has great ideas and a beautiful text but no vocal or performance skills, these points aren't going to get across.

GP In the 1990s, particularly since we are living in an information-based society, a highly visual, mediatised society, intellectuals should understand that we all have to learn how to package our ideas, how to make them sexy and more accessible, how to present them in interesting ways. And of course this is dangerous, because if we take this task too seriously we might lose the complexity of our thoughts and end up creating inventories of sound bites, which seems to be the only possible way one can be an intellectual in US media. It's very sad. I'm not advocating for people to compress their ideas into one-liners, or to sacrifice their depth of thought for the sake of accessibility and spectacle. I am not advocating for a kind of pop intellectual.

Don't get me wrong. What I'm saying is that we do have to learn to compress and edit our ideas and present them in more exciting ways in order to have impact outside of our own fields, in order to have a voice in the larger debates. Otherwise we will be condemned to speak only to our immediate colleagues, to remain trapped in academia, a self-referential concentration camp of the mind.

LW What I sense running through this conversation as an almost unspoken but foundational subtext is an understanding that different types of communicative strategies function in different venues. In a spoken word performance, one kind of writing is going to be successful, in a critical text something else, in a radio piece for *Latino USA* something else yet again . . . Even though you recycle material and create different montages by creating various juxtapositions out of a certain set of building blocks, there is always in your work a sense of strategy. You know what is going to get across to an audience on radio, and you know very well how far you can push the envelope on *All Things Considered* as opposed to what you can get away with saying on *Latino USA*. This kind of strategic understanding of different media and format seems to me extraordinarily crucial, and yet in many ways not sufficiently acknowledged by a number of intellectuals. If you're going to operate in different venues, you have to know each of those venues very well and understand who your listener is, who your reader is, what the boundaries are in that specific forum, what kind of knowledge base and level of engagement you can presume.

GP This is one of the spooky by-products of globalisation. The more globalised the world becomes, the more unable we are to communicate across borders. But at the same time, performance artists have become extremely savvy linguistic alchemists. We understand the importance of cultural context and translation in the shaping of a message, and we know that art does not necessarily translate to different contexts and audiences in the way the art world wishes us to believe. As artists constantly presenting work in different communities and countries, we know this very well. We know that the meaning of our actions and symbols changes when crossing a geopolitical border, sometimes dramatically so. And since Roberto and I are hyper aware of not letting ourselves be exoticised, since artists of colour have suffered exoticisation for so long, we want to make sure that something of the context we're putting into place to frame our work does translate. We operate as border semioticians. So our performance strategies are different, for example, when we perform in Mexico as opposed to working in the US. The proportion of English and Spanish shifts. The amount and nature of humour shifts, the notion of transgression. The positionality we assume within the work shifts.

LW I can see these kinds of shifts even when you move from, say, a university campus to a prominent art gallery or a Chicano community centre.

GP In certain contexts, our politics become more present, more overt. In other contexts, we can be more formally experimental or more sexually explicit. In certain circumstances, we have to do pieces that aren't language-based. One of the reasons why *Mexterminator* doesn't have spoken text has to do with the fact that we wanted to take this performance to other parts of the world, so the performance needed to be more visual and experiential.

LW How do you contextualise the culturally specific imagery of *Mexterminator* when you move away from the Mexican border region? Here in Aberystwyth, for example, people can't be assumed to share the same points of reference as an audience in the south-west US.

GP The images of our diorama are strangely familiar in other countries because these multi-hybrid stereotypes have been successfully broadcast by US media to the rest of the world; the context for *Mexterminator* has become strangely internationalised thanks to global pop culture. But still, we have to make changes, strip the hyperregional specificities from the performance, and add some pertinent programme notes.

LW Or add local references that suggest an analogy between the situations you're dealing with and the experiences of European subaltern groups.

GP Sometimes. Now, when we deal with a language piece in Spanglish, the alchemy we have to engage in is even more complicated. If we perform a language-based piece in Hamburg or Helsinki, we definitely have to make major changes and strip the text of all its regional references, translate certain sections into their language, and also to create conceptual connections with local diasporic communities.

LW To what extent do you have to worry about context and the kinds of references people will bring to your work when you're dealing with radio pieces?

GP I have developed an interesting consensual agreement with my editors at *All Things Considered*. They understand the uniqueness of my voice: I am first and foremost a performance artist who also happens to be a cultural critic, as opposed to a performance artist trying to impersonate a journalist. They like that uniqueness, the fact that I speak as a performance chronicler. At the same time, I understand that I have to mimic the format to a certain extent. If I'm too

experimental and too crazy in one of my radio pieces, I know that my
editors will call me back and say, 'Gómez-Peña, it doesn't fly. It's too
weird.' There is a constant negotiation, and I don't always win. The
same goes for our work in TV. In order to operate in multiple realms
and cross over with dignity into more populist domains, we have to
be pop cultural semioticians before anything else, even before we are
performance artists, otherwise we are out of the game. I see a lot of
naivety in many of my artist colleagues. I know so many performance
artists who work in a very rarefied, laboratory way, and then one day
they decide to bring their pieces to the streets, because there is something romantic, tough and urban about bringing your work back to
the streets. But people on the streets are very tough with your work.
If the work is not strident enough, not iconic enough, clear enough,
it becomes invisible. If it's too rarefied, people kick them in the ass.
People leave or spit at them, and then these artists get heartbroken.
They don't understand that every context demands a different set of
strategies of communication and presentation in order to be effective. The same goes for US intellectuals who wish to become public
intellectuals in the best sense of the term, to participate in the
national debates. That it is as much a responsibility for the *Washington Post* and the *New York Times* to create space for intellectuals as it
is for intellectuals to learn how to write for these outlets. Because
even if that space was available to them, many of them wouldn't
know how to present their ideas in a more populist way. They would
feel that they were compromising the complexity of their ideas, or
that their colleagues in the field would criticise them for having sold
out. If intellectuals are going to have a voice in the larger debates, the
effort has to go both ways. Mainstream culture has to open up to
include critical intellectual voices, and we ourselves have to develop
populist strategies that don't compromise the complexity of our
ideas. There has to be a third option, something between Gayatri
Spivak and Bill Maher, *que no*?

LW Going back to what you said before about your editors at NPR
(National Public Radio) understanding your voice, that you're a performance artist who happens to be a cultural critic . . . You understand
that distinction very well because you've also worked as a journalist.

GP But there is an internal fight within me all the time. The kind of
lunatic performance artist inside of me is constantly telling the journalist, 'Don't be a wimp, transgress even more, even at the expense of
getting kicked off NPR.' And the journalist is telling the performance
artist, 'Cool down, have a drink, let's negotiate.' There is always that
struggle within me. Why? Because as a performance artist I am

allowed to have a frantic voice, to be as strident as I can, and to be as contradictory as I am. As a journalist, I'm not allowed any of these privileges, and it's very difficult for me. In America, there's still the myth of 'objectivity', the naive belief that we can document or chronicle 'reality' in some way that's beyond ideology, and also a sense that your ideas have to be narrative and monodimensional when it comes to journalism. Journalism in America is very poor. I am perplexed by how naive people are in terms of accepting this optical illusion of distance and objectivity. Journalists treat citizens as infants.

LW There's more awareness of the limitations of 'objectivity', what Donna Haraway talks about as a kind of 'God trick', in certain sectors of academia, largely due to the work of feminist and postcolonial thinkers. What I think still hasn't been called into question enough and what I find to be particularly dangerous is the quasi-colonialist model of performance criticism, of art criticism. I know this gets us off the topic of journalism, but I think this also has something to do with enshrining some myth of an impossible objectivity. Any model of criticism grounded in the notion that the critic occupies a privileged position and is supposed to have the definitive word about the meaning of an artist's work needs to be problematised. There's a kind of hierarchical structure involved in that dynamic that needs to be reconsidered, especially when white critics write about the work of artists of colour.

GP Here again, the model is one of extreme distance. What happens when I don't get to look in the critic's eyes, when I never get to speak with the critic, when the critic never gets to know me personally and I never get to know him or her? Why is it that so many critics never ask anything of the artists they write about? Because that has been my experience. So many theorists and critics who have written about me never bothered to call and invite me for a drink and a conversation. I guess they are a bit intimidated by artists who can theorise, and I wonder, isn't it better to know as much as possible from the artist about their working process instead of assuming so much? There are also those critics who become very present in your life for three weeks, for the duration of a project, and then they disappear for good, especially if what they end up writing about you is negative. So there's no continuity, no possibility to continue a dialogue.

LW Part of the problem might be a certain anxiety about being seen as compromised or as being in complicity with an artist if there's too much of an involvement in the creative process, much less any kind of personal friendship, and a sense that this stigmatises the writing.

GP In terms of theoreticians engaging in a long-term dialogue with particular artists, I can only think of a handful of examples, but that type of dialogue is exactly what I'm arguing for. I'm arguing for an ongoing, long-term dialogue where we are both generous and critical with one another and where we're constantly questioning each other. That is something that really doesn't exist. In many ways, the hypersensitivity in academia about scholars getting 'emotionally involved' with the subject matter has translated into extreme distance, and this distance definitely produces a kind of neo-colonial relationship. The critic is way up there observing us with binoculars, and we're way down here screaming at the critic, or not even realising that we are being observed. And I wonder if that distance and unidirectional gaze really signifies objectivity. I don't think it does. The logical result of not making the effort to engage in an ongoing dialogue with the artist is that inevitably you end up writing about a ghost or about a shadow. Another problem is that you can't imagine how many times a month I get requests for *Border Brujo* (1988), or an academician walks up to me after my talk with a copy of my book *Warrior for Gringostroika* (1993) under his arm to get it signed and they don't even know that I've done other things since. There is a kind of time lapse problem, a chronological gap between performance and theory. It's very scary, because of course looking at *Border Brujo* in the late 1990s can be dangerous. The world changes. We change. That piece has a very binary worldview, which was very much part of the Zeitgeist of its time and place, 1987–88 at the US/Mexico border. That performance responds to very specific historical notions of the border. Those were the pre-NAFTA (North American Free Trade Association) days. Since then, the border has shifted dramatically in its meaning, content and implications, so to look at *Border Brujo* in 1999 can be very disorienting. The nonsynchronicity between certain milieux of academia and the speed at which performance art evolves creates a very difficult misunderstanding that we have to find ways to bridge.

LW There's often a tendency to freeze artists at a particular moment in time.

GP Art history basically wants to list artists by tricks. You become known for a trick, for a style, for one piece you did, for a bombastic incident with which you were involved, and then your wings get pinned against the wall, you are given taxonomy and you become part of art history. Perhaps this was inevitable during modernism, but nowadays, an artist has to be constantly redefining him or herself and his or her strategies, metaphors and languages. Our capability to reinvent ourselves must be as rapid as the changing cultural realities we wish to address. Still the art world wishes to freeze us in one particular instance, put us inside an ice cube, and we're constantly fighting to get out of the ice cube. First in the late 1980s, I became typecast as The Border Artist par excellence, and I did everything I could to get out of that ice cube. And then I became typecast as a multicultural artist in the early 1990s. I hated that term, and I did everything I could to step out of that ice cube. Then I became the hybrid performance artist, and so on and so forth. In the performance art field, it is a particularly serious problem, because the speed at which the field evolves demands that artists reinvent themselves constantly.

LW   Artists have to negotiate contradictory demands. On the one hand, they're being pushed to change, but on the other hand everybody wants to see that one paradigmatic work or image for which the artist is known. You're luckier than many artists, because you tend to get frozen in three moments – *Border Brujo*, the cage piece, and if people are hip enough to keep up with things, the interactive pieces you've done with Roberto. There's the 1988 snapshot, the 1992 snapshot, and maybe the post-1994 snapshot, but even that's a little too much to hope for most of the time

GP   Now there's a fourth one that is the web-back . . . For a while, we were adopted by Ars Electronica, ISEA [International Symposium on Electronic Arts], and Cyberconf as supposedly 'the only Chicano artists involved with new technologies' dealing with activist concerns. How does a field that is supposed to be constantly reinventing itself nevertheless become engaged in petrifying and typecasting art production in the same way as other, more traditional fields? It has certainly been important for me and for Roberto to be part of these debates, but we are getting tired of being part of a handful of artists of colour invited to these conferences to bring up the issue of race and the digital divide yet one more time. Everyone always says that these issues are important, but then a year goes by, and you get to the next conference or the next cyber-biennial, and nothing really changes. We're still the only techno-artists invited who are dealing explicitly with racial and cultural issues. And as a result of this, I'm starting to lose interest in work that focuses primarily on new technologies. Perhaps as a politicised Mexican caught between a pre-industrial past and an imposed postmodern present, I cannot completely make the leap into the digital information era. Some part of myself remains behind.

LW   You've said as much in your cyber manifesto. I've always found it intriguingly contradictory in a sense that someone who's as explicitly conscious as you are of the limitations of communication by means of electronic media has such a central position in the techno-art movement. Still, the material you and Roberto have collected by means of the responses to your conceptual websites have fed into your performance personae in fascinating ways, and in that sense the internet has been a valuable tool for your artistic practice. I think the attraction of the internet for some people is that it opens up possibilities of playing with identity as masquerade, which is something that performance artists and even theatrical eccentrics don't have to limit to virtual space because they often exercise greater freedom in playing with identity construction in real life.

GP There is a fine line between our projected, mythical identity and our everyday selves. There is a feedback loop that becomes a territory of ongoing negotiation for a performance artist. The difference between performance artists and other people is that performance artists are very conscious of the existence of this territory and of the fact that we are not straitjacketed by our identities, that we can reinvent them at will through the use of costumes, make-up, props, language. And this doesn't happen just in the realm of the performance, but can also be extended into our personal lives.

LW What do you mean?

GP The fact that, for Roberto and me, it becomes expedient to grab a *mariachi* hat when crossing international borders in order to alter the hat the border patrol projects onto us. When we do this, we suddenly become friendly Mexicans and no longer potential drug dealers, and this to me is a performance art gesture. By hyper-intensifying or emphasising the mythical features of our projected identity, that doesn't mean that we're responsible for people's reactions and interpretations. This is one of the normal responses to our performances. Whenever audience members engage in extreme actions, or whenever authorities in the streets, cops or border patrolmen, engage in extreme actions against us, the response of many people is, 'What do you expect? You called for it by always engaging in extreme visuals and transgressive behaviour and by being so confrontational and so obsessed with opening the wounds. You are inevitably going to face danger.' I'm not sure that we call for that danger. We don't conjure it. We are just pointing at its existence, making it evident.

LW You provide a catalyst, but how any individual – whether a cop or a skinhead or a person in the street – responds to that catalyst is their own responsibility. Whatever comes out reveals the person who is reacting. You open the door, but whatever happens then is the responsibility of the other person.

GP If you invite an audience member to get undressed on a diorama and they are adult and they engage in the consensual act of undressing for other audience members in a performance, they cannot just turn around and blame you for creating an eroticised environment.

LW Plenty of people choose not to participate in that way.

GP Exactly, just as many people choose not to engage in racist acts if you invite them to do so.

LW Everyone still has free will, even if the performer initiates certain acts.

GP Of course. Our goal is to create situations in which people get to exercise their civic will, in which audience members face democratic dilemmas they must resolve *in situ*. That, to me, is truly political.

An advocate for change
Tanika Gupta in conversation with Caridad Svich

As a child Tanika Gupta performed Tagore dance dramas with her parents' group 'The Tagoreans' across the European continent. After graduating from Oxford University, Gupta worked as a community worker and in an Asian women's refuge for several years. She began writing drama in the early 1990s. Her plays *The Waiting Room* and *Sanctuary* opened at the Royal National Theatre, London in June 2000 and July 2002, respectively. Gupta's personal and epic exploration of the relationship among the individual, language and culture marks her as a significant artist, especially in Britain, where the voices of writers of colour have not been properly heard in the theatre. A writer of depth and imagination, Gupta's work transcends cultural ghettoisation, yet throughout this interview it is interesting to hear from her how difficult it still is to break out of the proverbial box when it comes to having work seen as part of a 'dominant' culture or not.

This interview was conducted via e-mail in February 2001.

CARIDAD SVICH My parents are from Cuba and Argentina, and my family line extends to Croatia, Austria, Italy, and Spain. I was born, however, in Philadelphia, Pennsylvania and grew up mostly along the US eastern seaboard. At home my family spoke Spanish, and outside the home we spoke English. My relationship to words is always split between the two languages with which I was raised, and this has necessarily affected my sense of identity as an individual and an artist. I cannot help but think of myself as a Latina even though at heart I feel ultimately that my work is about being an American. I am eternally having intercultural dialogues with myself as I write. For me, the foundation for the writing, its centre, is intrinsically connected to my immediate blood memory. Family inevitably shapes us. This is expressed to a great degree in the manner in which we use language, especially if you are born into one culture and your parents into another. This awareness of the effect of language early on stirred my interest in exploring an expressive form like writing, where the alphabet of the world is at your disposal, should you wish to use it. What has your experience as a bilingual artist been like?

TANIKA GUPTA I was born and brought up in Britain. Born of Bengali parents, who were Hindus, although not particularly religious ones. I am bilingual and in the home we always only spoke in Bengali. My mother was a trained Indian classical dancer while my father sang. So, I was brought up on a diet of Bengali poetry, music, song and the theatre. They imbued me with a strong sense of being Indian and although the first time I ever visited India was when I was nine, I had no doubt as to where my roots were. It is hard to separate a sense of home from a sense of identity. Now that I have been back and forth to India much more, the two have fused. I write in English and am illiterate in Bengali (well, nine-year-old standard). I love living in London and the cosmopolitan nature of the place. Yet, almost all my plays to date have been based around an Asian family/perspective/narrative. I use Indian myths and tales, imagery, poetry and language but I seem to often root my stories in the here and now.

However, I have often been struck by comments made about my writing. It has been described as lyrical or poetic at the same time as being 'soapy'. The Bengali factor does come into my writing. Bengali is a sing-song language with soft sounds – 'sh' instead of 's' and soft d's and t's. Because of the colonial history of India versus Britain, English is widely used so it doesn't feel odd that my characters would use English in the home. I know some writers who are Asian have tried using the bilingual form to write but I have never done this because it immediately excludes a lot of the audience. I use words like 'nah?' at the end of sentences quite a lot (like *n'est-ce pas*). I hate having actors and actresses putting on cod Indian accents when they read my words out loud. I remember this one time when I was auditioning for actors for my play *Skeleton*. One after the other, these young Asian lads marched in and read the lines with a strong Indian accent. I would ask – can you read that in your own accent? They would look at me as if I was mad and then do it again. What's amazing is that none of these actors actually spoke with Indian accents – they were like me, born and brought up here in Britain and therefore when they put on an accent, they were copying/mimicking their parents and it immediately aged them by about thirty years or they sounded Welsh!

CS The actors were behaving, in a sense, based on their own preconceptions of what an Asian writer would write and therefore what her characters would sound like, no doubt because, in addition, when it comes to casting these actors are expected to speak with a strong

Indian accent in order to get a job as an Asian character in film and television. This has much to do with the sad but true state of ethnic typecasting which exists in English-language films and TV, especially, although thankfully, if slowly, typecasting is changing. It is remarkable and more than a bit shameful if you look at the way negative Asian stereotypes have been reinforced through film, TV and the stage over the years. Artists have had to fight through so much to be heard.

TG The battle to hear one's voice heard as an Asian writer? Where do I begin? What's interesting is that in the field of novels, writers from the Indian subcontinent seem to have been welcomed with open arms – Salman Rushdie, Arundhati Roy, Vikram Seth, Rohinton Mistry, Anita Desai, to name a few. But somehow in the world of theatre, film and TV, time has stood still. I have no problems personally being true to my work and not becoming taken in by the perception of all writers of colour as being 'colourful' or 'exotic.' I get very cross when other Asian artists trade on this and believe me, they do it all the time. In that sense, things are moving on. More and more writers who are not white or male are refusing to be seen as simply Asian writers. I myself have written for TV extensively and have hardly ever written for Asian characters. If I do, I refuse to let them be stereotypes.

Tokenism is a terrible thing. It's deeply patronising and so short term. But what worries me is that while theatres/TV stations here have got wise to the fact that writers want to be seen as writers and not as Chinese, Asian, Afro-Caribbean writers – they are now commissioning and producing fewer plays by writers such as myself. So, we don't even have tokenism to fall back on. They're simply not producing our plays. Yes, plays get slotted into seasons but I think this is happening less at least in Britain.

CS Theatre in Britain is less racist than in other European countries. It is significant, though, that companies like Temba or Carib have disappeared, and certainly Tara Arts and Talawa, however formidable a presence, are still somehow considered token 'ethnic' theatres. Perhaps how plays are critiqued has something to do with how plays by writers of colour are viewed?

TG I always rant about the reviewers but I think there lies the problem. They are almost all white, middle-class male and middle-aged. They have a completely different life experience and I just don't think they get it. They are the ones who exoticise or categorise our plays. What upsets me the most is that more often than not, they refuse to learn from a play that comes from a different culture. They judge things on the basis of their own limited knowledge and don't seem in the least bit afraid to admit their ignorance. Perhaps it is because theatre in this country remains the bastion of the privileged. I know the mums in my kids' school don't go to the theatre.

CS   *The Waiting Room* is the first play by an Asian female writer to be produced at the Royal National Theatre. How did *The Waiting Room* come to be?

TG   I was given an eight-week attachment at the National Theatre Studio at the beginning of 1999 and told by literary director Jack Bradley to try and write a new play. *The Waiting Room* is based loosely around my experience of losing my own father years ago. I was very close to him and when he died, very suddenly, I was obsessed with trying to work out what had happened to him. So, as any good writer would, I drew on the experience of death and fictionalised it. I didn't want to write a play about my father because I didn't want to expose him. So I turned him into a woman which gave me the freedom to make stories up. Drawing on Hindu cosmology and Buddhism and making bits up along the way, I invented a journey. Three days to roam the earth, visiting loved ones through dreams and having to face your demons before going on. One of my big influences was Charles Dickens's *A Christmas Carol* (1843). I loved the character of Scrooge being forced to look at his life, refusing at first to recognise himself or his mistakes, fighting all the way but inevitably bowing to the ultimate truth. Most of all, I wanted the vision of the journey to death to be fun. Atheists and people who absolutely do not believe in souls or afterlives or reincarnation surround me, so I invented the idea of a guide in the shape of the Bollywood actor Dilip Kumar (India's answer to Robert De Niro – only Dilip Kumar came first!) When the play was produced, it was amazing to see American white pensioners sitting next to British Asian youths sitting next to white middle-class English folk all moved and weeping quite openly at the same places. Stories are universal. It doesn't matter where they're based, in which culture or language. People can all relate to a story that touches on human experience.

CS   I'm interested in the audience: who goes to the theatre, why, what speaks to an audience, etc. Why is it, for example, that the Asian theatregoers who went to see your play at the National don't necessarily show up to other plays there?

TG   I guess I would break this down into four broad sections:
    1] more plays by minorities should be commissioned and then produced;
    2] marketing strategies of theatres should be more imaginative;
    3] more actors and actresses should be employed from minority communities;

4] more directors, artistic directors, literary managers, technicians,
   etc. should be employed from minority communities.

I think things are changing slowly here. For example, Peter Brook's
Hamlet has a black Hamlet (Adrian Lester) and the National's most
recent production of *Romeo and Juliet* had a black Romeo. My own
translation of Brecht's *The Good Woman of Szechwan* has a very multicultural cast (Chinese, African, Rumanian . . .) and generally there
seems to be more openness to casting black actors in traditionally
white roles.

One of the reasons so many Asians came to see *The Waiting Room*
was because of the actress we brought over from India. Shabana
Azmi is *huge* in India. She's not a 'Bollywood' actress but is a very
respected Indian art-house actress. People came flocking to see her
and in the process, quite liked the play. It shows how superstars can
sometimes shine a positive spotlight on a new play and it was good
that the National were able to put resources into bringing someone
like her over. A smaller theatre venue just wouldn't have had the
financial backing.

In terms of why these audiences don't go to the theatre normally, I
think it's simply a fact of (a) the plays don't speak to them. They can't
relate to them, and (b) they're not targeted. Some years back, theatre
Royal Stratford East did a whole season of plays, comedy shows, etc.,
which appealed directly to the minority communities of the area
(East London). The theatre did a lot of research into marketing those
shows and as a result, got a hugely diverse audience. It wasn't a case
of tokenism – the theatre put on shows that the local people wanted
to see. Likewise the Tricycle Theatre puts on a lot of Irish plays and
Hampstead Theatre put on a lot of plays that appeal to a Jewish audience. But is this ghettoising writers and artists? There is, of course, a
danger, but it shouldn't excuse other theatre companies such as the
Royal Court or Soho Theatre or even Hampstead from attempting to
do some outreach work. I think they don't do enough – lack of interest and lack of minorities within the theatre structure make them all
lazy. Added to all this is the different style of theatre. Theatre companies crave fresh new voices and above all, contemporary issues. I have
been criticised for always 'looking back' and not targeting plays at the
here and now. Maybe it's something to do with me having been a history student or even my style, but I think possibly what it's really
about is that I like the storytelling tradition. And quite frankly, it's
not 'current' enough.

I went to see my old friend Sotigui Kouyate on Friday, who was in the
Peter Brook production *Le Costume*. It was an interesting experience.

An audience made up of every culture under the sun, whooping, clapping in between scenes, in the middle of scenes and generally being much more vociferous and participatory. The play itself wasn't fantastic, but it was a lovely mix of narration and dialogue. Afterwards, I had a nice talk with Sotigui. He is a Griot from Burkina Faso and therefore comes from a fairly ancient African storytelling tradition. He said that for him, that's where it all came from. The storyteller sat with his enraptured audience around a fire, bringing tales to life. It made sense to me. It made me think of the 'Jatras' and street theatre I had seen in India. Sotigui himself always speaks directly to the audience, looks them in the eye and involves them in the evening. This is something a traditional Western actor would shy away from. It works, though. People were queuing up to see the show.

I think theatre needs to take more risks, widen its horizons and look at different forms. Theatre is so magical when it works, and all too often, theatre companies are caught up with who is fashionable, who is in and what do the papers say. Maybe then, they'd get a more interesting audience in.

Communing with culture
Chiori Miyagawa in conversation with Caridad Svich

Chiori Miyagawa is an Artistic Associate of New York Theatre Workshop where she manages the Writers' Fellowship programme for emerging playwrights of colour. She is also a co-founder of the theatre company Crossing Jamaica Avenue, and an associate professor of theatre at Bard College. Her plays include *America Dreaming* (1995), *Woman Killer* (2001) and *Stargazers* (1999). Miyagawa is actively engaged in examining how cultural identity is formed, and how immigrant cultures make their voices heard once in exile or in a new country.

This interview was conducted initially over lunch in New York shortly after 11 September 2001, and completed via e-mail.

CARIDAD SVICH You were in Tokyo earlier this year for the 3rd Conference of Asian Women in Theatre, where your play *Stargazers* was presented in translation. What was that experience like for you?

CHIORI MIYAGAWA *Stargazers* is about a group of people in search of a paradise. They get on a ship and leave the old country with no luggage, carrying only a dream for freedom and prosperity. The play was inspired by the crash off the coast of New York of Golden Venture, a

Chinese ship that was smuggling illegal immigrants in 1993. The story, therefore, is uniquely American; when translated into Japanese, the context of the play changed completely. The presentation of the piece in Tokyo was a rather strange experience precisely because I understand the Japanese language and culture: so, the characters and events were recognisable to me, yet the play's tone and themes had become unfamiliar.

There were two things in particular that changed the nature of the play. In English, my dialogues are spare. I'm interested in what is not said and how silence impacts the emotions of the moment. It literally takes many more Japanese words to accomplish my poetic intentions. The play runs about an hour and half in English; when presented in Japanese, it ran two and half hours. Imbedded in the Japanese aesthetics are the sensibilities of stillness and simplicity, and I am certain that my writing is influenced by the ancient sand gardens, dark wood temples, and beautiful spare Japanese haiku poems. Yoko Totani, the translator, is someone with a sophisticated understanding of my work. Yet the exchanges of the dialogues felt cumbersome with necessary explanations of the characters' intentions already understood in English. My plays are always done with a multicultural cast. In Japan, the entire cast was Japanese, which gave a different meaning to this group of people with a common desire and destination. In the play, through the difficult journey, people's secrets are revealed one by one, and the weight of the sadness and regret sinks the ship. With a homogeneous cast, the secrets became a shared experience; hence, there was a feeling of inevitability of their fate. In New York, many have said that *Stargazers* felt Asian, even though the cast was diverse and the countries were fictional places. It is clearly about the American dream and the consequences of wanting. In Japanese, the story became even darker and seems to reveal an ancient suffering of the people of the land.

CS Translation changes the way a play is perceived. As a translator who has translated both my own work into Spanish and other artists' work into English, I often encounter the difficulties of transferring meaning and poetry into a different language for performance. At the conference, you also had the opportunity to exchange ideas with Asian women theatre artists. Were there common threads in your conversation with them?

CM There was much talk of claiming time, owning history. The participants came from the Philippines, Thailand, Vietnam, India, Korea and the US. The represented Asian countries, except for Thailand, have all been ravaged by war and made to suffer by Japanese and/or

Western imperial colonialism. Chin Woon Ping, a scholar and a performer from the US gave a paper on the 'History' panel titled *Performing History, Claiming Time*. Dr Ping grew up in Malaysia where she attended British colonial schools, learned about the glories of the British Empire, learned to speak English – her native history neglected, her native tongue forbidden. In response to Dr Ping's theme about reclaiming time, restoring memory and transforming the experience, Kirti Jain, a director from India, spoke of the time when the British government established Pakistan in 1947, partitioning the land that was once part of India. Many women died as a result. Hindu women were abducted by Muslim men, raped and forced to cross the border. Muslim women were abducted by Hindu men and subjected to the same fate. There were women who attempted to commit suicide by jumping into a well but survived because the well was already full of the bodies of women who had jumped before them. Such tragedies abounded, yet almost nothing about this time is recorded. An enormous amount of writing can be found about the tragedies that happened in Europe. But in Asia, bound by ancient codes of silence, loyalty and shame, aided by the selective memory of the West, history goes unclaimed, untransformed, unhealed.

I do not have memories of, specifically World War II. In my mind, I divide the Japanese people into two halves during that time. On one side of the story are people who lived in Japan and endured hunger and the loss of loved ones, while some of those loved ones were soldiers who rampaged South-East Asia, killing, raping and burning. On the other side are the immigrant Japanese and Japanese-American citizens who lived here, lost everything they worked hard for, who were rounded up like a herd of animals and placed in prisons called 'camps'. With a devastation so absolute, and Hiroshima and Nagasaki steeped in the ashes of human corpses, the war came to an end – while in this country, Japanese-Americans did not know what they could call home. These two different groups of Japanese people are both me (without actual memory, without being a rightful heir, as I have no family members who were interned in this country); I am still authentic, because I claim them. I'm sure all this is somewhere in my psyche and manifest in different ways in my work.

cs   You cannot help but see yourself as a point of convergence between Japan and the US, and therefore Japanese and Japanese-Americans because you are living in the US now with past memory inside you, and another 'found' memory before you. When I taught playwriting for two weeks in Havana, Cuba in 2000, I came to the island with the stories my mother told me of when she grew up there. These stories were dated through 1961 when she left the island. I had one set of memories that I inherited, and as I read about Cuba since 1961 and saw films, and heard contemporary music, etc., another Cuba began to live for me, but both existed only in my mind. When I went there, I suddenly had to test my mental pictures of the island, however well informed, against reality. And of course, there are so many realities: there is one that a tourist sees, another which a traveller sees, and quite another which a native experiences. I felt I had no choice but to claim both the imagined and real in order to establish some sense of authenticity for myself about the island. Of course, what is authentic? Are the stories my mother told me, transformed by her memory, more authentic than my own first-hand present-day knowledge of walking Infanta Street in Havana?

In regard to language and memory and how they are linked, much of my relationship with the English language comes from my relationship to the Spanish language, which is what I grew up with speaking, reading and listening to, at home. What is your relationship to language?

CM Language is sacred to me precisely because I did not grow up speaking the language in which I now write. I relate to Gertrude Stein's notion of caressing a noun; I am very careful with each word. It may come from a fear of writing in the language into which I was not born, but I don't want unnecessary words to muddy my writing. So I try to examine each word to see if they really need to be there, if they are taking up space on the paper or wasting an actor's breath.

What 'marks' me as an Asian writer (for myself) is not so much my subject matters, as I have not written anything that is thematically about Asian identity since my first two plays, *America Dreaming* and *Nothing Forever* (1996), but the subtle, yet unresolvable sorrow that comes out in my writing. I say this only for myself, of course, as not every Asian writer shares this quality. I think it has more to do with being an immigrant: leaving one culture and language at age fifteen and having a long period of struggle to find myself again in the new country. There lingers in me an uncertainty about destiny when my 'home' is floating somewhere between two cultures and languages. However, as far as making work in the US, that is all I know. *Stargazers* was my first 'foreign' experience. I grew up as a theatre artist here, and I have always considered New York City my artistic home, even if in other ways I occasionally feel homeless.

The concept of memory is essential not only in my work, but in how I understand humanity. I'm fascinated by how people remember events differently; there is no absolute truth in history, personal or global, so I give myself permission to play with my own memories involving people from my life or my past. Certain moments of my life appear and reappear in different settings; it feels like I'm writing them down in order not to forget. Also, I have a concept of memory that is mystical and magical. In *Woman Killer*, there are two memory scenes that in reality do not happen. By that I mean the memories that the three characters have are not based on actual events, but based on a possibility of those events occurring. In *Stargazers*, when each character's secret is revealed, the strangers step into his or her memory and act out the events. In *America Dreaming*, a woman travels back in time, but certain painful or guilt-associated events have been erased from the collective American memory such as the Vietnam War or the internment of Japanese Americans during World War II. All stories are memories. All lives are memories. All my work, in one way or another, is about memories.

CS Culture moves in degrees. We are in a period of great transition in the arts in the US. How do you respond as an artist in a climate of crisis or flux?

CM Your statement, 'We are in a period of great transition in the arts in this country' has a very different meaning now – post 11 September 2001. I am interested in how the arts will incorporate/embrace or reject/assert the tragic events. *Woman Killer* was in the middle of its run, when the World Trade Center was attacked. Because the play examined the nature of human violence, my company had a very emotional reaction to going on with the show. After musicals on Broadway had long resumed, guilt remained with some of us about doing a play in which a woman is a victim of senseless violence. Where popular art was seen as uplifting, the seriousness of my play was seen, by some, as dangerous.

I'm an old-fashioned playwright. By that I don't mean conventional, as my plays are often non-naturalistic. I mean that I believe in writing about issues that we have been struggling with from the beginning of time. It is important for me to keep asking questions about violence. I also write about sadness that comes from not knowing the meaning of life, loneliness that comes from living with mortality knocking on our doors. The un-hip, un-trendy nature of my work, I might call 'high art'. I am impressed and moved by many things that might be categorised as 'low art'. Sometimes I'm envious of stomping, Blue-Manning excellence, but I don't know how to incorporate the popular elements into my art. So I remain honest to my stubborn, poetic, old-fashioned memory, grief and hope. My guess is that artists will remain faithful to their own style when we heal from this tragedy and its consequences yet to come, and there will be made-for-TV shows about the event on the one hand, and paintings on the level of Picasso's *Guernica* (1937) on the other.

Crossing language

The Kitchen's production of *Chaos*, written and directed by Matthew Maguire

The landscape remembers you
A reflection by Hilary Bell from an interview
with Naomi Wallace

Hilary Bell is an Australian playwright and librettist, who currently resides in New York. Her plays include *Wolf Lullaby* (1996), which has toured Australia and been produced in the US by Steppenwolf and the Atlantic.

Naomi Wallace is from Kentucky. Her plays include *One Flea Spare,* which was commissioned and originally produced by the Bush Theatre in London in 1995, and *Slaughter City* produced by the Royal Shakespeare Company in 1996.

Although Bell and Wallace had not met before this conversation took place, they have much in common as writers, not the least of which is the fact that they are both writers who were born in one country but work primarily elsewhere. Both are interested in the citizen's place in the political world, and have a commitment to exploring cross-social, cross-cultural relationships in their work. The conversation between Bell and Wallace was held over the telephone in February 2001.

What does it mean, to be a playwright of a particular place? It is where your vision is formed. Its landscape is in your blood, its sounds and smells. Its ideology is one that you either consciously accept or reject. It is where you first experience a live audience and see your reflection in its light. You might adjust your mode of communication to reach this specific audience. It's also what shapes your sense of humour, of irony, the sense of your place in the world.

So the geographically transposed playwright must interface with a new set of elements. The obstacles seem obvious: cultural differences, lack of common reference points and above all, language. But what if you move to a country with the same language and ostensibly the same culture? What difficulties do you face? What advantages do you have? What changes do you undergo? These were the questions I was curious to ask myself, having lived in New York since leaving Australia in 1996. In order to find out what I thought, I decided on a conversation with Naomi Wallace. Wallace is the US playwright of, most notably, *One Flea Spare*, and *The Trestle at Pope Lick Creek* (1998). She has been living in the UK for four years. We are both English-speaking playwrights who moved to countries where the language is English, and the dominant cultures similar: first world, democratic, secular and founded by immigrants. Yet we have each found that the longer one stays – and works – in another country the more apparent the cultural divide becomes. This is not necessarily to say that one's personal division from the culture grows – indeed, some writers feel that they've finally 'come home' spiritually and intellectually – that they never really belonged in their place of origin. But the experience certainly changes your work, as well as yourself.

There is certainly the advantage of having fresh eyes when you alight. You take nothing for granted. I came to New York and was astonished by the spooky beauty of steam drifting up through subway grates. You have the opportunity to make the familiar strange, to enable an audience to see anew what has hitherto been unremarkable. You also gain a perspective on home that you find only through comparison: I had never thought of Australians as delicate until I encountered New York directness. One may also find liberation from home's sanctions and politics, whether national or simply familial. Many writers have benefited from the transposition: George Bernard Shaw and Oscar Wilde, to name a couple of Irishmen. Ibsen wrote his best work in Italy, though he continued to write about Norway. You also discover that the most sophisticated of cities can be parochial, and appreciate the greater worldview.

'When you return to the place you're from, it remembers you,' says Wallace. 'The landscape remembers you. In a new place, you have no history, no stories. It's not until some years have passed that you start seeing places that have personal significance: "That's where we went sledding a couple of years ago."'

I have heard the same point made as having no peripheral vision. It is this subconscious awareness that gives your work context and texture. Without it, you can find yourself trying to write in a vacuum. When you are not part of the context, when you don't know how to read the signs, when you're not plugged in, you can feel very much cut adrift. While observations are interesting, they alone cannot constitute a play. And the longer you are away from home the less relevant it is to you, and you to it.

I experienced a bumpy period in the middle of the past five years where I felt, far from the advantage of having a view into two worlds, that I was superficially part of both, intrinsic to neither. Good writing is so much about detail. The details of home had become blurred by the passage of time; those of my new country were too codified for me to understand. Wallace happens to be one of those writers who felt a measure of 'coming home', primarily because she has an ideological affinity with her adopted country. She found herself among like-minded thinkers. She embraced the cultural difference, primarily that concerning the importance of the individual.

'I very much question the (American) notion that as human beings our welfare and our health are about turning inward and finding oneself, and letting your inner voice speak. This notion is always a movement of the culture away from community, which is a real political issue and connected to capitalism. Whereas I am far more interested in the individual almost non-existent without their function within a community, and the idea that perhaps we are only individuals when in context with another human being.'

For her, the very tenet of American playwriting rests on this notion. (Needless to say, we are speaking generally and of mainstream contemporary work, rather than the more challenging experiments to be found on all levels.) What passes for political theatre in the US, she says, is very issue-oriented – an 'abortion' play, a 'death-penalty' play – without links being made to other issues.

'It's topical. While abortion is a political issue, it's often written about in a very personal way, looking for the psychology behind everything.'

'When I wrote *Trestle*, I wrote it very much against the whole idea of the dysfunctional family play, which is so much about blame and victimhood. That is not to say there aren't great plays about dysfunctional families. *Death of a Salesman* (1949) is very much about one, but it is also about America, about how the seam of the American dream influences a family. It's a big play about the whole nation, and about a little family.'

The differences become most apparent, says Wallace, in production. In the United States, *One Flea Spare* focuses on the sexual and personal; in the UK it is put in the context of class. The American proliferation for method acting, the need to rationalise everything psychologically does not serve her work as well as the British vision, which concentrates on community, class and politics.

What has been difficult for her in England is the predilection for world premieres. Her break there came from being championed as an American writer whom they 'discovered'. While America (and Australia) tends to catch British enthusiasm for an artist, the UK prefers maidenheads. For me, the difficulties have been the other way around. I experienced the same initial interest in my work when I first arrived. But once that wore off, I found myself in a predicament: it appeared that the qualities that had made my writing exciting to Australians were problematic for Americans. I was asked why I shied away from writing autobiographically, choosing instead to set plays in exotic climes and to people them with singing devils and child-giants, raising suspicions that I was afraid of self-revelation. I was admonished on the ways in which I chose to end plays: one being too ambiguous; another circumventing the retribution readers desired for the amoral characters. I became frustrated to the point where I began to wonder if I should compromise. Compromise what, exactly? To write about Americans, about places that at that point in time held no significance for me, would feel dishonest and awkward. I thought about dismissing any hope of being produced here, and just sending my 'Australian' plays back home. Yet the longer I was away, the less I knew about home. I was no longer part of that culture's fabric. Still, I had no personal history here, no context. Although I continued to write, I felt that creeping fear that I had Nothing To Say – or at least, nothing relevant.

Wallace responded: 'It seems to me that if one is not compromising on the emotional level, on place and time, and you have respect for the way people talk and behave, communication is possible.'

I realised that it's what I'd been doing – or trying to do – since I arrived. I had begun to ask myself why I couldn't write about the quotidian details of my own life. The answer: because I have no perspective on it. I can only examine my emotional landscape through the transposing of it onto someone else, somewhere else. And let's face it: the quotidian details aren't terribly interesting. What connects me with the rest of humanity isn't my skin colour or my politics, but how it feels to be jealous, to be in a moral dilemma, to justify a lie.

This discussion segued into the perennial question of who may write about what. Can a man tell a woman's story? An Asian tells an African's?

'I have never liked the idea that women can't write about war,' says Wallace, 'when we know for a fact that some of our greatest war writers never set foot on the battlefield.'

It's exciting to me, and this connects to my politics, to think that there is nothing we cannot write about. In a way, that is what theatre is about: imagining the other. 'Americans feel they can't write about anything else, because they have this attachment to authenticity, instead of allowing themselves to be freed from constructs which might liberate them, and they could write about anything they wanted. American writers are still very essentialistic. I am much more interested in looking at how we work, what we desire, how we think. For me, there's far more freedom in that. If one goes by the notion that we are constructed, perhaps even our deepest desires are constructed, it's not a journey of discovery but a journey of remaking. People say that's what American culture is about: about remaking itself. Not really. Only on the surface. It's a very superficial remaking. It's still about the individual's power to make themselves.'

Despite the discouragement I was getting in regard to the escape hatch from reality, I realised that since being in New York my work had in fact become more heightened, the characters and locations more exotic. And I see now that the move away from naturalistic dialogue into verse, or from a contemporary urban setting to seventeenth-century Amsterdam was my solution to the task of expressing the human experience.

Unless you are in imposed exile, you have chosen your new country for a reason. To write in spite of it would seem somehow ungrateful, and a waste of energy – this is how you end up living a half-life, refusing to enter a dialogue with the place you live in. And certainly one of theatre's functions is this conversation between play and audience. To not write at all would be worse. The dialogue you engage in with your new home may be a vitriolic comment on its society: fair enough. Express it, but express it persuasively and honestly. Any artist knows that to deny themselves expression can lead to ill health and a stunted soul.

And if you write truthfully – true to your experience of human emotion, human invention – with the requisite skill and art, you will be heard. What matters is that you find a vehicle for its expression, which may be historical, or musical, or versified, or stylised. You will always connect on the level of common humanity if the artistic truth is intact, and in fact, the more specific your elements of character, time and place – irrespective of their foreignness or familiarity – the stronger the bridge to your audience.

Perhaps it is also the displaced, the transposed writers who contribute to the evolving nature of a culture's psyche. Foreign artists increasingly populate America. Some will give in to the dominant demands; others will, through persistence, reshape those demands. Some will fall through the cracks, some will be hailed (pardon the sidewalk metaphors) as cornerstones.

'The grassroots movement in the US is becoming much more international. It's about making bridges and finding interconnections, rather than nationalism. The idea that experience equals truth is eroding,' Wallace says. 'If you were in the Vietnam War, for example, that doesn't mean you were seeing things right. You were only seeing what you were seeing at the time. And that's connected to the idea that if you haven't been somewhere, you can't know it, which I think is a strange idea, because it devalues the imagination and education.'

The discoveries I've been forced to make in order to communicate in a new culture are what I credit for becoming a stronger writer – along with New York's more concrete offerings: a plethora of theatre of every quality; extraordinary artists of every discipline. They have made me stretch beyond old boundaries, bumped me out of complacency. I will always be a foreigner here to some degree, which means I will always be struck by the musicality of a Long Island accent, the sight of people passing by, without a glance – something that astounds me. A writer by definition is both outsider and insider, so geographical transplantation is really a physical rendering of this state.

Light, memory and other questions
A correspondence between Jim Clayburgh and Matthew Maguire

Matthew Maguire is co-artistic director of Creation Production Company in New York. He was written and directed many works including *The Tower* with music by Glen Branca (1989), and *Chaos*, a science fiction opera with composer Michael Gordon (1998). He also created with Philip Glass and Molissa Fenley *A Descent Into the Maelstrom* for Australia's Adelaide Festival (1986).

Jim Clayburgh is a founding member of The Wooster Group, and has been their resident designer for scenery and lighting since 1976, currently emeritus.

This correspondence was conducted over e-mail May 2000–July 2001 while Maguire was in New York and Clayburgh was in Brussels.

MATTHEW MAGUIRE 8 MAY Hi, Jim, I have a proposal. Caridad Svich has started to gather participants for a book called Trans-global readings. Would you be interested in collaborating with me? We could exchange e-mails about the shape of the theatre. It was great to spend time with you and Johanne and Alban. He's a pretty fabulous guy. Mairead was really taken with him. Love to all, Matthew

JIM CLAYBURGH 8 MAY So flattered I might even have to learn to type. 1 a.m. and fading but you got my attention. Bought a new mattress. First night. Never bought a new mattress before. Now that's a crisis. More later and best to the fam, J

MM 30 OCTOBER Dear Jim; Here's a possible strategy. Why don't we use as a springboard Edmond Jabes's *The Book of Questions*? This quote delights me: 'The Jew answers every question with another question – Reb Lema.' So here's a suggestion for our modus operandi: (1) we generate questions that arise form our current obsessions; (2) that we do not feel bound to answer one another's questions. We might want to respond and should feel free to do so, but we may also respond with another question, and that question might be germane to the original or it might be a new direction. So, we'd be caroming off one another creating a constellation of ideas. I trust that after a short time a collage of a conversation would coalesce. What do you think? All best, M

JC 3 NOVEMBER I don't know Jabes's book, but a series of questions seems like a place to start, as long as we can avoid the Handke play where the questions become too too. You know this play? I forget the name in English. In German it's *Das Spiel vom Fragen, oder Die Reise zum Sonoren Land* (1990), or that's what this woman in the office here in

Cologne tells me. And what can be better than one Handke clapping? Went well last night, J

MM 4 NOVEMBER Hi Jim, Here's one I've been mulling over. Since my loft was once a textile sweatshop (lots of black antique sewing pins between the floorboards) I often wonder if the lives of the women and children who worked here are still floating in the air. I'm not talking of a 'haunting'. I've been wondering if space has a memory. As a designer whose medium is space and light, etc., do you ever feel the space you create develops history? An accretion of the events that have filled it? Traces? Or is it like a tabula rasa, forever erasing the events that pass through it? I had a big chuckle over your 'one Handke clapping'. Here's one: does a one-legged duck swim in circles? Warm regards, Matthew

JC 16 NOVEMBER Matthew, On the train heading for Hasselt to do a performance tonight with Johanne. I perhaps mentioned the train as it has something to do with memory and space and perhaps landscape. There is a danger of latent pantheism in all this, I admit. This train seems pretty old, been in service for awhile. Even here in first class, there is a sense of mustiness despite the reproductions on the wall of a forest fantasy of long extinct animals in the Ardennes done in the etched quality of Dubuffet. This is not virgin territory by any means. Brueghels are out the window; the mud is the same. If I was in the first run of a new high-speed train, would it all 'look' the same? Don't think so. Would it be the newness of the train? The filter in the glass? The speed at which I see it? Rupert Sheldrake has this idea about genetic memory where a flock of birds learn a behaviour and generations later after the actual behaviour has been stopped for some environmental reason (no more milk bottles with paper caps on doorstops), another flock in another country will recreate a somewhat aberrant behaviour.

I think in the case of your loft, there is certainly a memory; conscious history I doubt. Unconscious history certainly. It interests me as a designer: looking for subconscious memories of space. Small shared flashes. Did you ever see *Fanny*, a 1961 musical? When the man comes back from the sea, he sings, 'Hello, said the door, glad to feel your hand once more,' and the chair, 'Now you're back where you belong.' There's a slight border between things that 'talk' and things that talk. (going through Neerwindeen)

As to the duck, straight and true. You ask a canoeist. Do you think there can be something that has NO memories? A space? An object? Best, J

MM 7 DECEMBER Dear Jim, Since Beckett's *Embers* (1959) is now open and I'm in actor mode, I've been thinking a lot about transparency.

I've always been convinced that the best actors can drop the masks that socialise us and allow the audience to view their thinking process. An actor's face is a transparent window. I haven't forgotten your definition of a good actor, and I often pass it on to my students: First and foremost a good actor has to be an interesting person. It seems bone simple yet it's passed the test of time in my experience. If the actor has the gift of allowing us to see inside, then hopefully they reveal a complex vision of a life lived fully. I've been thinking about space in the same way, wondering about transparency. Are there degrees of space that reveal their true natures more transparently than others? Are some spaces opaque even if you can see across them? Are some spaces transparent even if they seem dense with walls and objects? I have the feeling about Joseph Cornell boxes that my vision entering their field could go on forever, and yet that perception may not come from an absence of barriers. Could some forms of transparency emanate from density? Might density create an illusion of transparency by triggering an infinite caroming of associations within a closed field? Might that be the same mechanism that evokes in us the perception that we are entering an actor's mind? Looking forward to the next salvo. Warm regards, M

JC 9 DECEMBER Dear Matthew, Transparency, in my lexicon, has become synonymous with 'not attracting attention to itself.' Is this the condo/co-op dilemma? Do I own the walls but rent the interior volume or is it the reverse? However that works. I think this problem of ownership exists for actors in relation to text and a pre-established series of demands. Transparency in the dialogue between these. A glass elevator shaft? The paradox of density and transparency in regard to some actors. Maybe density and transparency exist in different degrees in opposition to each other where, as with most damn things, a perfect balance must be found. Not so sure in design where certain minimalism assists projection and clutter can focus. You know my long association with neutrality as a starting point of designs, and I'm not sure whether that is transparent as we are using it or reflection. Live amplification is perhaps an example: where the technology can be an invisible conduit. Good acting for me has to do often with multi-track reality: I see the person, and I hear/see the text/movements and I fill in the gaps between the two. Perhaps it's a method for me to avoid boredom. I found myself referring in conversation to a lighting design that I felt was dishonest. I hope this had nothing to do with belief. Did it have to do with the relation of the lights to the designer or the lights to the piece? The lights to the space? Perhaps it had more to do with a bag of tricks and the assignation of them. How dishonest can someone be with lighting? Can there be honest architectural lighting? Is the same degree that might be interesting for an actor be so for a designer or is it proportionally reversed? Is dishonesty a form of deception or is it just self-delusion? How dishonest can this same actor be and remain an object of desire? At what point does a dishonest situation become more humanly relevant or perhaps emotionally appealing than an honest one? Is that the same place for a dancer? Is the point in between an honest actor and a dishonest actor the most or least interesting? Jim

MM 12 DECEMBER Hi Jim, I'm intrigued by your concept of a *dishonest* lighting design. Can there be honest architectural lighting? I'd say yes. If the architect wants to guide our experience of the space with light, then I think that gesture could be integrated with the whole design. For example, the light through openings in the top of rotundas. I see no difference between the way an architect or designer shapes artificial light and how he/she shapes natural light.

I'm waiting to hear the Supreme Court arguments later today for Bush vs. Gore. David Bois meets Goliath. The soiled veil has been lifted from the illusions of our 'democracy' even higher this time. It's a bald seizure of power. With the pace of technological change so rapid, how is it that the rate of political change is devolving? When will the pendulum swing again? What is it like to live in Brussels and watch this disgrace from a distance? Yours in the thick, Matthew

MM 9 FEBRUARY Hi, Jim, Last night I went to see Julian Schnabel's film *Before Night Falls* (2001). Powerful. It's based on the memoirs of the Cuban exile poet Reinaldo Arenas. On his deathbed he says to his friend Lazaro, 'You are the most *authentic* man I've ever known.' I've had this idea of authenticity on my mind lately and references to the concept keep popping up. This film has authenticity. No corporate barcodes.

I'm wondering if there is any other quality more important to an artist than authenticity? In our culture images of authenticity have often been revealed as illusions. I'm wondering about the paradox of authenticity in the theatre when so much of our craft deals with illusion. How does one traffic in illusion authentically? When an artist is concerned with nothing other than their pure vision, that is authenticity. However, as theatre artists how do we factor into that our need for an audience? It seems as difficult as the Zen idea of non-attachment. Yet, what propels theatre if not the desire to reach out? Love to you and Jo and Al, Matthew

JC 23 APRIL Matthew, This now. With different texts of the many personalities of Pessoa (Pessoa and his heteronyms). Ring a bell? Jim

MM 26 APRIL Hi Jim, Are you suggesting that we inlay Pessoa's poems in between our exchanges? One juxtaposition came to mind when I encountered his *Alentejo Seen From the Train*. I associated it with your account of the train to Hasselt. Are you suggesting that you and I adopt heteronyms like Pessoa and add three more personas for you and three more for me to our conversation? Yours in Portuguese, Jorge

JC 27 APRIL M I can't remember how much coffee you drink, but that really was just a question, unrelated, but now part of the soup. It came from a descriptive metaphor for a composition of music which would be sung as/by a faceted personality. An experiment in the multiple-form (with different music) which is neither a synthesis, nor eclectic. A new form of One-and-Multiple. Or this is how it was mentioned to me. It had to do with designing, perhaps staging, an oratorio, a tricky thing. Classical and, by default, contemporary music have some tight boundaries around what gets accepted, although the boundaries often get stretched. The distraction of a twenty-minute light change in a concert setting seems to block the ability to listen for some. I find it a form of relaxation, a second track of active involved meditation. I'm surprised how few people shut their eyes when listening. Should I approach this as a question of necessity? Illuminate and go home? Jim

MM 30 APRIL Dear Jim, That was some heady soup you tossed me into. Nothing wrong with that, though. I'm with Yogi Berra, that dazzling proto-pomo philosopher who said: 'when you come to a fork in the road, take it.' I felt the stinger of your insinuation. I was hyper-caffeinated. Did you know that the honey bee is the only bee that leaves its stinger in its victim? The only bee to sting and then die. Kamikaze bees. [Why did kamikaze pilots wear helmets?] Well, I'm relieved it was just a miscommunication because that fork would have been a lot of work. We would have had to travel to Lisbon to study the original manuscripts . . . not such a bad idea. Ciao, M

JC 3 MAY M, I'm still wrestling with an earlier exchange: Do I own the walls but rent the interior volume or is it the reverse? This problem of ownership can exist for actors in relation to a text and a pre-established series of demands.

   Transparency in the dialogue between these 2/3: one, text; two, demands; three, ownership/occupancy.

   What do you think of this? J

MM 7 MAY Dear Jim, I understand that you're observing how the ownership of living space is like an actor's inhabitation of a text. It's a striking analogy. Let me respond to your question: Is it Condition A (we own the walls and rent the interior), or Condition B (we rent the walls and own the interior)? If a person can own the walls of their loft but only rent the interior volume, then that suggests an actor can own the shell of a text but only rent the interior volume. This posits that the walls of a loft are like the words on the page, fixed and immutable. The interior volume of the loft is constantly in flux like the experience generated by the actor's inhabitation of language. My problem is this: I don't believe the actor can ever own the walls, the shell of the text itself, for the text will forever *belong* to the author. Of course, in actors' parlance the actor can *make it his own*, but that describes a temporary inhabitation however convincing the illusion of bonding. Eventually, the actor will move on to another role and the ownership of the walls of the role – the text – will revert to its original owner. In this sense, the actor is a renter. Like a hermit crab, he finds a home that allows a tenant and, like the opportunist he is, he moves in as if it were his own.

This suggests that Condition B (we rent the walls and own the interior) is the easier analogy. The actor can only rent the walls but can own the interior volume, because the interior volume is his own experience catalysed by his entrance of the text. This evanescent yet real volume is composed of his ideas, memories, and emotional and physical choreographies, and he can rightfully say that he owns them because, whereas the text will never change, no other actor will perform the role in the same way. Now . . . another layer you're adding to your analogy is the relation between ownership and transparency. You're suggesting that true ownership yields a condition like transparency. When an actor owns a role we see the character, perhaps the whole play, through him as if he is a transparent filter. If he has any problem owning (truly absorbing and channelling) the role, then degrees of opacity will rise, and we, the audience, will fail to see the play clearly.

Off to do some plumbing with my landlord, Wish me luck, Matthew

JC 5 JULY M, Oddly enough it's the wide range of our conversation that makes it more about lighting than if it were 'more to the point'. These are certainly the ideas that go into lighting design, the rest being a series of answers to these questions, and others, that were raised in our ramble. This instrument here, this cue there. As we continue we should add a discussion on time: importance of, length of, passage through (remember *Einstein on the Beach* (1976)? Light moving at the speed of time). However memory touches on that. Oddly the frontal attack on 'what is light?' is too daunting.

I have spent a good part of the afternoon trying to draw the placement of the light switches on a stairway. I'm told dark stairs are not permitted. Why not?

MM 7 JULY Dear Jim, When we first started this project I mentioned Edmond Jabes's *Book of Questions*. Now that we're looking for our endpoint I'm reading it again. I found a passage I thought you'd enjoy since you're a master of light:

'What is light?' one of his disciples asked Reb Abbani.

'In the book,' replied Reb Abbani, 'there are unsuspected blank spaces. Words go there in couples, with one single exception: the name of the Lord. Light in these lovers' strength of desire. Consider the marvellous feat of the storyteller, to bring them from so far away to give our eyes a chance.'

[And Reb Hati:] 'The pages of the book are doors. Words go through them, driven by their impatience to regroup, to reach the end of the work, to be again transparent. 'Ink fixes the memory of words to the paper. Light is in their absence, which you read.'[1]

What a great thing to be able to ask such a simple question as *what is light?*

Love to you and yours, Matthew

---

1   Edmond Jabes, *The Book of Questions Vol. 1*, trans. R. Waldrop, Hanover: Wesleyan University Press, 1972, 25.

Evanescent truth
Erik Ehn in conversation with Caridad Svich

Erik Ehn is a playwright and librettist. He is co-founder and co-artistic director (with Lisa Bielawa) of the Tenderloin Opera Company in San Francisco, and an artistic associate of San Francisco's Theatre of Yugen. Ehn's works include *The Saint Plays* published by PAJ Books in 2000, and *Heavenly Shades of Night Are Falling* (1999). In our conversations over the years, he and I have shared our obsession with myth and restaging/reimagining ancient stories for a new age, as well as the making of a new language for the dramatic stage. His relationship to landscape through mythological, political and religious concerns marks him as one of the most influential and underrated dramatists in US theatre.

This interview was conducted via e-mail from May to August 2001.

CARIDAD SVICH Myths unlock origin, and in contemporary culture: desires, morés, or even unresolved roots of crisis.

ERIK EHN Myth language, being better worn (stronger and more economical), is better suited to action. Present language is necessarily a lot of noise – hasn't yet grown into the courage needed to name things in a transformational way. Older language (Grendel, parables, gossip-patterns, jokes) provide real working words; words that name complex states of being (worker, mother, coward, victim – each ambiguously singular) in ways that give us dominion (with collateral responsibility for stewardship). We can move these words around. We can be bound by them. Contemporary language has onerous responsibilities to inform and explain; a heavy tendency to move towards story. Experienced language is more spatial: states/figures are set relative to one another against a ground of pure velocity, not so much to explain or convey as to create a new tension (there are at least four gospels so that there may not be one story). The more expressive language is, the less informational it is, the fewer connections it makes – the event is a starting place and an ending place; a landscape, not a map. (The location and speed of a particle – one is known at the expense of another . . . and yet the matter is. Let the matter matter.)

cs Myths are what we carry inside us, in our bones and blood, which is why they resonate so deeply when we read them or stage them. I have often said 'we are Euripides' children', by which I mean we all have Clytemnestra as a mother and Agamemnon as a father, and we are still living out the stories he laid down, as we are those of Homer and so on. In making work for the stage, there is a movement against realism, which has existed ever since realism held its claim on the audience, and a movement toward reconnecting with ritual, myths, Greek drama (i.e. work that is presentational and non-realistic). These movements have yielded change, some more significant than others. For example, in the 1960s in the US, Joe Chaikin and the Open Theatre, the Living Theatre, Grotwoski's work at La Mama, etc. paved the way for The Wooster Group, Mabou Mines, Sam Shepard's writing and Maria Irene Fornes's writing to alter the way we view drama. However, for every step forward in US theatre, it seems several steps are taken back. How do you present ideas and shape stories for a new audience? What are your strategies for navigation?

ee We move as slowly as we always have, with our very few flowerings. Slowness stands out against a monstrous new haste. We have always taken a long time to come up with our cultural-statements-of-purpose, developing just a few artefacts per century, and then settling on just a few defining centuries. Today technology is booming and population is booming; the proliferation of artefacts overheats, but the real process of selection happens at the customary rate. English (for example) probably won't have its next Shakespeare until the next radical change in the way our mouths make language. We work slowly and in silence in the middle of speed and noise – to participate atomically in the running of the culture-clock according to the discrete tempo, knowing that one day our vowel will shift to the global sound. I write for specific local audiences, and try to put these localities in contact with one another (local means of production, global distribution – at hyperbole). The cultural rate is intact; the noise around it is screwy.

CS Would you describe some of the experiences you have had in working with specific local audiences? What unexpected dynamics have yielded poetic acts for you?

EE I have trouble with the biographic angle, but looking at the résumé as an anthropologic bone chip bag, here goes. A process worked out nicely in Dallas, Texas. I had been working with Undermain Theatre for a few years, and we got along well, artistically and personally. Randy Parry, the co-artistic director (with Katherine Owens) got it in mind to create a dramatic map of Texas – to do a series of performance pieces informed by the various regions of his home state. We set up a fairly long (eighteen-month) development process, the keystone of which was a series of road trips through Hill Country and down across the border with Mexico. The purpose of the trips was the trips. We didn't talk about story, theme, or business... We ate fried pie and took pictures of each other in front of red, red walls; picked up handfuls of tiny shrimp from small pools on Enchanted Rock when a light rain fell... After the trip was over, we did some writing to discover what images stuck, and how the images related. I went away with the information and deduced narrative from the logic of our collective collage. We made ourselves audience to the natural performance. We made an ensemble of our audience. We made a natural performance out of our shared dream-life and intuitive understanding of each other's talents (the way rain works).

Another time I lived with the Jesuits at St Michael's Institute, Gonzaga University in Spokane, Washington. I prayed with the priests and novices, cooked food, washed dishes and was generously welcomed into the life of the varied, thoughtful and intensive household. This particular community was built to serve other communities and the dramatic project we devised mirrored this; we opted to mix plays I had already written, relevant to themes of spirituality and social justice, with new plays on similar themes devised through exercises with the religious, students, and the homeless. We conducted workshops at a local free kitchen, where I worked as a dishwasher and counter help. I edited the fruits of on-site writing exercises into two short plays. We repainted the kitchen and performed four pieces together in that space after hours (Jack Bentz, SJ directing). Time and trust yielded a close-knit company; whatever meanings were construed by our crowds was secondary to this shared sense of time, of trust (which, in the end, is all I'm after).

cs   You referred to 'noise' earlier. The 'noise' around the cultural work and in society. Inside the noise of present language, is it possible to decode aspects of society and the self which have been forgotten? I think of automatic culture, where actions have become/are routine and therefore alertness is lost or neglected. How to counteract such automatism with art?

ee   To paraphrase John Cage, 'Language is the cure for noise and it restores silence. Silence requires listening.' Commercial culture requires capital (signifiers). Live, lived culture requires significance, meaning. Language controls meaning; consumption controls fashion. Deconstruction made spaces. Deconstruction is over, swamped by our persistent, long-suffering faith in communication. New narrative/expressive forms work their way up from the grassroots, along veins of live performance (punk, hip-hop), synthesising deconstructive energies to create room to move, then insisting in the wind that something worthwhile waits in the still spaces between surprises. In the hollow made by a strangely timed rhyme, unexpected dynamics, formal dexterity . . . are dark-night shrines to secrets clear of words – between and behind words, the *hecho poetico*.

  'How to counteract such automatism with art?' Assault surfaces; be faithful to the darkness in the cracks. Form over content and the purpose of form is to make something to break/break with.

cs   Linking of mythological influences from one culture to another is part of trying to find lines which unite rather than divide, to make an audience see rather than enclose themselves in one cultural experience.

ee   Travel is key – the aesthetic experiment (good globalisation) has a physical mission: to cross literal borders. Travellers' rules: go light, pay attention, listen more than speak. Learn local nuances of smiling and physical contact. Arrive in strange places with strangeness and need available, so that work you bring requires completion by local players. When developing work from scratch out-of-bounds, guarantee a place for your invention (your problem) as much as for your mediation. Fear and humiliation are powerful meditative tools.

cs   The traveller is always in motion. But a script, although living, stands still as a record of a time. What does publication mean for you?

ee   The fact that scripts enter history, or seem to, or may – separates writers from other collaborators, slows down or mis-weights the creative process and is holding back the development of script-based theatre, which is at the rearguard of experiment now. Documentation/information is too cheap (promiscuous, tatty); our pricelessness is in our unrepeatable immanence. Published work is literature, a separate field – and all I really want is theatre. I get more work and more play out of handshake deals and ill-advised beery potlatches. Playwriting is more than a writer's job and paper can't contain it (more, not better). A script, always an inaccurate document, seems increasingly a cynical sham when excerpted from context . . . a bid for permanence when evanescence is our glory.

Reshaping myth
Joanna Laurens in conversation with Caridad Svich

Joanna Laurens studied music in London at the Guildhall School of Music and Drama before moving to Belfast to study English at Queen's University, Belfast. Her first play *The Three Birds* opened at the Gate Theatre in Notting Hill in October 2000, winning her the Critics' Circle Theatre Award for 'Most Promising Playwright'. Music informs the shape of Laurens's work, and the way she not only imagines the spatial relationships in her plays but also how she designates place on stage. Her work is designed to explore in a deeply felt, unselfconscious manner the absolute limits of language and form for the dramatic stage.

This interview was conducted via e-mail in January 2001.

CARIDAD SVICH As a playwright, my own concerns are primarily musical, especially in regard to thinking about structure, and about rhythm and tempo for the stage. Federico Garcia Lorca, for example, a dramatist whom I not only greatly admire but have also translated (and one who also re-examined theatrical form and content), had a very clear and defined musical sensibility which he brought to bear in his playwriting. How does music inform your work, and your approach to language?

JOANNA LAURENS Music has influenced my writing to a larger extent than any writer – excluding maybe Garcia Lorca. I originally intended to become a musician – I play the French horn, and I went to a conservatoire in London where I studied for two years on a four-year degree programme. I left because I wanted to write. But music remains very important to me; both my parents are musicians and I was brought up in a house where there was a continual flux of pupils, records/tapes played, etc. Whenever I write, I speak out loud; I hear the rhythms, or beat them on my desk, and I like to play with the sounds of words – to collapse words together and then pull them apart. I am very influenced by minimalist musicians, such as Terry Riley and Steve Reich, which I discovered whilst I was at the Guildhall – especially Reich's earliest tape works of *It's Gonna Rain* (1965), for example. I often discard words because I don't like their sound on some level – often they mean, semantically, the same as the word I replace them with – I think I would find it very difficult to rationalise or explain why I select one word over another, or what it is about the sound of a certain word in a phrase which I like or dislike – it's not something which happens on a conscious level; I often think that language is only another form of music. And I love listening to the pitch of people's voices, and to the intonations of different accents.

As for my relationship to language, i.e. coining new words, using inversions frequently, etc., for me that's all part of the theatrical world of the work; it's a way of achieving some sort of distance from reality, a way of making people see the origins of words in a fresh way; it's also part of the sense of fluidity and flexibility which I value so much. For example, breaking the boundaries of what 'should' be used as a verb, and what as a noun – defying categories and playing with the audience's expectations; I think maybe that's part of what I mean when I say that language is another form of music. Music doesn't have those rigid categories; it (conventionally) has key centres and form only so that it can 'play' with these and move away from them to create tensions. I like to use language that way: to use convention only to move away from it and deny expectations. But always to be careful that this doesn't become self-indulgent or there 'just for the sake of it'; there must be a narrative and evolving action happening within this language at the same time.

CS *The Three Birds* is a play that is not only alive musically but is grounded in a strong mythic narrative. There are an increasing number of playwrights turning back to classic texts and myths as a way of responding to the chaos of contemporary life, and trying to make sense of it. How did Sophocles' *Tereus* find you?

JL I first encountered the Tereus myth when I was in Stratford during summer 1999. I went to see Tim Supple's adaptation of Ted Hughes's *Tales from Ovid* (1998), and was taken aback by the earthy, primal lust of the myths; the Tereus story was just one dramatised snippet within the production, lasting about five minutes, with a narrator reading Hughes's verse while the cast acted the scenes in conjunction. What really struck me about the myth at that stage was Tereus unwittingly eating his own son – and enjoying him. I could tell from the narrative that there was potentially an entire play within this snippet, and on further investigation discovered that Ovid's version of the myth in his *Metamorphoses* was based on an older text by Sophocles – of which there are only fifty-seven random extant lines. After a taxing library search, I found these fifty-seven lines, which, although interesting, were comparatively useless for writing an adaptation of the play; they weren't fifty-seven consecutive lines, but taken from throughout the text. So, I returned to Ovid's *Metamorphoses* and worked to a large extent from that. I wanted to remain faithful to the myth: to see if the same heightened sense of blood/lust/earthy desire would work now, for a contemporary audience, confronted directly with that, unable to escape from their seats. Theatrically, such points either generate the requisite emotion in the audience – or they fail, and cause the audience to back away, thus rejecting the drama.

Theatre is created by humankind to explore, criticise and comment on human life. And the concerns of contemporary man have changed very little from those classical times. That is how a play like *The Three Birds* can even make sense to an audience who has no knowledge of Thrace, of Greek wedding traditions or culture; we have all been in love, and we all know what it is to love and not to have the object of that love – that basic human experience has remained the same. Emotions are inseparable from the human mind (lust, love, death, betrayal, desire, greed, revenge) and there are certain taboos which occupy a similar place (incest, rape, murder of innocents, etc.).

CS How do you identify yourself culturally, or does that enter into your identity as a writer at all? Some writers, for instance, see themselves as only Irish or Scottish or North American, and others regardless of where they were born or raised view themselves in a more global manner, or sometimes align themselves with a different culture altogether than their native one?

JL My parents, my grandparents, my great-grandparents, etc. – have all come from Jersey (UK) – a small island nine miles by five, just off the coast of France. However, I was born in Bristol, UK, where my parents happened to be working at the time. At a few weeks old, I moved back to Jersey, where I lived until I went to the Guildhall at age eighteen for two years. I now live in Belfast, but don't envisage remaining here for longer than another year or so, after which I will probably return to London. Jersey is the place which cuts through a lot of my writing; the island is a place of sea, wind, sky and sand – it can be very wild and beautiful – and I feel a particular affinity with the place because, in a strange way, my family tree, for as far as we can trace, comes from this single island. Having said that, I don't feel any desire to relate this imagery to Jersey overtly in what I write – I just use it as a source of inspiration.

cs But there is clearly grounding for you in responding to the island. Do you as you write sometimes wrest yourself away from this foundation of senses, smells, etc.?

JL My second play, *Five Gold Rings*, which I finished just a few weeks ago, has a different geographical placing which has come entirely from my imagination; it's set in a dry, arid desert which is suggestive of Australia. In the distance are green mountains, which each character would love to escape to, but no one does. It is the unattainable ideal. Yet the characters have come from 'the city', which is a grey financial rat race, probably based on my experience of how the finance industry is destroying Jersey, and combined with having lived in the City of London for two years! The desert, where the action happens, is a sort of limbo world between these two alternatives. But I find that I need some sort of grammar of physical materials to work from in my writing.

For *The Three Birds* this was very much Jersey-influenced sea/water/sky based: I would hold the concept I wanted to communicate in my head, then flick through these objects which arise; for example, after Philomela is raped, I wanted to depict, visually, her state, so I held that picture of her in my head until I found the 'lowtided limpet, left sucking at the air' line. For *Five Gold Rings*, I have a grammar of dust/sand/heat, which functions in a similar way. The voice of the character arises from what they want in the fictional world, and who they have to be in order to want it. The world of the play is more complex, and fundamental to the writing – it is more a flavour of the world – something in the writer's mind, rather than something which can be located at specific places in the text. I like to create worlds that are theatrical, in that they are not realistic or naturalistic theatre; I believe television and film are the genres where realism works.

cs Making art is a struggle, a free and liberating one (depending on which society you live in) and an aliveness to the struggle, its nature and its necessary tension are what make us have these grand affairs of the heart, and I think writing a play is that: a grand affair of the heart, mind, body and soul.

JL Art depicts conflict and the best art will do so without trying to resolve such conflict: just depicting it in totality. Being 'alive to the struggle' is more fundamentally about listening – to yourself –which is what art is really about; listening to the world around you, and then listening to the reverberations from that world inside yourself. And then creating something unique and beautiful from those. And the more closely you listen, the more beautiful will be that which is created, the more detail there will be and the more unique will be the end product.

I have just finished reading Edmund Burke's *Enquiry into the Origins of the Sublime and the Beautiful* (1757) and his concept of what constitutes the sublime is something greater than us: bigger, vaster, something which approaches infinity, or which has indistinguishable limits. And for these reasons generates terror in the perceiver. To me it suggests artistic inspiration: the times when, writing, you forget yourself and your immediate environment and somehow are taken outside of yourself. I find it more beautiful and moving to create something that says 'OUR lives are like this', which then reflects something back to the audience that their whole self can identify with and recognise as true. I think that should be the primary aim in art: not to communicate any specific political message or moral, but to move people; the morals and messages arise themselves from that.

In search of a common language
Susan Yankowitz in conversation with Caridad Svich

Susan Yankowitz is the award-winning writer of *Terminal* and *1969 Terminal*, a collaboration with Joseph Chaikin and ensemble. Among her other plays are *Phaedra in Delirium* (1998) and *Night Sky* (1991).

This interview was conducted via e-mail in April 2001.

CARIDAD SVICH How did your work with Joseph Chaikin and Open Theatre shape your vision as an artist?

SUSAN YANKOWITZ I was very young and unformed when I encountered the Open Theatre, but their explorations confirmed my instinct that theatre was more than a story acted out on a stage: I was liberated to write out of bounds, against convention. Chronology, character, psychology, narrative were all thrown open (hence the name 'Open Theatre') to investigation.

For a long while I sat on the sidelines and watched. When, after I left Yale School of Drama, I was offered the opportunity to write the text for *Terminal*, I kept learning on the job. In particular, I came to love the collaborative enterprise itself and to embrace the myriad ways in which actors, designers, researchers and of course the director – especially one as brilliant as Joe Chaikin – could contribute to the creation of the work rather than simply realising the finished product of the writer. I saw that movement and vocal stylisations could sometimes substitute for words and that a surrounding silence could charge words with intensified meaning. I apprehended that a play could be built around a theme rather than a plot, that past, present and future could coexist on stage, and that a heightened fragment could be a synecdoche for an entire scene. As *Terminal*'s writer, it was my job to originate material as well as to help integrate the ensemble's improvisations into a structured and coherent work for the stage.

During this period, our audiences comprised musicians, visual artists, dancers, etc. We were part of a community that was proud of creating art as opposed to entertainment. As we discovered, our 'art', unusual as it was, was neither high nor low, elite nor popular, but had the capacity to touch a vast spectrum of sensibilities. I will never forget an inmate in a prison where we performed who stood up after the (wildly applauded) performance and said something like: 'You're not telling us everything here; we get to be part of the play because we have to fill in the gaps.' That may be the most important thing my years with Joe and the Open Theatre taught me: that questions are more important than answers, that a writer can write silence and movement and image as well as language, and that words in and of themselves are not always the most dramatic means of communication.

cs And yet still today so many years after *Terminal*, in a US culture that is highly visual in terms of the way it receives information, and one in which the fragmented narrative actually overrides the nonfragmented one, a conservatism toward nonlinear text on stage is increasingly the norm. A suspect eye is cast toward trusting silence and movement and image to communicate. Producers such as David R. White at Dance Theatre Workshop, and Ellen Stewart at La MaMa continue to believe in and support work that breaks boundaries through form and content, but they are producing at a time where there is a considerable shift against such support both from the private and public financial sector in terms of funding, and from the general theatre audience as well.

sy I can point to my tribulations with *A Knife in the Heart* (1983, revised 2001). They stand in bleak contrast to the exhilaration of my earlier experiences. The play was inspired by the Hinckley assassination attempt, the shooting of John Lennon, and the multiple murders committed by Gacy and Williams in the South, among other similar atrocities. That the United States has produced in the last few decades an alarming number of such mass murderers, serial killers and assassins, almost all of them young, white men in their twenties, seemed to me a fascinating subject for exploration. What had possessed them to feel that only an extreme action and public attention gave them distinction? What role did society take in the creation of these lost and alienated kids? And why, in every instance, was the mother immediately, almost reflexively, condemned? (We are seeing this recapitulated, horribly, today, with the children of Columbine and Jonesville, etc.)

I approached these concerns from the mother's point of view: *A Knife in the Heart* opens with her nightmare about the future of her newborn son. Then, in a series of heightened scenes that move backwards and forwards in time, her nightmare comes true. The play is not at all documentary and has nothing of the case study about it. On the contrary, it is fragmented, surreal and imagistic, with a rapid-fire structure that veers wildly between past and present, comedy and pathos. Scenes are shorn of the usual developmental build and stripped to an essence; many moments are dramatised visually or metaphorically instead of through naturalism, e.g., a hail of letters shower down on the mother and father trying to achieve intimacy after their son has committed murder. The piece poses theories, knocks them down and ultimately refuses to provide an answer. As Chekhov contended, the playwright is not obliged to furnish answers but only to pose the right questions. The audience, like that prisoner watching *Terminal*, is meant to carry those questions away from the theatre and into their lives. Here, as in much of my work, I keep trying to narrow the distance between *them* and *us*, to forge out of words and gestures something that brings us together in our common humanity, which is transcendent and bestial, perfumed and rotten, triumphant and despairing all at once. Why else have theatre if it doesn't influence the way we live, if it doesn't move us, literally, from one mental place to another? And how is it we have any problems (much less tragedies!) if the mysteries of the human heart can be resolved in the two or three hours of a performance? But Americans have always been afraid of the dark.

cs   Your play *Night Sky* confronts the dark in a very different way from *A Knife in the Heart*. Both plays deal with profound loss, but *Night Sky*'s singular focus on the means by which we communicate (how we form speech, share it, understand our world, etc.) forces an audience to face themselves with a degree of intimacy and pain that is rare.

sy   For me, communication has always been not only an inner compulsion but a central theme of my work. In 1985, Joe Chaikin suffered a stroke during heart surgery and became aphasic, that is, he lost his ability to speak grammatically. Joe wanted to make theatre out of that condition and asked me to write a play about it. In our original discussion, he gave me a series of givens: that the play have a narrative line; that it educate as well as dramatise; and that the central character should be a female astronomer who becomes aphasic as the result of a car accident rather than a stroke. When I questioned him about his reasons for wanting an astronomer at the heart of the piece, he said something like: 'Stars, stars, so many. Infinity'. I grasped that he was talking about the wonder and mystery of the cosmos, but had no clue, really, as to how this would mesh with the subject of aphasia. Joe and I conducted several workshops with actors to investigate the basic assumptions. In addition, I engaged in a good deal of research, as I knew little about aphasia except what I had observed in Joe, and less about astronomy. To my giant luck, I discovered an amazing connection: that the theory of black holes in the cosmos had a metaphorical counterpart in the black holes of the brain, where light or intelligence existed but was trapped. From this insight, the strands and structure of the play began to coalesce.

Joe directed the first production in New York, produced by the Women's Project, with Joan MacIntosh in the role of Anna, the astronomer. The rehearsal process was extraordinary, alternately painful, funny and upsetting, as Joe presided over a piece in which his own, still raw, affliction was probed and exposed. Joan was intrepid and brilliant in her ability to learn from him and yet create a character who was her own. The play has been produced throughout the world and translated into French, German, Catalan, Japanese and Spanish. That a play about communication can communicate internationally is exactly the kind of gratification that a playwright most wants.

cs You work as a novelist, screenwriter, librettist and playwright. Would you speak about the differences in those media and the nature of your new collaborations?

sy Writing a novel requires solitude and introspection: it also allows for total control over the creative process and outcome. What it lacks is the collaborative, democratic, tumultuous, live atmosphere of the theatre. Alternating between the two is, for me, essential; two different kinds of breathing: one, within the familiar privacy of home and mind; the other, outdoors, where the air is always a surprise, sometimes an assault, sometimes pure oxygen for the imagination.

Recently I've been trying my hand at writing librettos and lyrics, mainly because music creates possibilities for stylistic innovation, elevated or playful language, and drama that is inherently non-naturalistic. In daily life, people don't suddenly burst into arias or duets – and especially not with orchestral arrangements! What pleases me most as a writer for opera or music-theatre is that all disbelief is a priori suspended: characters can sing their thoughts and no one else on stage can hear them; a woman can play a male (the trouser role) and the reverse (the counter-tenor); an emotion can reveal itself, explode and subside within a single aria; lyrics can say one thing and the music disavow it. For me, with my taste for extreme or primal situations (too often deemed melodramatic rather than metaphorical in today's earnestly literal, thuddingly domestic theatre) these liberties are glorious. Further, dialogue with a composer is a form of collaboration, not as intense as ensemble work, but a good means of opening up new veins of expression. I would say that the use of music is another aspect of my ongoing search for ways in which to write dramas that are transformed by the imagination, that belong on the stage and not on television or the news or radio, and that bring the theatre into vital conjunction with an audience and with contemporary life.

Whenever possible, I look for collaborative situations and partners in art. On my own, I do what I can. Influences from my formative period shape aspects of many subsequent plays. *Phaedra in Delirium,* for instance, breaks gender and age stereotypes, allowing one actor to play both Theseus and Hippolytus (father and son), and another the dual roles of female friend to Phaedra and male friend to Hippolytus. But without the vigour of a group or the security of a theatrical home, it's difficult not to grow stale, at least to oneself, much less to keep going. I am always on the lookout for collaborations with composers, directors, other writers, artists, actors, designers, any person or group who can serve as energiser or irritant to my habits of mind. One sees differently from year to year, as well as in travel from New York to Madras or Barcelona. A new perspective, whether occasioned by a death or love affair or change of geography, always influences my writing. Before I was a mother, for instance, I unconsciously adopted the attitude of the child in any scene involving a family dynamic; afterwards, my understanding and concerns shifted, so that I saw also through the eyes of a parent. *A Knife in the Heart,* for instance, could not have been written were I not the new mother of a baby boy. My sensibility expanded and it softened; I felt more tender toward my characters. Living in Japan expanded my love of stylised high jinks (as expressed in the Noh, Kabuki and Bunraku); five months in Barcelona made me think about laughter, which is epidemic in that

city, and therefore comedy, which I am trying to write. What experience doesn't show up somehow – transformed, we hope, by art – in
the work?

cs New media affects the way we think about making work. How do
you negotiate your relationship to digital culture and performance,
if at all?

sy Thus far, I have not been attracted to or stimulated by the revolution
in media. Possibly that is because I don't fully understand it or its
potentiality; and possibly it's because I see the theatre as a shared
environment for actors and audience who can hear one another
breathing at the same moment. I am reminded of a judgement from
the last scene of *Terminal*: You are standing on a bridge. All around
you people move onto it and move off of it but you do not realise that
all those who walk upon it at the same time are not strangers. The
screen, be it computer or television, is a tangible intervention that
inevitably distances the viewer. There may be times when one wants
to play with that artifice, with detachment, changed scale, double
images, the grain of real skin and of celluloid skin, etc.; technology
can be artfully employed for such effects. For me, though, those are
best used as adjuncts to what is at the centre of our theatre and our
humanity: living bodies and voices making contact in the same time
and space.

IV

Crossing bodies

Junior by Stephen Bottoms and Julie Laffin

Strange behavio[u]r, Jr.
Stephen J. Bottoms and Julie Laffin in conversation

Stephen J. Bottoms is a senior lecturer in Theatre Studies at the University of Glasgow. He is the author of *The Theatre of Sam Shepard* (1998) and *Albee: Who's Afraid of Virginia Woolf?* (2000), both published by Cambridge University Press. He has written numerous articles on contemporary theatre and performance, and also directs and performs.

Julie Laffin is a Chicago-based performance artist, whose durational performance works centre around the public wearings of huge gowns she designs and constructs. Her major works include *Redress*, *Various States of D(u)ress*, *Path of Most Resistance*, *Supine*, *Small Sacrifice* and the ongoing *Red Gown* series.

INTRODUCTION BY STEPHEN J. BOTTOMS In 1999 Julie Laffin and I began collaboration on a new performance project. In April and May of that year, *Junior* was performed on the streets of New York, Chicago and Glasgow. The piece involved the two of us dragging a small, child-shaped felt sack around parts of the grid plans of these cities. We were also dressed in and gagged with felt, and our sleeves linked directly to the arms of the child, so that we were literally all bound together in one continuous piece of felt – my coat, the child-thing and Julie's dress. The notion of 'transglobal exchange' was fundamental to this piece from the start. For one thing, the public reactions in the different cities were tellingly different. On a more personal, conceptual level, this is a piece which can only be performed when the two of us are physically just a few feet apart – although normally we are separated by 4,000 miles. The piece was devised through an e-mail exchange, but then could only be actuated by physical proximity. This conversation was conducted via e-mail between Glasgow and Chicago, from 9 February to 26 February 2001, while 'Junior' himself (we always felt it was a 'he', for some reason) sat in a bag in the corner of my office – waiting for Julie and me to be 'back together'.

STEPHEN J. BOTTOMS So here we go again. We resume our e-mail correspondence, this time in the guise of an interview. I, as the theatre critic in this relationship, shall perform the role of interviewer, and you, as the performance artist, get to be the interviewed. Maybe we should begin by talking about this trans-global idea – because after all the piece sprang quite literally from 'trans-global readings', as we read each other's e-mails and thought of collaboration. And yet the performance we dreamed up that way, an ocean and half a continent apart, is one which can only ever be actuated when you and I are standing right next to each other. So in a sense this is a piece about *physical locality* more than trans-globality – as indeed all your work seems to be, however widely you may travel. Perhaps you could say a few words about that first.

JULIE LAFFIN Some of the work I do is definitely about a place (a city, town, etc.) and my relationship to it. For example, I went to Berlin to finish *Various States of D(u)ress* because I believed one of my ex-loves was there and the piece was about my whole (love) relationship history. As it turned out, he was actually in Cleveland at the time but I didn't find that out until I got to Berlin. Incidentally, I had already performed the piece in Cleveland – a trans-global irony?

But that's just one way of thinking about physical locality. As performers, many of us address physical proximity as well. I do public work in which I aim to take up a lot of the audience's space, or at least be clearly *in* or *of* their space: the huge gowns, being on the floor or the ground, connecting the dresses to the architecture in ways that cause traffic reflow, etc., are a means to this end. My work is somewhat site specific and I am always hoping for a dialogue between the environment and myself. With *Junior*, the environment is ever-shifting and physical locality becomes a very unfixed thing. I find that exciting.

I have been in collaborations in which I was connected physically to another performer (collaborations with Dolores Wilber and the shared *Red Gown*), but what's different about the work you and I are doing now is that it requires our separation. I'm not sure we would have made this piece (although I think we would have made another piece) if we were living in the same city, able to get together and work on it. One of the enticements of the piece was that in order for it to be performed live, it had to be activated when we were together, which meant one of us had to cross the Atlantic to make it happen.

What I'm wondering, though, is how has the trans-global dimension of the audience played a part in its creation and/or reception? The UK audience felt very different than the US ones. Was that your experience, also?

SB I'm not really sure – it's so difficult to judge this sort of thing when you're actually performing the piece, bound and gagged and moving. My sense is that the differences are not so much national as city-specific. We should perhaps explain that for each of the three street-performance versions of *Junior*, our basic activity was the same: we had to 'activate the sculpture' by walking around a pre-agreed pattern of city blocks, as if we were spelling out the word 'BOUND' around the city blocks themselves. A trail of sand leaking out of

Junior's torso or belly was supposed to be the 'ink' in this large-scale lettering, although of course we had some engineering problems with getting the sand to flow evenly sometimes. I also marked each corner we turned with a single chalk arrow, so there are ideas of inscription and mapping and family journeying all 'bound up together', if you'll excuse the terrible pun.

But to me the interesting thing is that the districts we chose for this large-scale writing were all quite different: to perform in Greenwich Village, starting out at Judson Memorial Church and moving through Washington Square, etc., immediately implies quite a different vibe and audience relationship than does performing in the downtown Chicago Loop district during a busy midweek lunchtime. So in Chicago, people seemed generally more stand-offish (as they might have been in midtown New York, say), whereas the Greenwich Villagers seemed more relaxed about us and more willing to interact. In Glasgow it was different again, because the city centre seemed relatively quiet that day, for some reason, so I have a sense that we were viewed more from a wary distance, rather than as a strange image that just materialised in front of people from the crowd. (You can see the surprise in a lot of faces on the Chicago videotape documentation!) In other words, to me the distinctions in response were about immediate framing issues more than national differences – although we'd need to do more performances to gauge this properly.

In theatrical language, we might say that the question was: what is our stage set this time, and how many people are finding themselves centre stage, and how do they then react? This also ties in with the responses to the version of the piece we did in October 2000, when we abandoned the street performance angle in favour of staging set-up images specifically for camera, with an eventual gallery installation in mind. We were deliberately choosing empty, depopulated landscapes this time, but when we accidentally found ourselves trespassing at that US Steel plant in Indiana, it was an armed security guard who found himself 'on stage' with us, and he really was not comfortable with that at all! And thus was Junior held at gunpoint (so to speak).

But I'm supposed to be interviewing you . . . In what respects did you sense differences in nationality or locality with the different versions of the piece? And do you buy my 'stage set' analogy, or are we getting into linguistic differences here brought on by another kind of crossover between the disciplines of theatre (mine) and visual art (yours)?

JL I do like your stage set analogy and what you said about framing resonates with me. I do think the Greenwich Villagers were more comfortable with us because they already have a vocabulary for what we are doing and hence were more willing to enter into the frame with us. They've probably seen a lot more street art than the other audiences. For example, while we were shooting stills in small-town Michigan, people asked us what we were protesting about. They didn't look at us and say, 'Oh yes, that must be performance art.' I do think public performances like this are often investigations in demographics even if we don't intend them to be. In my experience, people in different locales behave differently when confronted with work such as this, although I would really hesitate to make generalisations about how or why. I suppose it could be purely situational, sometimes an audience might even read the behaviour of others in their field of vision at the time and make choices based on what other people are doing. However, maybe the most important thing is that people are making choices: to respond, not to respond, how to respond, etc. In most theatre set-ups the audience is conditioned to respond by the rules of the theatre seating and will rarely deviate from that behaviour on their own. With public art, the options are more varied because the rules are less clear.

The ironic part about the US Steel episode is that we were looking for sites that were void of audience so we could 'stage' images for the camera. Some of the other 'staged' experiences made me extremely uncomfortable. For example, the shots we did at the abandoned farm just west of Chicago. I felt as if we were really trespassing there even though the place was clearly abandoned and completely in disuse and we weren't really doing anything wrong. Maybe I didn't have a frame for it in *my* personal experience. I was in a film once that was shot in an abandoned building, but it was an industrial site, not a domestic one. Something about entering into the personal space that once belonged to other people unnerved me even though we were really only in what would be considered their 'yard'. There was a sadness to that site, and I felt like I was taking advantage, possibly, of someone's misfortune. The place was in disrepair and there were some belongings left behind. I was rather spooked by the absence of audience, one that might have made me feel more secure, or legitimised our being there. Without an audience, what we are doing just seems like strange behaviour!

SB It's interesting to hear you maintain the importance of the 'actor/audience' relationship in this way. And I love your last phrase. Strange behavio[u]r just about sums it up, with or without an audience. I guess I'm particularly interested in the extent to which public performances of this sort might or might not be dismissed by passers-by as 'merely' strange behaviour. With 'indoor' theatre, people know what they're coming to see, and they've probably paid to see it, and will sit and watch. It's safely contained, but there's also an agreement whereby the spectator is agreeing to try to *take it in* on some level, to *read* the piece with full attention. The same goes for any gallery installation we might make with the staged photos and other 'artefacts'. However, I have the impression that, at a certain point in your career, you deliberately chose to move outside those kinds of institutional framework (as a comment of sorts on those frameworks, perhaps?). Yet in placing yourself – as it were – in the quotidian flow of the everyday, do you ever feel that you run the risk of merely becoming an oddity for the 'accidental' spectators?

I often feel that way about street art, in fact – although one of the reasons I love your work is that the images are so vivid that people can't help but be struck by them – particularly the sheer scale and colour of some of your giant dress pieces. There really is an 'artistic' or 'sculptural' image which your average person-in-the-street can see and appreciate as such (as opposed to the kind of conceptual per-formance work which sometimes borders on total invisibility). For instance, in Cleveland with *Over*, I remember vividly watching this gang of street kids follow you in fascination around an entire city block, as you dragged that big heavy dress on your hands and knees. With those pieces, you really are (to borrow a phrase of yours) 'inter-rupting the everyday' on some level. Maybe, for some, you're even facilitating a moment of liminal awareness within the everyday flux. *Junior* seems a bit different though, because the image is of a smaller scale: it's two people dressed in almost normal-size costumes (OK, they're made of felt with long sleeves and we're gagged, but . . .), and we're moving much faster than you normally would with the big train dresses. We're just dragging the kid along the sidewalk; blink and you'd miss us. So I wonder if it *registers* in quite the same way as your other pieces (in which stillness is often such an important factor). Is it more dismissible as 'strange behaviour' this way? There again, this more fleeting image is also possibly more *disturbing* than some of your others – thanks to the straightjacket quality of the cos-tumes, and the gags, and the blank-faced beat-up baby. Maybe you'd like to say something about this comparison.

JL I think *Junior* functions in the same way for the audience as the big dresses, even though we are simply passing through an audience's field of vision. They are still making a choice about how long to view us in some sense. They could choose to follow us – and some did! – although most people wouldn't. But it's often not that different for my other work. The ambient audience encountering the work might only spend a few seconds absorbing the work. I think the main difference is that they can choose to come back and view it again since it often has a static and prolonged structure.

My husband told me someone did a study of people viewing paintings in galleries and museums and the average time each painting was viewed was something like six seconds – which is quite different than the captive audience contract with the audience you mentioned. The reason I moved away from institutional frameworks such as the seated audience is that the *form* of the work was always predictable. No matter what happened (unless there was an emergency in the theatre) people bought their tickets, took their seats, and at the designated time, gave their seats back. No matter what interesting things happened during the piece, those rules never changed. Even pieces that were highly audience-interactive followed the same pattern. First, I began trying to subvert those rules, which was really fun. I did a version of *Various States of D(u)ress* in Philadelphia where the audience came, purchased tickets and sat in their seats and during my performance I asked them to follow me out on to the street for a tour of Philadelphia. At first no one believed we were actually leaving the theatre with me in my 60 ft dress to 'navigate' our way around the city. The interesting thing is that most of the audience was from Philadelphia and had seen it as part of their everyday experience, but not while carrying a 60 ft train of a performer from Chicago. Incidentally the piece was a somewhat spontaneous reaction to not being able to do the piece I came to do; one that involved my painting myself during my performance. The presenters were afraid I was going to ruin the pristine dance floor and be liable for it. When I tried to restructure the piece into another familiar incarnation of *Various States* by painting (with tempera paint) names (of my ex-loves) onto neighborhood property I was almost arrested.

Another example is a piece I did in Cleveland around the same time. I sat in the audience completely unclothed throughout the evening of performance events waiting for my allotted time to do my piece. Frank Green, a performer/writer remarked that my onstage piece (painting clothing onto my nude body) in front of the lights was one of the shortest pieces ever done at Cleveland Performance Art Festival. But my piece really happened while I was installed in the audience – not performing at all. There was also a period where I was doing pieces in cabaret venues that were more like installations. I really loved subverting the rules of the theatre. What makes it so easy is that they are so entrenched in our consciousness. I must admit, when I go to the theatre myself as audience I love being a passive spectator. It's a very pampered position to be in. To be able to sit back, absorb and enjoy, judge in a sense . . .

Yes, I think it's easy for an ambient audience on the street to be dismissive of work they can't find a context for. But that's true of all things we humans can't or aren't willing to find a context for. I see myself as an educator of audience. I expose them to work they would not seek out. I try to be democratic about it. I try now not to put myself in situations where the audience is 'in the know'. I avoid exclusively art-educated audiences because they are not representative of our culture at large. The world of the accidental audience is a much more interesting place to be in terms of being a performer, even though the work may be less legitimised and offer fewer rewards in terms of recognition, payment, etc. The responses are more varied (dare I say more authentic?), and unmediated by a body of knowledge that we are all cloned to have and rely upon, by virtue of our educations.

SB What you're saying makes complete sense to me – and I think also says a lot about the differences in our outlooks. My practical performance experience is mostly as a theatre director, which tends to make me something of a control freak: most directors are control freaks, no matter how generous they are with their performers, because in rehearsal you're trying to create an event which will then be reproduced as you envisaged it even when you've had to let go of it (directors don't get to *conduct* during performance, unless of course they're Tadeusz Kantor). The appeal of the static theatre audience is that they are the 'all other things being equal' element: they sit still, and the performers can get on with doing what you prepared, as accurately as possible. *Except* of course that this is always a delusion, because the audience are anything *but* 'all other things being equal': you never know who is in on any given night, or what the aggregate of their experiences or tastes or opinions or politics or incomes might be. There's no way on earth that you can control what they are making of your lovingly prepared *thing*, as they conduct a private conversation about it in their heads, all in relation to what they did that day at work, what dinner was like, whether they're fighting with their partners, or whether they saw a show that was kinda like this just last week. So what I love about experimenting with outdoor, 'accidental audience' pieces (which I have been inspired to do largely because of exposure to your work), is that in a sense the dynamic is much more honest. Nobody feels obliged to sit and watch if they're not enjoying what they see. Often you hear very vocal responses. The piece changes markedly depending on where and when you do it; it's constantly in flux. And that is scary, because in a very real sense it means that the event is *out of your control*. But that can also be a curiously liberating experience.

In fact, recently I've begun to try to build something of that sense of chance into my more controlled directing work: *nationspace*, the collaborative performance which my company created last year, began as a promenade piece in a disused warehouse in the dock region of Glasgow, and then mutated – in relation to the site-specifics of different tour venues – into a proscenium arch piece, a traverse piece, etc. We found that in each new situation, audiences were able to pick up on different dimensions of the show, because of this transformability (seated audiences laughed more easily at the show's humour, for example, because they were more relaxed and comfortable; but the moving promenade audiences had much more of a physical awareness of the piece's spatial fluidity). The performers were also responding to these shifts by moving spontaneously with the show's changing dynamic, allowing different sections of the piece to be improvised around or cut out altogether in a given performance. As a director it was hair-raising to watch, because you never knew quite what was going to happen next, but as a result there was an *edge* about the piece every time out, a sense of risk which was literally unrepeatable.

I mention this by way of indicating how opening myself up to your kind of work has allowed an evolution of sorts in mine, and that exchange element really interests me. I mean, in most respects *Junior* is obviously a Julie Laffin piece – the image is yours, the costume design yours, you even did the sewing. Plus we were out on the street, where you seem most comfortable. And yet this was/is also a collaboration in some sense. Perhaps we could talk a little about that – not just to prop up my ego, but because the whole topic of collaboration seems like a vitally important one. In theatre of course you can't avoid it (although the nature of producer–writer–director–designer–performer hierarchies often preclude real two-way exchange). Yet I'm also aware that, as a solo performer with a fine-arts studio training, you're extremely wary of collaborating with others, and that your past experiences in this area have not always been positive.

JL I was thinking a couple of days ago how our collaboration on *Junior* has healed me from other attempts at collaboration gone wrong. (This statement is not meant to blame anyone. I am only too painfully aware of my own severe limitations as a collaborator.) I suspect somehow the strength of our personal friendship has been a contributing factor, and maybe also that we are coming from different disciplines, the literary and the visual. Or perhaps we just had the right chemistry and enough 'space' (did you say it was 4,000 miles?) to make it work. But seriously, I've always felt, and hope you do too, that we've been able to share the work and also retain our own identities in the process.

It has never occurred to me that the work as a whole is more 'mine' somehow than 'yours', although we can both cite which parts look more like my previous work and which things came from yours. I agree that the images we are making hearken to my earlier work with garments outdoors, but they also call upon your earlier use of the gag, an image that is critical to the work because of the various interpretations it evokes. (Not to mention that it also gives the act of sandwriting more conceptual weight because we are unable to simply speak.) The (very crucial) spine of the work came from you, and your knowledge of literary texts, in this case, Paul Auster. Although I sometimes rely on creating my own minimal text and remain interested in it, my solo work has never been based on interpreting or invoking a pre-existing literary text. I find this excursion into the literary exciting, and would never have attempted it on my own. Finally, the parent/couple and the child images are very new territory to me and seem to have evolved spontaneously via our e-mail conversations about what we might do. *Junior* is not a piece I ever could have conceived independently of our process together and it has expanded my notions of what my body of work is.

I can't emphasise enough how much *Junior* feels distinctly different from my solo work and very much an equally shared creation between the two of us. What we ended up with visually or conceptually that came from our individual bodies of work, overlapped both of them, or sprung newly from this piece, is perhaps even incidental. I think the most important aspect of what we have is due to two things. Firstly, that we made decisions together. In my experience, we were striving for a consensus at each juncture, and most of the time achieving it. And I'm not even so sure if that's artistically desirable-decisions by committee only! Secondly, that our contribution and commitment to the project felt equal. Perhaps these dynamics are what makes it so worthwhile and so 'ours' in retrospect.

SB I really never realised the extent to which you see *Junior* as something very different from your other outdoor work. With *Junior*, I guess I've always felt that I was getting to participate a little in your kind of process. I've felt this as a great privilege, and perhaps I needed to feel humble about my involvement (you invited me to collaborate, not the other way around) in order to avoid getting 'directorial' ideas above my station. But maybe there always needs to be at least some sense that one person (for me, in this case: you) is ultimately in charge. Perhaps this is relevant to the caveat you've thrown in, about you not being sure if a consensus-based creative process is even desirable. Could you address that a little more?

JL At the risk of taking a fascistic position, I am not sure the best artistic decisions are made by committee! I mean, you then run the risk of always ending up with a piece that essentially is a bag of compromises. I guess that may be the visual artist point of view – most painters wouldn't even think about collaborating with other painters on a painting. On the other hand, theatrical groups have been working successfully in this collaborative way more and more. I can think of several Chicago-based groups who work like this that I admire: Goat Island, Theatre Ooblek, Curious Theatre Branch. It's something I have to rethink and learn about each time I collaborate. My solo work is very much about the creation of a single image – one I've already conceived and let brew before I ever set about making the work. That seems, and can be, antithetical to a collaboration of any kind.

SB Your mention of the 'single image' brings up something else – our use of the parent–child imagery in *Junior*. It's clearly the core of the piece, and yet neither of us seems to know where it came from. Neither of us has children, and neither of us even talked about this as a 'theme' for the piece. Yet that is what emerged, almost accidentally it seems, from the e-mailed to-ing and fro-ing, almost as if it crept up on us. This is 'our baby', I guess. And the nuclear family image is what people are seeing the piece to be 'about'. When I showed Lin Hixson (director of the performance group Goat Island) photographs of the piece, she was fascinated by it, and asked, 'Have you and Julie talked about having children?' Then of course she realised what she'd said and we fell apart laughing. But the fact is that we *hadn't* talked about it. As I recall it (my e-mail back account was eaten by a virus so I can't confirm this), the image simply evolved from the initial idea of having some solid object in between us and attached to us, and at some point that object became a small figure. Yet somehow the image *does* resonate with me, on levels I'm not sure I even want to talk about. On an analytical level, I could maybe point to connections with family-based dramas I've written about like those of Edward Albee and Sam Shepard, where the fate of the kid (real or imaginary) is always being fought over by the parents. The *Junior* image suggests to me something about the way families are tied together whether they like it or not, perhaps about how children can become a burden to their parents, and certainly about the way children's personalities develop as an accumulation of the ideas imposed and the scars inflicted on them by their parents. Junior himself has now been repeatedly torn, patched and re-patched as a result of all the dragging around on his knees in different cities – so that even the traces/residue of the performances seems to add something thematically: the older he gets, the more he experiences, the more *damaged* he gets; and yet we also seem to become more attached to him in a way, because he somehow seems more 'human' to us as a result. Is this just fanciful? Maybe. (And why are we so sure he is a he?) I mean I could analyse this all day, but the fact is that none of this was ever intended. It just happened. Have you any idea how?

JL The child imagery seems like a foreign land to me. A real departure from the other work I've done. I have a lot of personal feelings against the abuse of children, as most people with any conscience do, but this has nothing to do with that. I like what you said about our developing relationship with the personified object of Junior but my reading of the piece is different than yours perhaps. The potency in the image for me lies in the ambiguity of it. We're tied to this child-thing for better or for worse and what does it mean? It's absent, vacant, void of child actually.

It has occurred to me that Junior does not actually represent a child. Junior, the object is actually not an object or persona but a metaphor. Junior is simply the circumstance of our union. Junior is more of a dynamic – the thing that obviously makes us linked and legitimises our writing the word BOUND all over the streets. Oh, I think I'm backing myself into a corner here . . . It's this thing I deny personhood, that keeps us together, that can only be understood as an extension of ourselves, that I feel completely ambiguous about, that creates tension and weighs us down. Well, I guess I just killed my whole argument about Junior not representing a child. Sadly, I think many children find themselves in the circumstances I just described, with unfit and desperate parents.

What I'm trying to get at, I guess, is that there is something going on in the piece that goes beyond the literal reading of what we look like – a nuclear family made of felt. There is such a huge disjuncture between what we look like and what we are actually doing. Pacing around city blocks, trying to create letters that spell a word that no one can read because a lot of it is invisible. Junior is at once both the agent of our writing (the sand spilling from his wounds) and incidental to the process.

SB I think you hit the whole thing right on the head with this, although I wouldn't have described it in quite these terms. Incidentally, what I said about Edward Albee bounces right back here: you could almost have been describing the central relationship in *Who's Afraid of Virginia Woolf?* (1962) where a childless couple invents a narrative for a child they never had: he's a metaphor, a cipher, a blank, whatever they want him to be, and they fight over the terms of the narrative constantly. Although we're not fighting, of course, more politely seeking consensus . . . (or are we?) We're unfit parents, certainly, but apparently not desperate ones.

But returning to this lettering, which you've raised again. The action of several of your pieces has revolved around the writing of a single word – although never on this scale (as you say, that's an idea I stole from Paul Auster's 1994 *New York Trilogy*). I'm trying to remember some of the other words you've used – WOUND as well as BOUND, for example. They always seem to be words which can be read in more than one way, and don't give themselves up to single readings: you opted for BOUND in the context of *Junior* (vetoing my suggestion of FELT, as I recall, because you wanted that for another piece), but I was never sure exactly *why* that word. It could, perhaps, suggest either family bondage or that the kid will grow up to be Superman ('he leaps whole city blocks in a single bound!'). But I've a sense that it's the act of writing which is of more interest to you that the word itself.

I remember the first time I saw you, in *Path of Most Resistance* with Dolores, at two ends of a narrow, double-headed tube dress that only allowed the two of you to move on your elbows and butts. And you were gradually creating the word CASUALTIES (or CASUAL TIES) by spreading earth in patterns down a sidewalk. The final word is suggestive for an audience, but the real fascination of the piece was the mystery of not *knowing* what the word was until almost the very end. I guess, with *Junior*, we simply took that principle to an extreme, so that nobody but us knew the word BOUND was being spelt, and even we couldn't actually see it when it was written. To me, because of that, the spelling of the word was never more than a pretext for our travelling (because it's so conceptual rather than theatrical, perhaps), but I'm sensing from your last comments that the act of inscription really is of central importance for you. And while you've attributed the gag image to me, our enforced silence while writing the word is entirely consistent with your previous work. Over and over again, you seem to have used a combination of physical writing and verbal silence. Could you talk about this a little?

JL The unspoken word is important me. It may be my overreaction to what seemed to me to be too much reliance on spoken text in

American performance art. At one point I was trying to separate myself from performance poetry, monologue and stand-up comedy and arrive at something that could not be associated with those forms. So I made a decision I would only use language in a way that felt unique to me. Also, when I was working on solo pieces that involved visuals (always) and text (sometimes) the level of my writing could *never* rise to the level of my visuals. Instead of improving my writing, I abandoned it. Then it became silently central as the unspoken but written word in my work. The visible and the unspoken combined to form a language of their own.

The word, the appropriate word for each piece is critical and of extreme importance. The double entendre is essential. The act of writing is the speaking. In *Junior* we had the visuals before we selected the word. In some of my work the word came first and performances sprang up around them. I've had a word for several years I've been wanting to do a piece with but all of my best ideas for this word are physically dangerous. But, I've been carrying the word around with me for a long time like a little stone in my pocket waiting for the right moment for it to emerge. I had already planned to use the word FELT for *You are the Salt of My Earth* when you suggested it for *Junior*. And to this day, almost two years later, I cannot imagine having used a word other than FELT for that piece. In fact, it's hard for me to think of having used a word other than BOUND for *Junior*. Maybe it's just a sign of rigidity on my part. What seems written in sand is really carved in stone! But these words have now transcended being simply utterances or ink marks on a page. They are now physical facts, and I love that.

The scale of the word BOUND in *Junior* is, as you say, what makes the project of writing more conceptual than theatrical. While the word is mostly invisible since the residue is only partially evident, the making of the word BOUND has still gone through the process of having been physicalised, not by the voice but by the whole body that has been invested in its making. So the walking becomes speaking (and writing). The word has been enacted, literalised through the body. But not like in a play where the words often do not move beyond illustrating what the performers are saying. Speaking is a predictable way of using words in performance art, in my opinion. Talk is cheap . . .

SB Of course you're right. So maybe it's time to start thinking about winding up our 'interview'. We've covered a number of bases, and while we certainly have not 'captured' *Junior* or anything else in words, I feel like we should let go now before we 'talk it to death'. This is, in fact, an issue I feel very strongly about: I remember when writing my piece about your dress work for *Performance Research*,[1] feeling an enormous sense of responsibility because – for many people – my writing would be the only way they had of making contact with your work (thanks to its very ephemerality, and to the fact that it is rarely even advertised so that people know where and when to find it). I felt it was important that more people knew about your work, but I was also worried that what I set down on paper might simply become a restrictive or even misleading set of ideas through which your work was viewed. It's that age-old problem of how to talk about something that is primarily visual: as Roland Barthes says, 'every decoding is another encoding', and critics always run the risk of encoding their own preoccupations and prejudices in anything they write. So perhaps there comes a time to stop.

JL   Yes, I'm with you. Time to be fading back into the visual and silent realm once again . . . See you in Glasgow.

POST-SCRIPT In June 2001, Flexible Deadlock Theatre Company presented Shakespeare's *Pericles* (1608) in a site-specific promenade production in Glasgow's Botanical Gardens, as part of the city's West End Festival. The production was directed by Stephen J. Bottoms, with large-scale 'gowns' for the female characters designed and created by Julie Laffin. The collaboration continues.

1   Stephen J. Bottoms, 'Subsoil on the Sidewalk: Julie Laffin and the Chicago Underground', *Performance Research*. Vol. 3. No. 1 (1998), 73–81.

A sense of place
Peter DuBois in conversation with Caridad Svich

Peter DuBois has been artistic director of Perseverance Theatre in Juneau, Alaska since 1998. In 1992, he moved to Prague where he co-founded Asylum, a multi-national 'squat' theatre which gained public notoriety, the support of the professional theatre community and, eventually, official recognition by the state.

This interview was conducted via e-mail and telephone from November 2000 to March 2001.

CARIDAD SVICH Alaska is often perceived as 'another country' even though it is part of the US. It is a state which for many citizens still feels like the 'purest' of social and ecological environments, which is one of the reasons many people go to Alaska to find themselves and/or escape where they are. Yet, it is also a state that has a conflicted relationship to its colonial history, and to the use of its natural resources for commercial profit and gain. How do these factors affect making art there?

PETER DUBOIS Juneau is an isolated community with no roads in or out. You come and go by boat or plane. We live in a rainforest that is surrounded by Pacific channel waters, mountains and an ice field. In July, there is always a little light in the sky, and in December the sky never quite achieves full daylight. And so the feeling here is different from anywhere in America. And these extremes affect every aspect of making art here. In particular, the unforgiving landscape and the geographic isolation from the lower 48 has led to a psychological distance from the rest of the country. We are Alaskans first and Americans second. Also, many of the contemporary characteristics of American culture – speed, convenience, globalisation – aren't really a deep part of the Alaskan identity.

At the same time, however, so much of what is fabulous and what is ugly in America's mythic identity exists here in epic proportions: the notion of frontier, the presence of diverse first nation native cultures, the quest to conquer nature, transgression, and the pursuit of God. So, at the same time that Alaska feels like the least American place one could be – another country even – it also feels like the most American, but in a mythic sort of way. This tension is exhilarating to create within.

As a theatremaker and an artistic director, ultimately it comes down to this: Perseverance Theatre is a theatre of place. The landscape, the isolation, the cultural diversity and the disorienting political and psychological extremism become incredible source materials. As a theatre artist, my job is to look at the world around me, and, by dreaming myself into that world, find what is revelatory. Creating in such a way in such a place like Alaska is exhilarating. Also, the audience is central to a theatre of place. I have never felt so accountable for my work as I have in Juneau. People will stop me in the supermarket, the post office, or the gym and want to give me notes on Act Two.

CS The notion of being accountable for your work, where the community actually has a profound investment in its theatre throws light upon artistic responsibility. How do you please yourself and your own enquiry/quest for making and producing work, and respond to the community as well?

PD Relating to audience in this intimate way can be terrifying. I learned a lesson the day of my first preview for Chekhov's *The Seagull* (1896), the first show I directed here at Perseverance in 1998. I brought my designer with me from Prague, Maria Illum Ciccia (a Danish-Italian expatriate from the Czech Republic) and an actor I had spent the past two years working with, named Stephen Hallam, who is now in London. I brought them into collision with the most exciting artists I discovered in Juneau – my past and future as an artist were coming together. The fact of the audience is different in a community in which you are rooted because they will come back again and again, and together you will develop a relationship. As a by-product of our isolation, Juneau gazes inward, and what I realised at that preview was that my work would now be a focus of the gaze. This terrified me. My audience had previously been in transient communities, constantly changing except for a faithful core – like creating at an airport gate. And I realised that I actually wanted to reach my new audience, that I wanted a deep connection. I wanted to challenge them, but also to win them over, to steer them away from the familiar and towards art and revelation, but also to discover catharsis and whatever good storytelling could mean to me.

However, ultimately as a director I respond to the place in which I am creating. My work in Prague, in Providence, in New York, is very different from my work in Juneau. I try to let location and audiences find their way into my process. Sometimes that means challenging them, and sometimes it means challenging myself. I try to give my community keys to the work without erasing the question mark that I need to live in as an artist. One way of doing this for me is by creating lobby installations that disorient the material on the main stage through visual arts, poetry or video. This sends the audience into a place where they are trying to understand meaning through abstraction, before the house even opens. They are then in a different headspace; their horizons are wider, when they enter the theatre. Another way of creating a key is by curating seasons as journeys with an arc around a certain idea or place or question. The whole season becomes a story with a beginning, middle and end.

I constantly ask myself, how do I give the community keys to the more challenging and artistically daring work, and at the same time make the work that is more accessible, more familiar – and generally more popular – full of risk and integrity? Ben Cameron (executive director of Theatre Communications Group in New York) recently told me I had two voices inside me – one insists that I constantly challenge my audience and find ways to push them away from comfort and agreement, the other expresses a populist urge for everyone to be in the room together. I am interested in fostering a community that encourages disagreement, while finding ways for us to live together. For me magic happens in the struggle. Art happens in that struggle.

CS And that struggle can illuminate where we are. The volatility and complexity of the contemporary sociopolitical world forces us to rethink where we are and where we have come from and how we exist within our immediate as well as larger community.

PD Artistically, I think cultural collision mirrors this struggle. I have this same desire for the forms to challenge one another, but to live in the same room together, like when something distinctly Alaskan Native meets Chekhov. An example: Ekaterina Oleksa, the actress playing Masha in *The Seagull* – who is of Y'upik and Russian descent – was performing the opening moment of the play, 'I am in mourning for my life', and she arrived at this magical moment of truth physically. It was exciting and it communicated the moment clearly, dramatically. It was a Y'upik dance gesture signifying grief. It met Chekhov in such a profound and melancholic way. These sorts of cultural collisions, these moments of contact were exciting to me.

CS Your staging of Shakespeare's *Romeo and Juliet* (1595) at Perserverance with a Serbian dramaturge Sodja Zupanc in your 1999–2000 season is another instance of your ability to create a complex mythical space by juxtaposing cultural collisions.

PD Working with Sodja Zupanc was indeed remarkable. It was a way for me to return to Central Europe in my mind, and to allow for the war in Serbia to resonate in my work and in my life in a meaningful way. It was also an opportunity to create collision between something emotionally, politically and artistically volatile in another part of the world with Shakespeare in Alaska. With *Romeo and Juliet*, my decision to do the show came out of a conversation online with Sodja during the NATO bombing there. She 'virtually' dramaturged the show.

    We communicated online several times a week, visited sites together, exchanged source materials. I didn't locate the play in Serbia – I try not to locate things like that. But Sodja's thinking on Serbian culture was in there, and so resonances of the conflict existed. But it was also bound to something Alaskan. And this all-Alaskan cast was Y'upik native, Tlingit native, Gwichin Native, Inupiat, Filipino, African-American and white. It complicated the racial politics in the play. Sometimes it neutralised race in the play, which may have been problematic. We played archetype and stereotype off of each other in the play – ancient images against the iconography of popular culture.

I find in Chekhov and Shakespeare this theme of not being able to live in the world your parents have made for you. It is everywhere in their plays, especially in Chekhov: *Uncle Vanya* (1899), *The Three Sisters* (1901), etc. I am directing a production of *Waiting for Godot* (1953) with young people to keep exploring this idea of what happens to people who cannot live in the world they inherit, which many of the characters I have directed in Alaska (Konstantin, Romeo, Juliet) seem to be dealing with on some level.

cs What happens when you're born into a history of which you are inevitably a part, and yet you wish to break free of where you're from and what you've inherited? How do you make a self, in other words? And sometimes you have to leave where you're from to find out.

PD That is what I experienced when I left the US. I began my work in central Europe as an acting coach for a company doing a production in English. I then joined a group of Czech, Danish and American squatters and helped create an illegal, multinational squat theatre called Asylum. I directed image-based theatre – choreography, mask, ideas from my fascination with performance, ideas from happenings – and I performed. My artistic partner at the time, a Dane named Morton Neilson, and I were holding all-night rehearsals, with the thought that fatigue might help us break into new creative frontiers. Milan Maixner, a lighting designer from the National Theatre's Laterna Magika, came to one such rehearsal, and came to us crying afterwards. He said, 'You are creating art from the inside. I have not seen art from the inside since before the revolution in 1989. I want to help.' He donated nine light instruments and a board to us. And for a while we kept making art from the inside. We were eventually shut down for operating a café without a liquor licence. People saw my work at Asylum and eventually I was hired to direct both original, non-text-based work, as well as English translations of Czech plays and Czech premieres of American plays that I thought would go over well there.

I felt as though I was part of a generation that was creating within a gap in Prague and Czech theatre culture. Prior to the revolution in 1989 the really good theatre was all about subverting the government and making the revolution happen. I directed an English translation of a play which originally premiered the month before the revolution, called *A Small Czech Macbeth*, about a man who created calamity and chaos, and eventually killed his own wife, because he was afraid of power. After the Velvet Revolution, theatre had lost meaning for many of the playwrights and directors. The revolution had come. I found myself there at a time when the Czech theatrical identity was at a nadir. My work there at that time seemed to make sense to me, and to my Czech colleagues. As soon as I saw the work of Czech director Petr Lebl, I thought it was time to leave. I suddenly felt out of place. Petr's work had such an aesthetic intensity that was clearly wrapped up in his identity as a Czech, I felt I needed to go home and investigate my identity as an American.

CS Where do you see yourself in your rediscovery process as an American artist?

PD The hard part about creating theatre in America is that Americans are uncomfortable with tragedy and ambiguity. This is the big difference between making work in Prague and in Juneau. In the Czech Republic, there was an encouragement, and even an expectation, in audiences and artists, to move towards what is tragic, what is perhaps melancholic, and, of course, what is absurd, and to find theatrical value in that. Not so in America. Here we take our right to pursue happiness to extremes. Americans are losing their capacity to engage with tragedy and to find it cathartic and liberating. What I learned in Prague was that you can watch something sad, and leave feeling energised, like something was grieved for you. Or challenged. Like something was left in you. But either way, there is growth. So, I miss that, the encouragement to make tragedy or absurdist work.

I still have the freedom to do that, but not necessarily encouragement from the audience. It is more like I am trying to convince the audience to go on the journey.

CS In the US where freedom is a concept often taken for granted, there is such a fear to push at the boundaries of theatre. It is almost as if we are clinging to an ill-remembered vestige of the nineteenth century.

PD 'Ill-remembered' is a great term for what has happened to Americans' understanding of its past. Americans tend not only to forget, but also to remember wrong. Stanislavski, for example. What we have is sense memory, but sense memory is something that by the end of his life he rejected. We also fail to remember where his thinking went by the end of his life – towards the physical and away from the internal. Also, melodrama is a great thing Americans have failed to remember correctly. Europeans, as well as South and Central Americans, have 'remembered' melodrama in a way that allows them to use it profoundly. Acting in melodrama is heightened, larger than life, and operatic. It is very beautiful, sweeping, and requires virtuosity – a good sense of rhythm, gesture, fluency and the capacity to understand the power behind the tableau. Americans understand melodrama as hammy overacting, so they will never realise the full potential of the actor's, the writer's and the director's capacity.

CS How do you work with actors to break through fears and educate/train an audience as well?

PD I try to contextualise things with history. With actors I talk about American realism as a dominant acting style in a period in American Theatre history, then I talk about other acting styles in other periods (periods which saw much larger, more involved audiences). And we explore acting styles and vocabulary from those periods. And we apply our artistic values to those acting styles: What can clarity mean in vaudeville? What does rigour mean in melodrama? What separates good style fusion from mud? Finding ways to fuse what we know about psychology and good moment-to-moment emotional work with style and external form intrigues me. I may look at a script and decide that Commedia, drag and vaudeville is the right combination to explore in finding a performance style with balance. Or, when staging Chekhov, I may turn to melodrama, vaudeville, and something gothic. Without theatre history I feel as though I'd be nowhere as an artist. It is so rich with signals and signs, paths to walk down. Sometimes I imagine them in the room with me, like ghosts. Chekhov has told me things I have never imagined were in Chekhov, right there in the rehearsal room.

As a director I am very interested in what happened in American theatre in the first half of the twentieth century – Black Mountain College, American expressionism, early O'Neill and Williams, vaudeville, burlesque, the birth of the American musical (such a potentially dangerous form!). Anne Bogart talks about how McCarthy's blacklists stopped the flow of interesting and political art in the 1950s, and how we haven't recovered. I think she's right. But I am not against realism in theatre as an ingredient to the total act of telling a story. What I am against is privileging realism over the creative capacity of the imagination. Right now I am interested in storytelling. How do we tell good stories? I tend to begin with interesting visual language, and with creating universes that intrigue, and move from there. Realism can help with storytelling, but it seems like a cop-out to go there right away. Realism should be a place to arrive at, not to begin with.

Working in partnership

David Greig in conversation with Isabel Wright

David Greig has been Writer-in-Residence at the Royal Shakespeare Company, and Vice-Chair of The Scottish Society of Playwrights. His plays include *The Architect* (1996) and *The Cosmonaut's Last Message to the Woman he Once Loved in the former Soviet Union* (1999). In 1990, with director Graham Eatough, he co-founded the Scottish theatre company Suspect Culture, which is dedicated to collaborative methods of producing work for the theatre. Their work attempts to integrate text, movement and music through the creation of innovative performance styles. Their show *Casanova* premiered at the Tron Theatre in Glasgow, February 2001.

This interview focuses primarily on his work with Suspect Culture rather than his work as a freelance playwright and was conducted in Glasgow in October 2000, as he was in pre-production with *Casanova*.

DAVID GREIG Suspect Culture is initially a partnership of Graham Eatough and myself and then a collective including Nick Powell (composer), Ian Scott (lighting designer) and Pamela Carter (dramaturg) as well as international associates (Mauricio Paroni de Castro and Andres Lima). This is not to mention those actors with whom we have regularly worked, particularly actors like Callum Cuthbertson or Jill Riddiford, or Louise Ludgate who contribute regularly to the general artistic movement of the shows the company does. I mention this because it is central to understanding the company. I have an overview and a guiding role within the company but Graham might give different answers and everyone has their own perspective on what we're trying to achieve and why. Primarily, however, Graham and I set the artistic direction of the company.

The company began in 1990 as a post-student affair that really was my baby. It was just a chance for me to direct and write. However, even then there was a vision of a collaborative way of working, there was the desire to push boundaries, and the feeling that theatre could be a more total, fulfilling experience than we were tending to get from British companies. But we were students and, in many ways, we were a bit thick. We didn't know what work people were doing and we didn't know that what we wanted to do was also part of an artistic continuum involving practitioners in Britain and the rest of the world. In 1995, after I had some experience of professional theatre, Graham and I decided to reconstitute the company as a professional entity, to apply for funding and be serious about things. At this point there was a two-stranded vision: First we wanted to be a European company, by which I mean we wanted our work to cross borders and to collaborate with artists abroad. We wanted our work to be seen in a European context, not a British context. Secondly, we wanted our work to integrate all the elements of performance in a considered and experimental way. That is to say, we would take nothing for granted.

We had been very fortunate to have available to us the incredible international programmes of the Tramway and The Edinburgh International Festival. We were hugely influenced and inspired by the work we saw (Pina Bausch, Robert Wilson, The Maly . . . etc.). In a sense, it was our arrogance that led us to think, unselfconsciously, that this is what we wanted to do. And it seemed obvious that the way to achieve that level of quality was to push harder, for longer rehearsal time, for higher production values, for more ideas within the work: to consider the 'production' as art and not 'the play'. As time passed, and we have done more and more shows, something else has happened. We have realised that we were very lucky in the coincidence of who we were and when we met. We're much less interested now in the theory of what we're trying to achieve and much more interested in simply pursuing our personal vision. Something inchoate and indescribable verbally: a response to our own lives, and our own feelings and an attempt to produce theatre which 'answers' our own personal needs. We still hold to one key principle: never go back. Each new show is a step along the road to a destination we will never reach, something always one show away, which is perfection. Each new show contains elements of every other show but is also a step in the dark, an attempt to find something out. Vitally, we're not comfortable with this step unless we're scared and think it's 'stupid'. That's what makes us decide some shows are Suspect Culture shows and others are not. The ones that contain genuine risk, risk that really makes you think this could be crap or it could be amazing and we're just going to have to go all the way to find out, that's what we aim for.

ISABEL WRIGHT Where do you look for inspiration for the company's working methods?

DG The working method is very much our own developed out of Graham's and my relationship and our desire to collaborate. Collaboration necessitates group-working situations like workshops and you slowly learn how to handle them to the best advantage of the work. My general artistic inspiration is more primarily Brecht. For Graham, Pina Bausch, Robert Wilson and many others. We've never really taken much direct inspiration from Scottish companies that I can think of because we feel as though we're ploughing our own furrow, although we've both admired Irina Brown's productions and we've learned a lot from Ian Reekie and John Herahty's outreach work and philosophies at 7:84. The influence of the Spanish and Italian actors with whom we've worked has shaped a lot of our thinking about rehearsal process and attitude: more passion, more relaxed; it's not a job.

IW A production of your company's such as *Timeless* (1997) used elements of music, gesture, lighting and text very effectively. In a workshop you led at the Traverse Theatre, which I attended, Graham Eatough mentioned that he felt each element had an equally important function, and that you were trying to find the best way to tell the story at that part of the show. Would you say this is something you explore in all your productions?

DG We're always exploring physically but curiously we're less and less attracted to the 'abstract' gesture within the naturalistic context. We're tending now to find physical 'languages' for whole pieces. So in *Mainstream* (1999) the characters appear to move naturalistically but they are within this very contained space and they are constantly repeating patterns of movement. In *Mainstream* also each 'gesture' was significant, however tiny. In *Candide 2000*, it was necessarily much wilder but it was still there in the way the kids were asked to move; we took the physical language from the kids and let that spread to and infect the actors. For me writing, it doesn't affect things much except that I'm always trying to say less, wherever possible, and to find ways of leaving space. It's too easy for writers to get caught up in trying to create a template for the entire stage picture. It's much better writing, to my mind, when your writing is at its simplest leaving space for a world to be imagined around it. This is very difficult to achieve, but you find it in Shakespeare or Brecht. It is a way of writing that suggests everything but limits almost nothing. It is solid and simple, but also poetic and abstract.

IW Is there a usual pattern to the creation process you use with Suspect Culture?

DG The method has evolved as we have grown up and done more work. Basically, the usual pattern is this: I will map out the process of *Casanova*, since although each show has its own variations, it is typical enough. It begins with an idea. In this instance, I wanted to write something about an immoral anti-hero and Graham was keen to explore a visual image of frames and sliding panels. During a chat in the pub this became a modern Casanova. It is very free at this stage and we let it lie for a few weeks. Then we spend more time talking about it and eventually conceive of it as a possible show. We start to bring in the company and discuss its parameters. In this instance, it was the dates, that it was a touring show, that it can have five actors, that the budget is limited. The next stage is to get the entire main artistic partners together (Nick, Ian, Pamela and some actors) and to do a wee exploratory workshop. At this stage we tend to play around with everything. I may write stuff, Nick will have his piano and samplers. We may improvise but it's all in the knowledge that nothing is likely to be 'used'. We're not trying to make the show. It is important that everyone contributes exercises and ideas. It must be open.

We'll then let that sit for a while and eventually we will have another workshop. This time it's getting a bit more serious. We will pursue things a bit more deeply, and then we will have a brainstorm session. This is where everyone gets together for a weekend in a hotel room and we just hammer out ideas and structures and possibilities. We set the parameters. Then I write. This is a pretty big step. In some ways I'm extremely limited. In others very free. I try to surprise myself, to bring something new to the work. That is the stage we're currently at with *Casanova*. When I have a draft, it gets shown around and we'll probably meet again to discuss it. Everyone else will begin to prepare their first drafts (direction, lighting design, etc.). The show will be cast. Then I'll write a rehearsal draft and we'll go into the rehearsal room.

Things will change a lot in rehearsal but usually it resembles a normal rehearsal process at any other new writing theatre. The only thing that is different is that we will still need contributions from the actors and technicians. We try to include them at every stage of thinking and decision making so they're never doing something they're uncomfortable with. In the rehearsal room we try to be relaxed but we're a benevolent oligarchy rather than a democracy. We know where we're going; we just don't know what it will be like when we get there. That way a team builds up and actors and technicians feel ownership of the work. It is theirs as much as ours and they're committed to it and will take risks for it. Then we have the first run. We let that sit for a while, digest our reactions to it, and then we'll do it again. We have never put a show on exactly as it was on its first outing. We always re-work and rewrite. It would be boring just to do it the same way again.

IW Do you think your work with Suspect Culture has changed the way you view writing?

DG Suspect Culture has been invaluable for me but it has also been a great responsibility. There is a lot of stress and misery attached to being deeply involved in a company in this artistic climate (that goes for everyone involved, not just me). So I'd definitely be a different writer but I don't know precisely how. I cannot imagine not pursuing collaborative work. I think, if it didn't exist, I would form it. That is all I can imagine. I sometimes dream of giving up theatre entirely and writing novels. So maybe I'd have gone that way.

IW Suspect Culture has toured and worked with non-British performers. What do you think can be learnt from working methods in other countries?

DG A lot. Everything. We should constantly be looking at the way other people and other cultures do things. In Britain, we're immensely complacent and we tend to think we do theatre better than everyone else does. I don't mean we should lionise everything foreign but we should be open to it.

IW What are the possible pitfalls of interdisciplinary work?

DG They are legion. In fact I tend to shy away from it these days. Video/dance and so forth . . . That is partly the onset of middle age. I would be disappointed if some young company were not already experimenting with internet/DVD theatre or some such. The main thing is defining the show. Audiences only come to see a show and it must have a point above and beyond its production elements. Also, for it to work takes time and effort. People often throw a dancer in a room with a writer and a video maker and say, 'Make a show.' It will almost certainly be banal, because when you collaborate across media, at first you have to go back to basics in order to communicate with the other people. It takes time to assimilate the possibilities of what they do and for them to assimilate the possibilities of what you do. And then, what do you want to explore? Do you share a vision? To find this out takes time and most often people don't take that time.

Dreaming out loud

Phelim McDermott in conversation with Caridad Svich

Phelim McDermott has been directing and performing for more than twelve years. Productions with Improbable Theatre, which he co-founded in 1996, include the award-winning *70 Hill Lane* (1996), *Lifegame* (1998) and *Coma* (1999). With Julian Crouch he co-directed *Shockheaded Peter* (1998), a junk opera collaboration with The Tiger Lilies, for Cultural Industry.

This interview was conducted on 14 January 2001 in Columbus, Ohio after the run of Improbable Theatre's show *Spirit* at the Wexner Center for the Arts.

CARIDAD SVICH You just staged *Shockheaded Peter* in Hamburg, Germany. What was it like to bring that piece 'home'?

PHELIM MCDERMOTT We did a German version with a German cast at the Schauspielhaus. The Tiger Lilies were not in the show for the first time, so the music was orchestrated for five musicians rather than three (the musical director was the same who did Robert Wilson and Tom Waits's *The Black Rider* in 1990), and the MC character was played by a woman named Wiebke Puls. Basically it was the in-house company of the Schauspielhaus, so we were given a cast to work with, which were selected by the artistic director Tom Stromberg. It was a fantastic company who were hungry to work in a different way than they were used to. It is, however, a different show. I don't think it is as spiky or scary as the British version, but on the other hand it has a grandeur to it. It's not as claustrophobic, partly because the Schauspielhaus has a bigger stage and the set is bigger. There are also bits we reworked, and there are new puppets for the Bully Boys. It was quite exciting to do new sections of the piece, but on the whole it is the same show, although the company has the same kind of freedom to play with it.

In terms of the difference of how they were working with the material as opposed to the British company: *Shockheaded Peter* is about unashamed theatricality. One of the things it seems to me about German theatre is that it is not about being theatrical and charismatic, being over the top and doing big acting. It's almost obsessively the other way. Contained and cerebral, and about small things taken to an extreme. My guess is that historically there's a kind of edge to being charismatic with an audience and whipping a crowd up into a frenzy. Some of the German actors were resistant to saying, for example, the line 'I am the greatest actor in the world!' because it's not the sort of thing you are supposed to say. Of course the irony is that the character in the piece means it, but at the same time he is the worst actor in the world. It is exactly the kind of paradox that makes the show work. We created a script from it, which has been given to German publishers, and a lot of German companies are doing totally different versions. There's a version in Dusseldorf where there are robots and rabbits and all sorts of things. Producer Michael Morris (of Cultural Industry) went to see it and said it was strange to see because it is so very different. In Germany, of course, these stories are part of the culture in a way they were not in Britain.

CS Has the element of improvisation always been in your work?

PM Even when we've worked with texts. Julian and I directed a production of *A Midsummer Night's Dream* with the English Shakespeare

Company 1996–97 shortly after *70 Hill Lane*. Julian said, 'Maybe we should do the whole thing with Scotch tape.' So, we did this large-scale production where we used the tape to create the forest, and the fairies were like insects, and built the bowers, etc. That was a situation where we were working with a text and a set design element, which was somewhat fixed, but still we encouraged the actors to play the text in any way they wanted, so they played it differently every night.

On that production I became interested in the work of Jeremy Whelan, who wrote a book called *Instant Acting* (1994). In it there is this great technique for working with text where you sit down and record the script with the actors, and then you stop it, wind it back, and everyone gets up and moves about in the space as the tape is playing. So, for example, an actor will hear his words and interact with another actor. What this means is that you can improvise straight away. You are immediately engaging with inner impulses before you decide how you might speak any of the lines. Then you go back and record again, and you do this process five times or so, and after you've done this, you tell the actors to 'do the scene', with the assurance that if they need prompting it will be given to them. It's astonishing how much they remember. The main problem is that actors don't quite believe that it is possible. The biggest block is their intellectual mind saying 'it cannot be', but when they give up, the words just pop out. It's a real body-based way of working. We kept that going into the show, and we told the actors to keep playing with it, even if it was Shakespeare. It was a scary and exciting process.

CS How did your work with Keith Johnstone come to be?

PM Keith Johnstone has been an amazing source of inspiration for Improbable and perhaps the improvised show which has had the most influence on our work has been *Lifegame*. I first did Lifegame when Keith Johnstone was beginning to play with the idea in 1987. I did a ten-day workshop with Keith and it was the beginnings of my interest in improv. It took me about ten years to be in a position to persuade the Arts Council to give us money for an improvised show. It is very simple on one level because it is merely an interview about someone's life. However, it is in fact incredibly sophisticated and lay-ered as a theatre experience. The guest chooses a performer to play someone for the evening and the other players play other characters from their life. The process of seeing the stories dramatised seems to have an amazing effect on the guest. One of the possibilities is to involve the guest playing people from their life, say, their old school teacher or their parent. Memories emerge for the first time in years. Over three years we interviewed nearly two hundred people and it totally changes your view of people and humanity. To play someone from a totally different culture and learn about their story can be a real honour. To be able to say to an audience, I'm playing a six-foot tall, black American police officer and for the audience to be totally happy to go with that is an extraordinary experience.

CS *Spirit* is such a new piece and already it has undergone such change in process. How did co-director Arlene Audergon become involved with *Spirit*?

PM It began with the last show we did called *Coma*. It was based on the work of Arnold Mindell, who does Process Work, which is basically his development of psycho-therapeutic work, but it had expanded into different areas: into work with people in altered states, people in comatose states and communicating with them using minimal signals. It is what he calls 'world work' centred around conflict resolution, and field issues like racism, etc. Before the peace process in Dublin, Mindell did Process Work there, for example. I did a workshop with him which was about coma work, and as I watched him I thought, 'he's doing improv', because a lot of the work he does is based on play and what we would call 'the game', picking up signals that would normally get missed and amplifying them, and also reading incredibly sophisticated signals from the body through different channels – vocal, physical, sensory. I started studying his work because I found it useful in working with actors.

Coma was the story of Mindell working with a man in a coma and my own story in relationship to that work. Arlene Audergon trained with Mindell and also had been doing work with puppetry and we started talking. She had been working in Kosovo and Croatia doing postwar trauma work and democracy building with groups in places where people had been killing each other. Her job was to try to get them to talk to each other and to try to process the conflict so they could interact – how to buy bread at the bakery from someone who had just killed your brother? That became the seed of the idea for *Spirit*. And while we began with war as an idea, in the end, what we know best is our own conflicts because the conflicts are inside of us – Lee Simpson, Guy Dartnell and myself – and that is something we can work on.

One of the ways you can deal with conflict is to go into it with awareness, so that even though you go in, you are also outside of it. Mindell calls it 'stepping off the wheel'. It is the Buddhist idea that you can be within and outside at the same time, which means you can support your own enemy as well as stand for your own side and then be outside both positions in a place of awareness. You become free of just being identified with your own role. By doing so with awareness the potential to transform the conflict into something positive becomes possible. The opposite idea is that you can create wars by trying to make peace happen. One of things we developed in *Coma* or from years of being on stage as improvisers together is a kind of possibility to stay in something: to stay in the silence which might be uncomfortable, to go into a difficult interaction within an improvisation. There is a search for beauty in that, which is alchemical. The beauty is in the dirt, grit and in owning up to being terrible to begin with and then transcending it.

cs How do you build a piece?

PM We build them together and usually from an idea. We are getting braver, though, about sharing our ideas and obsessions. In making a piece there is the sense of following something and not quite knowing what it is until it presents itself. In making the decision for the set for *Spirit*, it happened from the space where we were rehearsing. There was this little ramp in the corner of the room and we ended up improvising on it and we just decided to make a big version of that for the set. There's a sense of trusting the wonderful unexpected things that happen, the Tao, that says, 'This is what we are supposed to be working on. The strange flirts and impulses which we could ignore, trust them and the answers will present themselves.'

cs How do you stop for dream time, or do you steal it?

PM You have to do it on the hoof. At the moment I would say we need time for other people to have ideas for shows. One of the things I get frustrated a bit with is that you can categorised. I remember, before we brought *70 Hill Lane* to the US, I really wanted to come here. Part of this was the dream of being alongside Spalding Gray or Laurie Anderson. There seems to be a kind of respect for people as theatre artists and as creators, which doesn't really happen in the UK. You have one or two, but on the whole these individuals are not treasured or looked after in the UK. In Europe, though, as opposed to how England sees itself, there is a respect for these artists. You see, the UK has this massive weight of tradition that is a text tradition. I mean, we do carry Shakespeare on our backs. We are doing *Spirit* at the Royal Court when we complete our US tour and the Court is a text-based building. Yet one of the people who inspired me is Keith Johnstone, who started there with the writers' group, but that legacy isn't there any more. When I left college there was a whole band of companies like Impact, for example, companies who were experimenting in a radical way. Now all the people who were in Impact are either TV actors or film directors. They've all gone on. And the next wave? Well, there's Forced Entertainment, who were inspired by Impact, and Frantic Assembly, but there are few and far between. There's not much of a sense of a community that is supported. It's strange for me to find myself in a position where people go, 'Oh yes, Improbable . . . I'm excited about their work' when I'm still looking for people to inspire me. It's an odd situation, and sometimes quite lonely.

CS Because you feel a lack of support?

PM Because the work doesn't seem to relate to the buildings. The repertory system is fucked in the UK, because that transition never knew how to incorporate what might be called 'alternative' work and to educate an audience about other possibilities. So, if you're someone like Rose English, what do you do? You're a performance artist. How does that fit into a rep theatre? It doesn't. In some ways it's about control. You're allowed to do your work, but only in one place. And you're given money to do it as long as you don't go somewhere else and muck up.

The route I should have taken officially was to do my fringe shows, then direct in the reps, then direct at the National, then be given a rep to run, and then be considered a proper director, and then get to do a musical in the West End, and then make movies. It's part of theatre in crisis because people don't stick around. One of the things I'm lucky to have is a kind of support. One of the major funding bodies has been The Comedy Store. It's been a training ground because if you can deal with a hard-nosed, cabaret club audience, it teaches you a lot. It teaches you about fluidity of roles and reminds you the work is about the audience and not the critics or a building's reputation.

CS I think artists have a responsibility to be alive to those voices which are being ignored or left behind on the planet, because then these voices will come into the work and maybe communicate something else to an audience outside of what they usually experience.

PM There is a racism against dreaming, in this world there is this marginalisation of the experience of dreaming and these people are doing necessary work for us. If you work with the person who is in the coma, for instance, be with them, go into the same kind of state as them, pick up their signals and communicate with them, they can actually process what is happening. What then happens is that they go on their journey and often come out of their coma and perhaps have visionary messages for us.

I think when you talk about the artist being responsible, that is what they are responsible for. They are responsible for the dreaming and bringing the dreaming to the people so that it is not left. One thing theatre can do is honour that part of life. More than cinema.

Because in the process of being in the theatre, there's the possibility of what you described before: to watch something on a stage, to be somewhere else, to be in all your memories, and still be present at the same time. In cinema it tends to happen less, whereas in theatre you have people on stage and then these images and dreams happening on top of it and that's where the beauty is, in that potential. I don't see it that often in theatre but the potential is still there. That's why I think I still do it. I feel I have to. I don't have any choice. It was decided by the gods.

A fixer between living and dead artists
Nick Philippou in conversation with Caridad Svich

Nick Philippou is co-founder of the NYC-based theatre company The Art Party, which produced the English-language premiere of Genet's *Elle* in 2002. He was Artistic Director of Actors Touring Company (ATC) in London from 1993–2000. His productions for ATC included Mark Ravenhill's *Faust Is Dead* (1997), and a radical version of *The Tempest* (1999) with new music by Laurie Anderson and featuring the eminent British performance artist Rose English. He also directed Mark Ravenhill's *Handbag*, commissioned by ATC, which opened at the Lyric Theatre, Hammersmith, in London in 1998. He is currently collaborating with Caridad Svich and actor/writer Todd Cerveris on a multimedia piece entitled *The Booth Variations*.

This interview was conducted via e-mail from August to October 2000.

CARIDAD SVICH Has working with 'dead' texts as opposed to 'living' ones redefined your thoughts or practices?

NICK PHILIPPOU When I first took over the Actors Touring Company I was interested very much in uncovering old plays. I believed (and still do in a way) that we could use those texts as mirrors to ourselves – albeit fragmented ones. After productions of plays by Sartre, Genet, de Rojas and Strindberg, I decided that I wanted to use the text itself as one of a series of components that would be 'introduced' to each other through a workshop and development process. I feel more and more now that my job as a director is as a fixer between the living and dead artists. That those artists come together with some archetypal story as a playing ground, which becomes the theatrical or filmic project at hand. Sometimes there is no living writer. When I adapted Shakespeare's 1593 text *Venus & Adonis* in 1995, I was interested in the music of Madonna and a radical Irish dance group called The

Hairy Marys. Through this process we retell old stories for our time. We're part of a continuum of reinterpretation that – with the story of Faust – goes back through Thomas Mann, Goethe and Christopher Marlowe to a strange little Middle Ages puppet show. In our Faust we ended up with a piece written by Mark Ravenhill called *Faust Is Dead* about a Foucault-like philosopher set in Los Angeles. The work developed through an extensive series of workshops that lasted up to a year. But sometimes there is no text before we start.

cs Would you speak a bit more to how you develop work with writers in a room? For example, with Mark Ravenhill's *Faust* . . . was actor Alain Pelletier in mind for it before you began working?

NP The project began in 1994 when I began exploring ideas of Foucault with designer Stewart Laing, and researching in Paris, San Francisco, Los Angeles and Death Valley (where Foucault used to drop acid). The project was an experiment. I played Foucault and we called it *Brainy*. We jumped through various texts – Beckett, Goethe, and the 1980 film script of *Cruising* – and we presented it in Glasgow in 1995 at the Centre of Contemporary Art. I then met Alain at the ICA in 1996. He had just made a film called *Faust Meduse* (1995), which I saw there, and so I asked him to play our Faust/philosopher. I was sent Mark Ravenhill's play *Shopping and Fucking* (1996) at the same time, so I asked Mark to re-examine the material I had developed in Glasgow. The cultural experiences of the group certainly created a mythological Los Angeles. Mark had never been there, and Alain as a Quebecois was innately critical of that culture. It was never conscious, though. It was like osmosis. Otherwise, you get that terrible tokenism. I call it 'cultural shopping', a kind of faux-Peter Brook-like attitude that says, 'we're universal because we've got lots of different people from different countries in our show'.

cs When you worked on *Handbag* by Mark Ravenhill, weren't there audience preconceptions going on in terms of Oscar Wilde's *The Importance of Being Earnest* (1895), and even to some extent Mark's own previous work?

NP Those preconceptions were very strong. Wilde's play probably contains the most famous line in any play in the British psyche – 'A handbag!' – and we wanted to play with that and actually confound those preconceptions. Getting Mark Ravenhill, one of the UK's great mannerists, to dialogue with Wilde was the point. Of course when you are dealing with a play that people think of wrongly as effete and you have someone deal with that play that people wrongly think of as a social realist dramatist, then you've got something very interesting. Mark is a great dramaturg. I think, he wanted, in *Handbag*, to write within a literary tradition that spanned back to Euripides' *Ion* and included T.S. Eliot's *Confidential Clerk* (1954) and Joe Orton's *What the Butler Saw* (1969) along the way. We are always playing with our own stories and traditions. The act of theatre to me is centrally about that – principally because theatre, unlike cinema, has such a long and ancient tradition. Maybe in a thousand years, film will be able to do it as profoundly. The play was developed, like most of my work over the last ten years, over a long period of time. We worked intensely on the back-story of the play by Wilde. Miss Prism's speech at the end became infused with the most sinister tone and the choice between the manuscript and the baby became like a version of *Hedda Gabler* (1890) and *The Caucasian Chalk Circle* (1948)! The play became about means of parenting, the need to be looked after, the need to turn the most inappropriate people into parents and the strange needs that the most inappropriate people have to become parents. That is voiced in the ancient Greeks as explicitly as it is in our culture. Mark developed five drafts in our eighteen months of work-shopping and then the play also changed after we'd opened.

CS In Michael Wynne's *The Boy Who Left Home,* which you staged for ATC this summer (2000) there are points of intersection between the British social realist tradition and grisly German fairy tales. Not unlike Cultural Industry's *Shockheaded Peter,* which also is a piece, that has a dialogue with the past as part of its framing device.

NP With *The Boy Who Left Home*, we were looking at the precise intersection between Grimm's tales and now, the year 2000. *Shockheaded Peter* was not really about that intersection, it seemed to be a reinvention of the Victorian Grand Guignol. We wanted to reform the images of fairy tales in our work, to wrest them away from the physical theatre, the cliché of grotesque and eccentric and, more insidiously, the Disney horror of antiseptic and controlled stories. It seemed one was obsessed with fear, and the other with wonder. We wanted to try and put real figures into the tales. Michael Wynne was a writer I had always wanted to work with. He seemed while being still quite young to be able to write to and from that position which I found really exciting. We began working on the piece two years ago when we went to schools in north London and ran a series of workshops with sixteen-year-old students (tough, inner-city ones) on what their memories of fairy tales were. The extraordinary thing is that we all have memories of them. We asked the students to bring in objects that reminded them of fairy tales. We then made a fairy-tale landscape on the floor of the studio – a strange place populated with dead parents, horrific weddings and ghosts in photographs. It was very powerful. Then we started working with professional actors about a year ago. We retold fairy tales and tried to imagine the truth that the stories had come from. *Hansel and Gretel* is obviously about hunger, but what is *Cinderella* really about? It seemed to imagine the orphaned girl that has to grow up too soon. Those rites of passage became very important to us as we worked on text.

CS   In your deconstruction of Shakespeare's *The Tempest* (1611) for which playwright Steven Sater did the adaptation, you were working with a known text and turning it upside down, and then working with Rose English, who is from the world of performance art but not an 'actor' in the conventional British sense, and then with Laurie Anderson, who wrote the music for the production, who intersects so many worlds artistically. What was that like?

NP   My objective with that project was to bring together two great actors, albeit not conventional ones, and ask them to meditate within *The Tempest*. I'd known of Laurie's fascination with the play and the meditative themes of water and transformation for years. She had already set *Full Fathom Five* on an earlier album and was about to complete *Stories from Moby Dick (1999)*. I had imagined her as a Prospero energy until we met, and then I realised she was Ariel: all thought and narrative, mercurial and prone to disappear at any moment! With Rose, I wanted her to contemplate the nature of seeing in British culture. She has very strongly held beliefs in the corrupted nature of seeing in this puritanical culture we are resisting. The act of imagining her as a Prospero figure was easy. She began as a man and ended as a woman, which Rose does quite often in her work. It was one of many transformations in the piece. Rose and Laurie never met, but the collaboration was one of the most interesting I'd effected. I would read the contexts of Ariel's songs to Laurie, who I think worked with a sense of what came before or after. We spoke a lot about what things looked like, and spoke with Laurie about what things sounded like. I suppose it is how we ended up with expressions of Caliban as just a mouth (*à la* Beckett) and Ariel as just eyes . . . This seemed to say something about music and language, which I think the play addresses profoundly.

CS   But what is the role of the critics in receiving radical work in what seems to be an increasingly conservative theatrical climate in England?

NP   Well, there you have hit the nub of the problem. Critics who have no vocabulary to fall back on in observing non-character and narrative-based work in the UK are now reviewing us. The climate is not just conservative among critics, but also among the circuit of small-scale venues where experiment is only measured in box-office returns. The need to experiment seems to be being forced once more into the domain of the un-funded, post-student-theatre-company world.

CS   Where do you see your work going in the next few years?

NP   At the moment I want to find a way of exploring mythology, our own mythologies. In *The Boy Who Left Home*, we are playing the fairy-tale narratives and horrific modern non-fictional narratives of child abductions and murders. These things exist in us simultaneously. In a sense I think I want to work now with non-English, English-speaking actors for a while. Actors who I can read in a vacuum for a while.

There's a tradition of Stanislavski-based naturalism in England that is all encompassing. That's not to say that there is not that tradition in the US, but because there are more actors, there are more ways of working. The act for me of finding out how actors work is fascinating, and with my work in Cuba, Greece, Ireland, the US and the UK, it has become even more significant that actors carry culture in their bodies, and you've got to begin to understand how to read them. The vacuum for me is one in which our cultures differ but our language does not. I'm not American and never will be so that things seem strange to me that may not to an American director. When you work with actors in Cuba and Greece, you have these actors who work on Passion, with Passion. They shout. They roar. That tells you so much about their theatre and their politics. If they are disorganised, that tells you about their social systems. They are not systematic. That can be a relief after years spent with English actors who quite often deal with acting as a science . . . and that also can be very interesting too!

CS   Although you are beginning to make films now, do you still find theatre exciting?

NP   There was an article published in the *Guardian* not long ago that spoke provocatively and ridiculously of closing down all theatres and turning them into bars and bingo halls. And part of you is furious and outraged, and part of you, secretly, wishes it on us. Our audiences are part of a tradition that is so ingrained in the morés of theatre-going that you suspect that our minds are equally entrenched. But then again theatre is such an ancient art form that our body-knowledge of why it is needed is also very strong. I think what I'm saying is that theatre in theatres is becoming less interesting to me – or should I say, theatre in theatrical contexts, and that could be within a theatre or not. The idea of reclaiming theatre outside of its context is fascinating. I had a daydream for a long while that I would develop a form of 'guerrilla theatre' in which I and a company of performers would turn up for one night in a disused theatre, break in, alert the audience, perform and then be gone before the cops arrive . . .!

Hidden worlds: on artists and collaborators

Peter Sellars in conversation with Maria Delgado

Peter Sellars's recent work includes *The Merchant of Venice* (1994), *Peony Pavilion* (1998) and *The Screens* (1999). In opera he is best known for his collaborations with composer John Adams: *Nixon in China* (1998), *The Death of Klinghoffer* (1991), *El Niño* (2001) and for his work with Handel, Mozart and Stravinsky.

INTRODUCTION BY MARIA DELGADO One of the most interesting and least commented-on areas of the work of American director Peter Sellars is the long-term collaborations that have shaped his productions. Throughout the 1980s he worked consistently with a floating ensemble of singers which included Susan Larson, James Maddalena, Sanford Sylvan and Frank Kelly and the conductor Craig Smith on a series of productions which decisively dispensed with the period settings located by Edward Said as promoting 'the usually unstated ideology of authenticity'[1] in favour of clashing anachronisms which positioned performance as the site of vicious contradictions and, at times, irreconcilable polarities. Perhaps best known are his notorious relocations of the Mozart/daPonte trilogy, developed, produced and revised during the 1980s with *Don Giovanni*, *Così fan tutte* and *Le Nozze de Figaro*; each set in the late-twentieth century in Spanish Harlem, a seaside diner and Trump Tower respectively.

In the 1990s Sellars went on to forge key musical relationships with Kent Nagano, then Music Director of Hallé Orchestra and L'Opéra de Lyon, and composer Esa-Pekka Salonen, Music Director of the Los Angeles Philharmonic Orchestra. Both have worked with him on the Salzburg Festival production of *St François d'Assise*, Salonen in 1992 and Nagano in 1998. Just as Smith, Nagano and Salonen have remained constant companions in Sellars's operatic quests so have his design collaborators remained almost unchanged. George Tsypin and Adrienne Lobel have worked with him on almost all his productions over the past ten years – the most prominent exceptions being painter Elaine Spatz-Rabinowitz's sets for *Orlando* (Cambridge 1981) and *Giulio Cesare* (New York 1985), Coop Himmelblau's set for *Oedipus Rex* (Amsterdam 1994) and Diane Gamboa's designs for *L'Histoire du Soldat* (Ojai 1992).

1   Edward Said, 'The Barber of Seville. Don Giovanni', *The Nation* (26 September 1987), pp. 318–20.

Tsypin, also known for his work with Joanne Akalaitis and Robert Falls, first trained as an architect in Moscow before studying set design at New York University. Although very much viewed as a designer who orders and orchestrates stage space architecturally, like Sellars he crucially views theatre as a synthetic art form. Their collaboration began when Sellars took up his appointment at the American National Theatre where Tsypin designed *The Count of Monte Cristo* (1985). Three other productions at Kennedy Center followed. Tsypin has subsequently worked as production designer on Sellars's debut film feature, *The Cabinet of Dr Ramirez* (1990) as well as a succession of stagings, which include the more recent *Theodora* (Glyndebourne 1996, 1997) and *Le Grande Macabre* (Salzburg 1997, Châtelet 1998). All their work has been epic in proportion, giant structures of staggering beauty, which brilliantly layer what Ronn Smith locates as 'various historical references and/or scenic elements within a single set'.[2] Significantly Tsypin views directing as an intrinsic component of designing a set, while Sellars has acknowledged how his shows are often 'saved' by his costume, lighting and set designers: 'If the audience gets an impression of theatre as three dimensions, as something that impinges on the lives of real people, it's the designers who are responsible for that'.[3]

Lobel met Sellars through Robert Brustein and they have worked together since 1980 when she designed *The Inspector General*. Her work is perhaps best exemplified by the Chicago Lyric Opera 1983 production of *The Mikado* reset in contemporary Japan complete with Honda motorcycles and Datsun cars. Here images of contemporary globalisation abounded. The emphasis is often more obviously horizontal than Tsypin's structures (although *Le Nozze de Figaro* and *The Rake's Progess* [Châtelet 1996] defy this generalisation), and has a greater reliance on realistic props and furniture. The visual environment provided is concrete; painted and projected backdrops proved a feature of both *The Mikado* and *Die Zauberflöte* (Glyndebourne 1990) respectively, but these, like the celebrated replica of the jet in *Nixon in China* (Houston 1987), have given the impression of being larger than life. Designs for *Così fan tutte* and *Die Zauberflote*, were conspicuously adorned with the detritus of contemporary America.

The Czech artist and UCLA Professor of Design Dunya Ramicova has been Sellars's regular costume designer since 1980, providing

2 Ronn Smith, *American Set Design 2* (New York: TCG, 1991), p. 159.
3 Peter Sellars, From a lecture delivered on design at Northwestern University while Hope Abelson Artist-in-Residence, 17 February 1990.

functional attire capable of operating both on a realist and conceptual level. James F. Ingalls, Sellars's lighting designer for over seventeen years, is similarly admired for his ability to use colour to evoke characters' emotional states, veering between arrangements which operate within seemingly realist codes while drawing on the expressionist and surreal. To talk of a Peter Sellars production is to acknowledge the crucial role that all his collaborators play in shaping the products seen by audiences. As David Littlejohn concludes: 'they have all been able to realise, perhaps even to inspire, his most unusual and provocative fantasies'.[4] Here Sellars discusses their different collaborations in what is habitually perceived as 'a Peter Sellars production'. This private interview was conducted on 17 September 1998.

PETER SELLARS I don't see my work as the imposition of a single point of view around the material; it is really the opposite. It's always a conversation. I'm not interested in a single viewpoint. Master productions where you solve all the problems just aren't interesting to me. I'm not interested in solving all the problems. I can no longer accept a master narrative. In my productions you cannot say that this is Peter Sellars's view on this or that topic. For me it's all about dialogue, about inviting all these different people into a room to see what kind of a conversation we can have. Theatre is about having a conversation that society is not having. And communication has to be reciprocal. It has to go in two directions.[5]

MARIA DELGADO You work very closely with a team of regular collaborators. You've been working with lighting designer Jim Ingalls and costume designer Dunya Ramicova for eighteen years, and with set designer George Tsypin and Adrienne Lobel for thirteen and fifteen years, respectively. I wonder if you could talk about these longstanding creative relationships.

PS George Tsypin came to the final performance of *St Francois* in Salzburg and was so overwhelmed by Jim's work. He said: 'You can't even see the light cues. It's just pure feeling. The entire stage is bathed in pure feeling. It's not about lights, it's about feeling.' That was George's understanding of what Jim does. It's like Turner watercolours. It's in three strokes. An entire seascape is there: the clouds, the time of day, the climate, how warm or how cool it is, the light on the water, the light in the sky, the sun, the slight mist of rain. And that's three strokes on a piece of paper with a watercolour brush that

---

4   David Littlejohn, 'Reflections on Peter Sellars' Mozart', *The Opera Quarterly*, 7:2 (Summer 1990), pp. 6–36.
5   Arthur Barstow, *The Director's Voice: Twenty-One Interviews* (New York: TCG, 1988).

took less time to make than to describe. Jim works that quickly and that impulsively. He watches the show and reacts. His skill means that he can do it so breathtakingly quickly.

Also, it's always so personal and emotional. It's never a decision about a look. It's the emotional life of a piece. A lot of the shows we do which are about issues of spiritual awareness or struggle, have as their subject the entrance of life. Each person comes into the world bearing light. In *Peony Pavilion* you see the women when they're ghosts carrying these lights. In the programme of *St Francois* we call these people 'light bearers'. The two key scenes of *St Francois*, 'Healing the leper', and 'The stigmata', are entirely lit by six people holding light instruments. They're in contemporary robes, like young Franciscans today – whereas the robes in the rest of the show are historic. The light is moving with St Francis and with the leper and following them everywhere. So you get this glow around St Francis. The three lights lighting the leper – two on one side and one on the other – have green gels in them and the lights lighting St Francis – two on one side and one on the other – are without gels. The healing when St Francis kisses the leper has the light bearers quietly lift out the green gels, and the man's skin is clear. It's so simple but it's also that they are in the scene illuminating it. The light has this personal active presence. 'The stigmata' is lit the same way with the presence of the people revealing. Light is a very personal and potent force in people's lives.

The wonderful thing is that I will ask Jim for something very specific and what he does is nothing like what I ask for. It's always so much more beautiful than anything I could have imagined. He really solves it in his way. Jim started out as the stage manager in Twyla Tharp's company. The show we first did together at La MaMa in New York in 1980 was his first show as a lighting designer and he's lit practically every show I've done since then. We really started together. He has a stage manager's gift. He's virtually a production manager for the whole show. When George is not around, Jim is keeping track of what has to be done on the set. He holds the company together. He's also really patient. The last two minutes of light in *St Francois* took eight hours to programme. He dedicates such incredible care to it. It's never too much. He's always adding one more thing. I'm forever calling him and he's changing the lights by telephone and fax. I try and stay around for all the performances and he usually doesn't. So we speak and he faxes the new cues to the stage manager and we put them in for that night's performance.

It's all part of his quality as a person. He's such a generous person and so much part of the total project. It's never just about lighting and his work reflects that generosity and that interest. You really feel he's offering that to people. They experience it as some kind of gift rather than as a condition. It's always a sort of state of grace that's bestowed the minute the light appears.

MD And always unobtrusive.

PS You can't spot the cues. He's doing things that are so subtle. You wouldn't know that they're happening. What I try and do a lot in shows is use light and sound in very cinematic ways, so that it's like a movie. We may have a close-up and then a wide shot so there are a lot of cues. With some shows we do, the light cues operate like cinematic cutting. *Electrification of the Soviet Union* was like that. It was like an Andrei Tarkovsky movie and Jim was the film editor. You knew where a cut was because of the lighting but you were also aware of what it meant to flow through a cut. But inevitably the most beautiful things he's doing are the things you're moved by and yet you can't tell what it is that's creating that moment.

MD And yet the relationship's evolving and creating work that always looks very different.

PS *Peony Pavilion* doesn't look like *St Francois*, which doesn't look like *Nixon in China*. Jim enters each world completely and creates it.

Dunya, I always think, is the most profound artist I've ever worked with. We don't talk a whole lot. She's a great teacher and every project she takes so personally and so far. George's sets you can't miss but the most impressive thing about Dunya's work is that halfway through the evening you're not aware that people are wearing costumes. You really think people came in their own clothes. While George calls your attention to the fact that this is an artistic event of incredible magnitude, Dunya actually makes sure there's nothing between you and the people. Her costumes draw you so close to the people that you're unaware of any mediation. You feel people living in them completely. So, there's this tension between George's sets which are, on one level, so extravagant, imaginative and aesthetic, and Dunya's costumes which have all that same information but so deeply imbedded inside them. The surface is itself unremarkable. For the last ten years in most reviews Dunya's name is never mentioned, because people are not aware that they're costumes. You just completely believe that's the person you're looking at; it ceases to be separate from the person wearing it. It becomes one thing.

Yet, when you look at her costumes, they're so unusual. She particularly works at the emotional level of pure colour. In *Peony Pavilion* she's holding the whole production together with those costumes. They seem unremarkable but they're binding all these different performing styles. All these different worlds are touching because of those costumes. It's done very modestly. To get each of these costumes she goes through an elaborate hideous process. Some of these things are shopped, some are built. She has an amazing eye. Again, as with Jim, I will ask her for something very specific and she will just get it wrong. In *Giulio Cesare*, I wanted Sesto, who was played by Lorraine Hunt, to be a preppy kid – I went to all those schools, I know exactly what he should be wearing. She bought all the wrong clothes and it was fabulous, because Dunya knows that nobody is wearing the clothes they intended to wear that day. She knows that nobody looks exactly the way they want to look. None of her costumes have 'a look.' There's always something wrong. The image is always just partial. Most people don't know how to make 'an image.' It's always a little of this and something of that. So much costume design is a single statement about a person in a way that prevents us from having to look at them and noticing who they are. With a one-line statement you don't have to look for the rest of the night, whereas Dunya's costumes refuse to do that. You see someone walk on in their costume and you still have to look for who they are because you don't know yet. That is very rare.

Dunya's a very profound thinker and metaphysically inclined. All of her costumes have this extraordinary philosophical depth and theological inner life. She's constantly dyeing things until the colours are rich and layered. She then puts costumes next to each other that are slightly dissonant. In *Rake's Progress*, Willard White's Nick Shadow and Paul Groves's Tom Rakewell are both dressed in this blue. Willard has this turquoise which is both Caribbean – so you get Jamaica from the ocean in one of those travel posters – but at the same time that horrible institutionalised hospital blue-green. Paul is in the blue of a gas-station attendant. Right next to each other all night these two blues are impossible because they keep trying to cancel each other out. The colour shift is just close enough to clash permanently. So, you're never able to see those two men together and have your eyes be at rest. And those men are standing next to each other all night. In the simplest thing, just by forcing those two blues to live with each other, Dunya creates this constant tension which is unresolvable. Paul's blue has this melancholy. Like work clothes. But at the same time the clothes are just blue and what it means to be blue. So, you get all of that imagery in the simplest possible way – it's an unpretentious pair of pants and a shirt.

Dunya's attention to detail is very special. In *Oedipus Rex* where there is a chorus of 120, no two costumes are the same. She has designed every single one. She hasn't just gone out shopping. She has made a drawing, a beautiful watercolour of each individual costume. No two people are ever the same, or replaceable or extra, or unthought-out or unacknowledged. Every individual is present. The same energy goes into creating that as creating the costume for the principal. The stage is shared equally by all these people. That's Dunya. That's democracy.

MD   And yet, in the first instance, for a brief moment, she deceives you into thinking that the chorus's costumes are the same; that's one of the reasons they're so unsettling. They make you think about your mechanisms of perception, about how you're constantly deceived into thinking one thing when something very different is going on.

PS   Those *Oedipus Rex* costumes, like all her costumes, have such long histories. *Oedipus Rex* comes from a moment in Brazil, which then took Dunya to Benin. This is because black culture in Brazil came from Benin. The north-east of Brazil is Benin transplanted to the New World. Dunya researched all of these ritual costumes in Benin with these strips of cloth and the way they're sewn out of these patches of red and white. She then took people's Sunday clothes and began sewing in patches. She turns what people are wearing to the golf course into ritual clothing. But at the same time, of course, it's all Malevich and the constructivists. It's recapitulating avant-garde Russian art of the 1920s and 1930s. It's also giving you the Stravinsky mode of operation, which is permanent rhythmic syncopation. These costumes all viewed next to each other with their slight shifts create this permanent syncopation in the landscape. There's an image of diversity and yet at the same time everybody's going through the same thing. The bands of red that are appearing on everyone's nice white clothing are also an image of the disease moving through the play. Everyone is marked.

You never know where Dunya will come from. You see it in the holographic fabric, the bizarre Liberace stuff and especially the yellow chorus costumes in *Grande Macabre*. I had told Dunya I wanted nuclear protective clothing. Dunya, as she always does, researches things exhaustively. She sent away for the catalogue of a company that exclusively manufactures clothing for disasters: ecological catastrophes, oil spills/slicks. I forget what the company's name is but the emblem on every page of their catalogue is a piggy: piggies who enjoy being in dirt. She found these huge yellow nuclear protective suits but then she creates the yellow out of this delicate brushed silk. The slippers became like little bunny slippers and the protective hoods became soft drawstring bonnets. So, it went from an image of the most impervious clothing ever created to little kids with the most vulnerable possible clothing, like pyjamas. All this in just one image.

At the same time the yellow is this acid colour that you can't get out of your eyes. It's not banana, it's not warm, it's not tropical, and it's this nightmare sulphuric acid bath for the eyes. But against that the cloth is lovely and brushed so it absorbs light and is not shiny in any way. It's astonishing and yet very rarely does it get written about.

MD George Tsypin also seems to work in astonishing ways. I always admire the ways in which he constantly lifts my gaze upwards. He creates grand epic structures where past, present and future, exquisitely layered, seem to coexist. Even in *Theodora* where the set was less evidently vertical – the six glass bottles shifting to create different configurations, evoking both fragility and longevity, cracked by the ravages of time but still standing. We are provided with a sense both of the fluidity and tangibility of space. In a world where I am advised to look down and across, George's orchestration of space moves away from the horizontal focus of the television screen and encourages me to look up and beyond which is always a really uplifting experience.

PS My Russian professor at Harvard, Jurij Striedter, when he first saw my work with George was so excited. He told me that it was exactly the dimension that Meyerhold brought to the stage: up. You feel this vertical space, which is what then permits metaphysical topics, because then you're into vertical reality and not just horizontal reality.

George is a restless artist for whom self-satisfaction never intrudes. Also everything he works on opens and opens. Adrienne Lobels's entire work, on the other hand, is about closed spaces and sealed universes into which nothing can get in, no matter what. No one can get out and no one can get in. The rigidity and intensity of the proportions of the stage worlds she creates have been so carefully considered that every detail is engraved in their flesh. After two hours in *Cosi fan tutte*, the sheer intensity of the detailing on the metalwork in the diner lit red shows us that these people are living in hell. Hours earlier it was a perfectly entertaining bit of diner kitsch and then later it is absolutely the toothmarks of a demon. These people are living in an oven roasted alive for eternity. The moral force of Adrienne's work comes from the relentless perfection of the proportions and the insistence on how fine the lines are, whereas George is always dealing with really complex situations of equilibrium that could shift at any moment. The system is never closed and is forever subject to change; you're constantly on the precipice of something unknown or some major reversal. With Adrienne what's both wonderful and a nightmare is that you never leave the house. These people have laid out their lives and now they have to live them; they have bought into a self-image that is so limited and that's what's wonderful because they know exactly who they are, but it is also a nightmare because they're trapped forever in having to be that. Her sets deliver the way in which most people accept identities much too quickly and want to identify themselves all too easily with a certain image or a situation so that they can feel secure in it. Then it's about how that security then turns on you.

With George there's never a second of security. There's always some unknown, unfinished, unacknowledged future that you can't predict or foreshadow and just don't know how to deal with. Adrienne's sets are 'light'. All of the rigour and relentlessness of the proportions also gives it this eighteenth-century quality of a world of pure rationality, which oddly enough, if you blow the whole thing, will just collapse. George's sets have that sheer weight of real life – big heavy things, like bridges, which really weigh something. Adrienne's sets feel quasi-conceptual. The perfection is such that you feel it's the fantasy of an eighteenth-century encyclopaedist. The mathematic precision leads her towards fantasy. So, it's a fantasy diner in *Così fan tutte*; it's the hideous Donald Trump architecture in *Le Nozze de Figaro*, which is a fantasy that rich people have that life could be that simple – or it's a fantasy if you're not rich and you imagine life could be that simple. Once you live there, of course, it's unbearable. But you were imme-diately attracted to the clean modern lines that have no history and what you'd thought meant no baggage. But there's always baggage.

George trained as an architect, so his work has a sculptural quality and a special quality as a building and as a construction. You always feel it's a lived-in space. George always scales things so even in his mammoth sets, like *The Death of Klinghoffer*, a human being makes a tremendous impression. In *St Francois* the set is vast, but all the things that people are next to are slightly smaller, so that people seem large next to them. George will make doors far too small so people have to duck to get through them. The actors feel like giants and you are actually stunned by the power of a human being and how much presence a human being has on a George Tsypin set. Adrienne is always working with much more Palladian values where the whole thing is to human scale. With George you're constantly getting extremes because he both shrinks and explodes. Things are oddly small and oddly large.

MD Yes, and even within a single set the proportions always seem to be shifting. At one moment it may appear awe-inspiringly huge and yet inhabited by performers. I am struck by the intimacy of the environment.

PS That's because George is a poet. The sets are about him in many more ways than people may think at the beginning of the night. What's embedded in it is so much content that the longer you watch the more you see. This is different to the way most commercial theatre sets work, which is about giving you an image which tells you where you are in the first three minutes and then you can forget it for the rest of the night. You watch George's work all night long and the longer you look the more places you think you are. Frequently it's not that there's a big scene change, it's just that the set begins to reveal more of its secrets. George's sets are worlds where there are so many secrets and they only reveal themselves across time and that includes years after you saw the production. Adrienne's gift is to make an image that is so instantly recognisable that its very rigour gives you a lot of comic potential. That is because it's such a vivid emblem but then also, as I mentioned earlier, provides a merciless sense of entrapment which she gets in *La Nozze di Figaro*, in *Così fan tutte*, and in *Nixon in China*'s commercial postcard universe. Here, in order to take America's mind off its problems you're going to stage a made-for-TV spectacle of yourself going to China and then you're trapped in your own made-for-TV universe realising that you haven't a clue what's real any more. Where does the press conference end and where does your life begin? You've got the script written while history is unfolding; that's one of the things that's most compelling about *Nixon in China*. One of the things I most admire about Adrienne's work is the fact that she is always able to bring a lacquered finish to her sets, which is just scrumptious. You want to take it home.

MD You want to eat it. Her sets always look good enough to eat.

PS They're really scrumptious. You want one of your own. Yet, at the same time, there's this neurotic energy that's charging through it. The emotional mood swing is tremendous. You will something into being, and initially you think it's going to be wonderful because I'm having everything my way. Then later the worst thing that could possibly happen is that you had everything your own way. By the end of the performance you have a demonstration of the destructive side of human will-power.

MD This is very apparent in Adrienne's design for *The Rake's Progress*, where you have a huge pristine white penitentiary presented on stage. You admire the sheer scale and architectural majesty of it and yet you're constantly reminded that this is a prison that encloses, curtails, incarcerates and oppresses.

PS Adrienne's research for that design was this very luxurious architectural design book on new prisons which was put out by architects proud of their work. Here was a high-gloss architectural coffee-table book with lavish photos of the latest, most glamourous, high-tech prisons. It's all incredibly attractive and then you begin to realise what it's there to do and what the real motives are behind and beyond that gloss and modish smart exterior. This is why I wanted to set something there, because prisons are the budget priority of the future. It's the society that's under construction, a society where education is all about student loans which have to be paid back almost immediately at interest rates which are twice as high. It's all about a profit to the state. Art allows us to enter into a discussion with these issues.

Active sound
Darron L. West in conversation with Caridad Svich

Darron L. West is sound designer, director and company member of Anne Bogart's SITI Company. He has designed numerous productions all over Manhattan and US regional theatres, including the original production of *Rent* at New York Theatre Workshop (1996). He is currently collaborating on projects with Improbable Theatre Company, and the musical group The Rachels.

This interview was conducted online from May to September 2001.

CARIDAD SVICH You began to work with Anne Bogart and SITI in 1993. Since then you have designed every show in their repertoire. The commitment to a company aesthetic is one of the aspects that makes SITI so unique in a US theatrical climate where fewer and fewer ensembles can create and develop work over time and present it with integrity and focus. Your work as a sound designer with the company has truly made audiences listen differently and re-evaluate what is possible in the creation of sonic environments in the theatre. What has the process of working with Anne and her actors been like for you?

DARRON L. WEST When I first came on board with SITI I had found in Anne a likeminded idea about what the theatre is and the way in which it should and could be presented. The collaboration was instantaneous and that connection hasn't changed but only gotten deeper and clearer in its focus as we have grown together as friends and as colleagues. I had, as importantly, found in the company of actors she chose to surround herself with, a highly extraordinary musical sense about them so my designs became instantly more sophisticated than they ever had been. The company has an uncanny ability in timing text and the body to the music with ease and that allows me to be able to stretch out much more. In the first year with SITI, I was engaged in a deep study about how actors worked and what their process was in creation because frankly I had never spent that much time in a room with the actors as they struggled and experimented and kept things and threw others away. So my calibration, I think, in how I learned to collaborate was completely learned and crafted by my experience in the room with actors. The freedom that they had to follow down various paths to find the right one really rubbed off on me as a designer.

CS How do you work with actors in the practice hall?

DW One of the more important things I have learned from Anne was one afternoon quite a few years ago we got into a discussion about what it means to be on the other side of the rehearsal hall from the actors as they worked and she said to me, 'My job is to focus and give the actors my undivided attention as they work. My intensity of focus is what allows them to create.' I have the fortunate position to be able to participate in our work from both the perspective of an actor in the scene and as a director concentrating on the stage. In creating the soundscape you have to be dealing with the same issues that an actor has in their work: motivation, logic, clarity, subtext, situation, etc. So much of the time my collaboration with the cast is based on discussions about where they are and what they have to accomplish in the work of a particular scene and how can I help them or provide a hurdle for them. In addition, I'm also in the unique position to speak back to them as they work. A director sits and observes as a scene is being created. I have the advantage of reflecting back to them what I perceive they are saying to me with sound and music. I also have a theory that at any one time in a collaborative rehearsal hall the helm of the ship is manned by various people in the room – sometimes I'm the director, other times it's Anne, and again other times it could be a member of the cast. The way the SITI company works we are working on unlocking the question of the play. The play for us is always something that is 'out there to be found and discovered', which is great because it puts you in a position of being able to work without ego. I often use the example of a large stone of marble, that we all have hammers and chisels and as we work we are chipping away at the marble to find the art. The common mistake in creating theatre to me is that place where you aren't working towards a question which allows all sorts of assumptions about what the play is or means. The moment you assume in the collaborative process it dies because you confine and box in whatever you are creating. Working against assumptions is the biggest challenge for us, and something we still work at. We also say working on a play with us is a lot about following the Ouija board.

cs Do you go into the process with conceptual thoughts in mind?

DW I'm a research hound when it comes to my work on a play and frequently I do find myself swimming around aurally in unknown cultures. Keeping a finger to the pulse of high art and low art is necessary but I must say that the act of creation for me is a violent one. It is visceral and emotional and doesn't come from an intellectual place. Some of my first decisions that I make are based in the conceptual thoughts of what the space and the play need to sound and feel like and the negotiation between the two. Is this design about stage depth, as SITI's *War of the Worlds* (2000) was? Or is this design about width as something like SITI's *The Medium* (1993) was? In doing a show that was experimenting with cinematic techniques on the stage such as *War of the Worlds* it was of a great necessity to be able to do a long-shot or a close-up aurally. So, the design of the system was about corridors of sound on the stage, lots of deck speaker positions both low and high. With *The Medium*, the stage space used is actually very small so the audience got this feeling of being immersed in the play and the space because they were enveloped from all sides watching this little square of a play in the cavern of sound around them. You are really dealing with defining the aural frame through which you peer at the play. The moments that seem in my plays that the design explodes and takes the stage for a bit are soundly (pun intended) rooted in the bodies that are participating with the cue. It's like dance for me. I love to watch dance because it allows me to hear the music in a new way with fresh eyes. It's both things going on at the same time: the sound creating the space and the time and the act of the actors cutting through it defining it even further. I like silver platter designs, one that has a strong foundation and a logic of their own based in the play in which the actors can play and feel comforted inside of.

cs Soundtracks on film have conditioned audiences to experience the emotional journey of a story in an aural and visual manner. This kind of conditioning often makes an audience expect a sound score to cue them throughout the telling of a story in the theatre as well. However, one of the strongest elements you can work with in sound design is the use of silence. Where silence falls, how it operates juxtaposed to other types of sound is crucial to the experience of a score on stage and film. In what manner do you keep yourself alert to silence when composing a sound score for performance?

DW My process in beginning every play that I work on consists of reading the play in silence once a day for a full week and in that week I don't make any notes. It's about gazing into the text and finding the musicality of the text itself, the repetition of words, sentence structure, etc. In the first three or four readings, I'll skip all the stage directions to free myself up so I can think laterally. Only when I feel like my head is comfortable enough in 'lateral land', for the lack of a better phrase, will I begin to read the stage directions in the play. In the next week of reading the play I look for where there is no sound in the play and my first notations with respect to the play that I'm working on will be in fact where I believe that it's silent. I think it was Miles Davis who said that music is the space between the notes. I maintain that if you are going to begin to score a play the three most important things to keep bubbling on the surface, in order, are (1) where it is silent, (2) when a cue might start, and (3) definitely when the said cue ends. Sound deals with, defines and helps manage time and space in the theatre and silence is the palette that all of that rests on.

CS Does access to newer and newer technologies make your work more difficult? More exciting?

DW On the difficult side of the equation: This technology has tended to distance designers from the meat of creating sometimes; we have so many toys in our toy box that we get more concerned with what the toys are and what they can do than what story we are trying to tell. The technology, as Marshall McLuhan would say, has taken the art of a sound design more often than not into a hot medium, which provides all the information of a show to the audience in the sound design thereby alienating the audience from the stage and not allowing them to lean in and participate in the piece. It has the tendency to become hot because there is so much now that we have the ability to do to fill in the emotional blanks in a piece of theatre. The technology is so precise that focus on the whole is lost.

On the exciting side of the coin: the technology has allowed us to be more in tune with the creative process because the time spent cue to cue working on the technical aspects of our jobs have been cut to an amazing degree. The instantaneous access to aural information via the net has also changed the way a sound designer can research. While in Louisville KY working on Charles Mee's *bobrauchenbergamerica* at Actors Theatre of Louisville's Humana Festival in 2001 we came upon a section of the play in which we wanted a NASA space broadcast as part of the soundscape for the scene. Online in ten minutes with my Macintosh I-book I had found a desirable source from the NASA website and with the computer still hooked to the internet in the rehearsal hall I could stream and playback numerous files from the NASA communications site on the internet as we worked, enabling me to create from the sounds of the world in time as we staged the play.

CS Nevertheless, despite advances in the field, sound design is still very much the 'orphan' when it comes to professional theatre training programmes. The kind of work you do with SITI and with other companies and artists with whom you collaborate profoundly are testament to the sophisticated, ground-breaking possibilities sound design can offer to a theatrical production, and how sound is a live presence, a body interacting with other bodies, on stage. Yet, education is still behind. How will the next generation of sound design artists find their way? What would you like to see happen?

DW If I had the chance to create a dream programme in sound design? Classes in directing and acting, in both modern dance and ballet, in music and art histories. And most importantly collaborating with fellow directors, writers and actors on actual plays and workshops of plays that will be performed in front of audiences. One thing also I've found lacking is training young designers starting at the beginning with tape editing (the old-fashioned way). Many of the structures that get put into the computer now are in fact rooted in earlier analogue technologies. To understand the language of the faux buttons and knobs that you're seeing on the screen of your computer, it helps if you have some idea of what the mode was. It's the same as learning music. You don't start by writing symphonies. You have to know the scales first. I believe what I do is simply make theatre. The mistake that I think is often made by designers of any discipline is that they have been brought on board to simply design the show. In reality we are also there for the director to bounce ideas off of, and our jobs are to keep focused on the forest of the play we are helping to create, as the director concentrates on the trees.

Afterword: contemporary dramatic writings and the new technologies

Patrice Pavis, translated by Joel Anderson

We tend, and rightly so, to separate the study of contemporary dramatic texts from that of the media and new technology, as if the two were incompatible and unrelated. Indeed, the same people do not venture into these two domains: we either take refuge in the inexpressibility of poetry, or we succumb to the feats of the media (of which the internet seems to be the latest figurehead). But does this separation of these domains and their missions do justice to the complexity of the texts or the effectiveness of the media? Should we not make them communicate since the writings 'speak' of a world constructed by all of the media, particularly by the new technologies?

To test this it might be useful to go via the *aesthetics* of *mise en scène*.[1]

Indeed, they are applied in such an anarchic way that these two terms, *aesthetics* and *mise en scène*, are in danger of losing all theoretical relevance. *Mise en scène* is the last baroque metaphor, fashionably used to make believe that all cultural activity is theatre, theatricality or spectacle; as for *aesthetics*, it is supposed to ratify all practice of sense and meaning. As much for writing as for the media, the concept of *mise en scène* is threatened with the loss of all aesthetical function. In texts the *mise en scène* can erase itself in a literary and poetic reading that does not sufficiently recognise its *mise en jeu* and its relationship with the real, in particular the media real, therefore its aesthetic *mise en scène*. In the media, the *mise en scène* disappears 'in favour of' a technological functionalism of which the machine and computers are the zealous servants.

---

1 Kongress in der Oper Frankfurt: 'Ästhetik der Inszenierung', 22–26 March 2000.

Here we will take two examples of the flight of the aesthetics of the *mise en scène*: on the one hand the multimedia spectacle *Zulu Time* by Robert Lepage; on the other hand contemporary French dramatic writing (Koltès, Minyana, Novarina, Jouanneau, Durif).

Given the task of analysing a performance that uses new technology, and thus a task that seems far from my current work on contemporary dramaturgy, I have chosen *Zulu Time*, the latest work by Lepage, presented at Créteil in October 1999. My reactions from the day after seeing the play, here recorded without addition and in uncensored form, are rather negative, but as such they are the first step toward a more moderate evaluation of multimedia performance and they were also to alter my perception of plays up to the present.

Notes on *Zulu Time* from 24 October 1999

Every machine, every technology, every computer is a foreign body at the heart of theatrical performance.

The more complex, sturdy, omnipresent the technology, the more derisory it is to our eyes.

We impatiently search to find a living and speaking body, whatever it does or it says.

Technology has got the upper hand on the human for good. Alas, the human apparitions did not put this into reverse. The audience is sitting on either side of a stage, where a mechanical bridge goes up and down; above it, machines, identical on each side, move like robots, radio-controlled by an army of programmers sporting headphones who content themselves with carrying out the orders of the chief programmer.

The human body is no longer able to be itself, in particular to enjoy; it needs all the paraphernalia of sado-masochism (chains, gags, ropes, etc.) to feel pleasure. There is no way any more, it appears, to meet another body and to make love with it with no other aim than pleasure, play and curiosity. It is pulled into the machine, but this is no longer the infernal and amusing machine of *Modern Times*: in the cybernetic machine every action comes from inaudible orders from outside.

Is Lepage's performance not even a *mise en scène*, and more a lesson *à la* Virilio?

The transatlantic flight where you abandon your body to sleepiness, to a change which goes beyond it, becomes a machine that defies time, catches up with it, or at least neutralises it, a short moment of eternity.

The erotic fantasy remains without effect on reality. The hostess carries on serving drinks and ice-cubes, without realising the erotic annunciation of the male passengers. Moreover, it is not a question of fantasy: here in no time, gone in no time.

This time, Lepage has crossed the limits: the living, the human, the voice have all been engulfed by technological and computerised devices. Like the last time, in his Elsinore monologue, no human incident, alas, comes to jam the machine. He contents himself with farce: small morsels of human meat interspersing the technical device and taking up with what is human, which is comedy, humour and error.

The human is ridiculous, but human. This drugged-up woman listening to her erotic messages on her bed, very much alone, is ridiculous and pitiful; this old woman at the bar taking a twirl; these tango dancers attached to the ceiling by their feet and dancing with their heads on the floor; this muscled contortionist ready for any twist and for the erotic figures that are so complicated that we get lost and give up trying to follow . . .

All of this makes us miss the old formula of *boy meets girl* or else the purely erotic meeting of a man and a woman.

So much technology talks so much it forgets what it was talking about, it becomes an end in itself, and exhausts us. A performance conceived, created, understood and appreciated by computer scientists alone.

The people from *koken*, those men in black from the classical Japanese theatre, the machine operators are there too, with their pathetic rope, a kind of pre-emptive limb, to see that the trap door closes properly, without the rope getting caught in the mechanism. These zealous stage-servants, who are clumsy additions to the ensemble of the piece, become human and sympathetic to us again.

This foreign body in the living – this heavy technology or this fragile rope – will it remain foreign for a long time? Nothing is less certain, since everything seems to be organised and planned for the machine, in particular the computer, to the point where the last traces of life and humanity are made to disappear. Paradoxically, from this point on, the body and the voice appear displaced in this technological device; they are like a foreign body in steel and plastic, animated by an artificial intelligence.

Naivetry or sophistication? Both! Aesthetic naivety of observation, sophistication of production. We can no longer say what is technical and what is aesthetic, what is part of a giant Meccano set and what makes up the *mise en scène*.

Boredom of the solitary look, of the solitary crowd, of solitary pleasure (drugs, alcohol, technology, masturbation).

The machine, the new technologies and computers are foreign bodies, but invasive ones, which want to make us believe that they are going to assimilate themselves, or rather that humans are going to assimilate them. They intrude into everything, these foreigners blessed with bodies: the stage, the Créteil theatre and its idiotic machines in the wings, the ministry of culture, the city, the private lives of honest citizens.

Zulu Time has, nevertheless, a sense of humour, or at least some outrageousness. And is it not at heart a warning to humans, to herald the invasion and assimilation? Perhaps, but to mock technology and the media, Lepage is induced to try to outdo them, to sacrifice everything to this triumphant technology, to organise everything, to think, to arrange according to it, to cut short any critical or simply aesthetic *mise en scène*.

We no longer have the right to complain: the computerisation of our lives is for our own good. Science is automatic, food, screwing, work, meetings – all automatic. Survival in a state of assisted respiration.

Speech is over. Brook and his camp fires, his sand, his water, his fire, his velocity, his food from after destruction (epilogue of *Mahabharata*) seem archaic, cut off from the world, 'old-hat', like our poor human body seems ridiculous with its needs, hungers, desires.

The parade is over. We have lost the power of speech. Even so, we are not going back to Grotowski, his rituals, his chants, his naive homilies. Its origin is now so distant, so hidden, that we mock it like our first pair of trousers.

The only show left: a naked voice saying a text?

Such were my spontaneous reactions, from which I must now protect myself, and from which I must also distance myself, by inserting quotation marks, seals on the unsayable and the incorrect.

These negative reactions are somewhat excessive, and could easily be labelled as nostalgic, conservative, reactionary even – so I should nuance them. For *Zulu Time* is nevertheless a challenge to aesthetics and to *mise en scène*. The piece forces us to see performance in a different way; to distinguish for example between that which consists of foreseeable and mechanical elements and that which consists of unpredictable and human elements, and to evaluate their interactions. The spectator is constantly on the alert: he must judge if he is manipulated or not, and how, and if his attention is distracted and at what moment he could intervene with his aesthetic judgement. Technology and technocratic thought constantly put to question the notion of the author and of the authority of *mise en scène*. Not everything in the show has the same aesthetical function: sometimes it is only the technical functioning of the show that counts, but most of the time, the *mise en scène* and its aesthetic condition[2] determines the meaning. Differentiated aesthetic principles cross the dividing line between man and machine, animate and inanimate, voice and microphone, actor and puppet. But this dividing line changes and these old dichotomies are thrown into doubt; different fictional qualities apply themselves to the image and to the living actor, to presence or to repetition; different densities characterise all of the elements of the *mise en scène*.

The media are free electrons that threaten to blow up the *mise en scène* at any moment. Since it is no longer a homogenous mixture, controlled by a central creative subject, the *mise en scène* no longer guarantees the coherence of the aesthetic artefact: it is reduced to montage, construction, scenic practice, signifying practice, *encuentro* or installation.

The entry of the media into theatrical representation – in the example of *Zulu Time* – serves only to confirm and deepen the crisis of representation. The *mise en scène* is no longer allied to a central and 'authoritarian' subject: without an author, without a centre, without the capacity to represent, it loses its raison d'être. When certain directors escape into new technology, from the inside to the outside of theatrical performance, they no longer consider themselves as the central subject, artist or aesthetic subject, but simply as an organiser of functioning, a functionary of meaning. The crisis is all the more pointed that, from the 1960s to the 1990s, performance has been conceived as visual and spectacular, thus non-textual, while the dramatic text is seen as a banal subsidiary of the *mise en scène*. Moreover, this is the reason why we have lost the habit (after the experience of Brecht) of conceiving of and analysing plays as something specifically theatrical and scenic, allied to dramaturgy and the art of the actor. Thus it seems fitting to envisage the text as inscribed in the specific moment of its utterance, especially if it is uttered in a mechanism dominated by machines and automatism. We will examine the text not only, as before, philologically and hermeneutically, but also as a score or a sub-score for the actor, that is as a verbal substance carried by voice, intonation, gesture and rhetoric. But it is necessary to pick out, amongst the machines, videos, technology and other computers, some fragments of body and some scraps of text.

Now, it is precisely the unexpected emergence of the speaking body that we observe in *Zulu Time*. Despite the apparent victory of the computer operators over the directors and of mechanical function over aesthetic object, there is a moment where the repressed body and human presence, voice and text, make a return, like the devil locked-up in his box. What re-emerges is the body of the actor momentarily subjected to the

---

2 To use the title of André Veinstein's book, *La* mise en scène *et sa condition esthétique* (Paris, Flammarion, 1955).

regularity of the machine, the body of the operators, the desiring body of the spectator. The actor always causes a derangement of the scenic image, the foreign and invincible body imposes itself despite the aseptic mechanism of the scenic machinery, the videos, the computers; rediscovering its former powers: presence, voice, biological rhythms, physical performance.

The crisis of representation, the uncertainty of the notion of *mise en scène*, but also the rejection of an absolute mediatisation killing aesthetics as much as *mise en scène*; all of this leads to a re-evaluation of the role and effect of dramatic texts and, as a result, a revival of dramatic writing.

It is clearly no accident if, everywhere in Europe, and especially in France, the crisis of *mise en scène* and the end of a generalised aesthetics of theatre coincide with a flowering of strongly varied dramatic writing. These writings (the plural use of the word vouches for their extreme diversity) are, moreover, all the more strong and sure of themselves that they have perfectly assimilated scenic practice and the many paths of *mise en scène*. Our hypothesis: the renewed confidence present in these writings is made up as much of a reaction and defiance against the media and communication machines as it is of a desire to confront them, even to integrate them, even if it is *ex negativo* in a general theory. In writing the media is not, as it is onstage, a foreign body; it actually places itself in an intertextuality in the widest sense of the word, that is an intermediality,[3] which serves writing instead of marginalising or assimilating it.

Thus in the five chosen plays,[4] the relationship with new technology is highly ambivalent. The authors, frightened by the media, appear to exclude and reject it, but so doing they are no less influenced and transformed by it, almost without their knowledge. Here we have a contemporary version of the Pygmalion myth: hoping to ignore the media and the machines of theatrical practice, we turn to texts, but now the machines have come back, at the very heart of the lines and the words, and the conflict rages between a fantastical idea of pure textuality and a concrete reality of media omnipresence.

In analysing contemporary dramatic texts[5] the question of context and of intertext (A) and the question of a general theory of the media, where they

---

3 On this subject see: Jürgen E. Müller, *Intermedialität* (Münster, Nodus Publikationen, 1996).

4 Bernard-Marie Koltès, *Dans la solitude des champs de coton* (Paris, Éditions de Minuit, 1986); Philippe Minyana, *Inventaires* [1987] (Paris, Éditions théâtrales, 1993); Valère Novarina, *Vous qui habitez le temps* (Paris, POL, 1989); Joël Jouanneau, *Allegria Opus 147* (Paris, Actes Sud – Papiers, 1994); Eugène Durif, *Via Negativa* (Paris, Actes Sud – Papiers, 1996).

5 Patrice Pavis, 'La coopération textuelle du spectateur' *Théâtre public*, 152 (March–April 2000).

meet, occupy key positions in the diagram of the reader's textual cooperation. The difficulty is to establish a line between the play and the media, to imagine a theory of intermediality guaranteeing the accessibility of the play from our knowledge of the world that is shaped by the media.

In *Dans la solitude des champs de coton* by Bernard-Marie Koltès, a dealer and a client fight it out without our knowing what the object of their transaction is. The speech, the dispute, indeed the conflict itself become the object of desire, the only thing at stake in the confrontation. The convoluted sentence and the neo-classical rhetoric of the arguments are the only currencies; it is a fearsome textual machine which, in expending, excess and *potlatch*, places itself at the other side of the world from an exchange of information and from effective communication. The Koltèsian sentence, an illusion machine, has not so much to be understood by the reader and audience as to be *described*, commented on and travelled as one describes the landscape seen from the train that is crossing it. The trajectory of the sentences and lines describes a spatial and rhetorical figure, which does not penetrate the meaning, but crosses the contours of the textual landscape. It resembles the Cartesian machine: '*une gigantesque machine en laquelle il n'y a rien du tout à considérer que les figures et les mouvements de ses parties*'.[6] This war machine, whose operation is mastered bit by bit by the reader, becomes more and more rapid, simple and conflictive until the final confrontation: '*Alors, quelle arme?*' (p. 61). The sentence ends no longer referring to anything but itself as an effective, but empty, mechanism. The pastiche of classical heroic and mock-heroic forms and the crazy arguments of the classical rhetoric take us to a metatextual game and to an auto-*mise en scène* of language, no longer of the world and of fiction as in a baroque metaphor of the world like theatre, but more like a language game from the rhetorical period. This writing of excess and this preciousness of style, which is so mannered and torturous that it cuts itself off from all mimetic reference to the real, clashes with the standardisation of language and the indoctrination of the media.

The difficulty with the theory of intermediality is to pinpoint the origin of the influence of the media, notably the audiovisual media, in dramatic writing. Most of the time, the text does not in any way indicate the implicit presence of other texts and other media; for the theoretician any hypothesis is often untestable and is always risky. The risk and the game are always worth it, however, since it matters to understand with what and against what the play was written.

This forces us to go back to the written text, to imagine how the writing has perhaps been informed by some specific rules of one or more

---

6 René Descartes [1637].

media and to imagine how we recognise this influence. This genetic and cognitivist reflection is very delicate and we must stick to the most prudent suppositions. At the same time, the intuition of an intermedia influence will show itself to be of major importance in an understanding of the organisation of the final text. More than researching sources or direct influences, we make the hypothesis of certain specificities put in contact with one another and of a rewriting of other writings, particularly the most resistant, conflicting or dominant ones.

For solitude, audiovisual communication is clearly the enemy to be knocked down; the *disputatio* takes the opposite view from the televised political debate or the socio-cultural television series about young people in the suburbs: it is not so much naturalistic dialogue which is parodied and contradicted but television reports on a disadvantaged milieu and the lip-service of electoral debate. It is a great deal more difficult to prove the influence of Hollywood *Film noir* on the writing of Koltès (even if we know what a film-buff he was). Nevertheless, we can see the same art of evoking a taut situation and an atmosphere full of contrasts, and a revival of the same motifs in this high-level exercise in style. The lighting is chiaroscuro, the enigma is preserved at all costs, reality effects and the poetry of the real – all of these are characteristics of *film noir* that are applied to the play (a fortiori, since the play was written for, and directed by, Patrice Chéreau!).

Is it a question of these two possible influences (television and *film noir*) providing a component in the dramatic work? We perhaps cannot go so far as to say that. We can just suppose that Koltès uses these forms as a springboard, just as one uses the floor to push off and get as far away as possible from it.

It is the case that this pushing-off is more directly visible when the dramatic text makes reference to a medium, even if only to distance itself from it. This is the case in *Inventaires* by Philippe Minyana: three women confront each other in a radio or television marathon; they uninterruptedly tell their life story in a programme run by two hosts. Their monologues are being recorded and we are unaware whether this verbal material is to be shown, edited or adapted for the demands of the radio. What we hear seems to be the raw document, but their discourse indicates rather that Minyana has considerably rewritten their recorded monologues, if only to clear speech of its repetitions and silences or to remove what is incoherent. The author has reorganised, concentrated, channelled these verbal waves, not so much in terms of themes, of topoï, of common places but according to a quasi-musical score of assonance, repetition, acceleration, *glissando*, sudden ruptures. The rewriting of the raw document for the stage has punctuated the discourse in a way which is not necessarily in line with the demands of radio, those being more concerned with speed, the absence of silences, the musical breathing of the actress. We receive these testaments in the form of theatrical monologues written in an oral style, without punctuation, but with the necessity of finding a rhythm for them.

So we are witnesses to the difficulty of adapting popular speech to the tough laws of the media, as regards delivery, but also the norms of correction, standardisation of the raw, but always correct, message. Radio puts pressure on the contestants to confide without holding back, but also to do so without shocking or slipping into vulgarity. The text of the play, which is regulated on the one hand by the necessities of the radio, and on the other by Minyana's writing, gives a precious insight into the influence of radio speech on dramatic writing.

The influence is not unilateral, since, by an ironic twist, the three women take such pleasure in revealing their past and outdoing each other in the offering of intimate or spicy details, that the hosts have to constantly interrupt them, eventually shutting them up with a piece of cake. The stage and the live broadcast, improvisation and histrionics cheerfully cut into the well-established frame of media-correct radio. This unexpected counter-attack holds the radio to ridicule, limits its powers, relativises its processes. Popular oral character and theatrical verve hold media standardisation in check, the play becomes the battleground for this symbolic struggle between textuality and mediality, a struggle that Minyana referees majestically: his rewriting, lyrical and rhythmical meaning, resists the media invasion by making the last echoes of popular speech be heard.[7]

This kind of symbolic confrontation between individual speech and the media is frequent in theatre up to the present. It is a struggle between the media, notably audiovisual, and dramatic writing: crafted, individual, often held at bay on the defensive, and sometimes, as with Minyana, ready to fight back. But it is an unequal fight: writing believes itself to be unique, personal, untouchable while it is in fact already penetrated and filled with the other's discourse, invaded whether it likes it or not by the media and its economic and stylistic norms.

We notice this in a work that is apparently distanced, out of reach of the influence of the media: *Vous qui habitez le temps* by Valère Novarina. Against standardisation and repetitiveness, Novarina pits a language that is unique because it is invented, with all traces of the norm removed, used by him alone – and perhaps not even by him – since it is hard to imagine a translation into ordinary language . . . This is a language so strange and informal, compact and light, that we recognise neither plot nor fable nor traits of

---

7   Patrice Pavis, 'Sous bénéfice d'*Inventaires*: l'écriture retorse de Philippe Minyana', *Philippe Minyana ou la parole visible*, ed. Michel Corvin (Paris, Éditions théâtrales, 2000).

character nor dramaturgy in any position to integrate all the indications of the text to give the illusion of a fiction, a hidden sense, an intention.

Such qualities are worlds apart from effective mass-media communication. We find, far from psychological and mimetic exchanges, false replies, false dialogue where the speakers make do with making assertions, making lists of words or categories: names of months (p. 20), of weeks, of dramatic cases (p. 19). These endless lists try the patience of the listener. They are printouts, and constitute a challenge to computers, which are always inclined to churn out this kind of literature. But the Novarinian list is perverse, since each element has its own personality and moves away from the proposed norm: if we look at the '*liste de mes jours dépassés chez les Déroulés*' (pp. 20, 28) or the list of months (p. 82) we hear extreme variation and extraordinary originality in each invented word. The very idea of a foreseeable printout or of an exhaustive catalogue, things that a computer can prepare in no time at all, is perfectly foreign to the writing of Novarina. He uses the impression of repetition, of exhaustiveness, of mechanism to conjure up and parody the anguish of absolute mediatisation of the real and of language. The Novarinian accumulation, the infinite creation of terms and phrases that are barely legible (however evocative), the impossibility of making neither head nor tail of the 'dialogue', all of this comes from the same attitude of defiance, even vexation in the face of a normalised and simplified reality of the world and of communication. The theatre of Novarina responds homoeopathically to the computer's accumulation of information with a thesaurisation of verbal invention, with an inexhaustible supply of signifiers cut off, at least provisionally, from their signified. The poetry is the complete opposite of efficient communication, of accessible culture, of a rapid transaction on the internet. It is a counter program: what in the list is mechanical, interminable and neurotic, here takes on a playful, critical, ironic dimension. It accepts the battle against the anonymous and invasive enemy: the machine, the computer, fixed language, repetition. To better resist the heavy, ambivalent media machine, Novarina uses the same processes (repetition, systematisation, standardisation, exaggeration) but in an ironic, even deadpan way, he allows himself the luxury of outdoing these epic and poetic processes of exaggeration, after having definitively neutralised discursive, narrative, agent structures (plot, character, action).

In the diagram of the textual cooperation of the reader,[8] all that remains is the emerged part (in A) – semantic and lexical invention, the music and the material of words – and the most hidden part, the implicit philosophy of the play, notably the situation of man in language, a philosophy very close

8   Cf. note 5, p. 44.

to structuralism and conceptions of words and things, mirroring Foucault and Lacan. If the poetic surface of the signifier is open and overflowing, then, conversely, the linguistic philosophy is particularly implicit: 'l'homme est dans l'ordre des mots, et non le monde dans l'ordre des choses' (p. 16). This response to the media is paradoxical: the poetic form is multi-faceted and dense, the ideological message is univocal and almost simplistic. It is appropriate then to 'probe' the textual surface, to analyse first and foremost the poetic signifier. In the place of plot and fiction, we find a series of linguistic shocks, verbal inventions and polished routines, as we would find in a music-hall revue or an operetta. All that counts is the virtuosity of the performer or the occurrence of the author's verbal inventions, his 'witty asides,' which are stylistic brainwaves. We could discuss them, as for the signifier in general, in terms of auditory close-ups (like those used in radio and cinema even more than in television). These close-ups are 'microphone effects', which enlarge one property of the signifier, scrutinise the smallest out-of-place detail, highlight every auditory distortion, make strange this or that familiar expression (or the opposite). Novarina does with the text what the perfected tool of technology (micro, focus, linking, enlargement, distancing, collage, condensation) does daily and without effort on the chain of continuous communication. He innovates, one could say, but the renovation of language does not turn its back on the immediate world of the media: it takes nourishment from it – to take up the formula again – to 'mourir de force' (p. 27), he calls upon the most garish effects of the media to reinforce the poetry of his language and resist retrieval by computer engineers.

Nevertheless, writing's proud response to the computer printout, this response from the sheepdog to the shepherdess, this extraordinary and stubborn comic effect, this pleasure of articulating and hearing words lacking immediate meaning or where the meaning is hidden – all of this is not without its risk: the risk of playing to the crowd with this virtuosity. It also runs the risk of irrevocably spoiling theatrical pleasure, since there remains neither action nor fiction nor character to attach oneself to. There is the risk of killing the patient in the course of this homeopathic treatment for ambient media reality with these drastic remedies. While, like poetry, the play is delectable and subtle in small doses, sustained reading, or a three-hour performance, quickly renders it sparse, or even unbearable.

There is no such danger in Joël Jouanneau's play, whose title, *Allegria*, completely corresponds to its general sense of *joie de vivre* and of playing on despite the pangs of artistic creation. We see Dmitri (Shostakovich) give his student, Virginie, a final cello lesson and, in the process, create, thanks to his interpreter, the last movement of his sonata. Should one perform or interpret? The composer gives contradictory instructions: after having told her to just play the notes, without interpretation, he reproaches her for limiting herself to going through the motions: 'Vous vous contentez d'exécuter, vous n'interprétez pas, résultat c'est très plat' (p. 79). The alternation of playing and interpreting, technique and inspiration, mechanics and invention, maps onto the choice between a life without surprises, but without passion and creativity, and a life open to creativity, but also open to uncertainty. The artist, the composer, like the interpreter, does not content himself with perfect technique and identical reproduction. Art is not mechanically reproducible; it is precisely about an irruption of the unexpected in the middle of repetition and routine. This irruption is the inspiration that gives the master his last note and the certainty that the piece is finished, and is ready to leave the nest. This inspiration is eventually a question of unforeseen personal events: the suicide of the well-loved grandfather, the chance meeting with a woman in Cordoba, the abandoned child who he is to take in as his next student.

How do we escape repetition? How do we escape the grip of the media? The answer is clearly not given on a plate, but it is audible in the technique and in the way that the text is delivered, in distinguishing the accentuated passages and the less focused and more developed ones. We see this in Dmitri's first short monologue (p. 66). To set the textual machine in motion, phrases must be made rhythmical, to bring out the exclamation and the writing at the same time: an affirmation, then an explanation, an attack then a retreat, an affirmation then a doubt, a cry/a phrase, a motif/a variation. So it is a question of picking out the following accentuated terms around which the reasoning is organised: une nuit blanche (. . .), un enfant (. . .), le progrès (. . .), du banania (. . .), le sixième (. . .), l'approche des vacances (. . .).

Individual interpretation as much as rhythmical reading, decision, creativity, the irruption of desire always take place to a background of the repetitiveness of media programming. They are certainly painful, like life and love, but they also constitute a defence mechanism against mediatisation and stereotype.

Jouanneau's writing, the joy of creating in the face of adversity, routine and the fear of disappointing is marked with the irruption of rhythm, of intonation, of the voice in textual structures, including established structures of discourse, of plot, of fable, of action. It is the irruption of the body into too-fixed textual structures.

But is it not metaphorical to only speak of textual structures as mechanisms, as machines that create meaning? It is probably necessary to single out these textual structures of the media, of which the exterior existence is undeniable and whose impact on writing can be easily shown. But textual structures are also literally invaded and threatened from outside by the media, which imposes its perception of the world and its way of telling it. But the media does not content itself with just going very fast (getting ahead of the rhythm), it also changes our perception of the world, our divisions of feel/see/know/experience/become, etc. It is this modified perception that places the spectator (the user) on different ground and in a different world from those of the old world. And thus we understand that authors are always on the defensive, and that they are always writing against or *at least in reaction against* the media, and that they fall back – as in Koltès, Minyana, Jouanneau or Novarina – on their own self-referential mechanisms.

But what happens then, if the media and the communication machines are no longer either visible or locatable in the exterior world, if they leave no trace in the body of the text, like an undetectable drug? What happens if they are in tablet form, anti-depressants, for example? Is it still a question of the media when we take downers or uppers and our perception of the world finds itself clinically modified? '*Tu m'aimes, chéri? – Attends, je prends mon médicament*' – this is the kind of question posed by Eugène Durif's *Via Negativa*.

In this work, a group of depressed intellectuals, veterans of 1968, in a psychiatric clinic, test different anti-depressants that the pharmaceutical industry, represented by the head doctor and 'la killeuse', wants to put on the market. The effects of the anti-depressants are varied and unexpected: neutralisation, aggression, deliriousness, lamenting the past, demands for love, suicide. Durif's art is to vary the styles of speech according to the particular obsession and to the medicine of the moment. Hence extreme variations of delivery and concentration; each scene presents a point of view on the illness and a discursive method of treatment. Conversation, dialogue, dialectic, monologue, brooding are no longer enough to appease the patients, obsessed with the obligation to communicate, to define their neurosis, to seek treatment, to place themselves in the universe of advertising, information and political debate. The ways of speaking correspond to the stereotypical discourses of Marxism, Lacanian psychoanalysis, advertising or to the discourses of the pharmaceutical industry.

The narrative and discursive structure, that is to say the way of linking ideas and relating events, borrows a great deal from classical filmic narrative. The 'camera' easily takes us from one place to another, keeps us very close to the evoked event, gives the multiple perspectives of the characters, without ever privileging any one of them, giving an impression of polyphony, and, in the details, of contrasts and effects of dialogism. This gaze, which belongs to the 'grand imagier' (Laffay) of the filmic account, to the organiser of meaning, ceaselessly changes object and visual and auditory scale. The editing makes us aware of the contrast between one scene and another, but connects the dispersed shots that allow continuity in the dialogue. Each short sequence resembles an extract of video surveillance that records and archives the least reaction of the patients. It is as if the spectators are placed on an overhang, keeping an eye on the monitors to follow the experiments from a distance.

In the example of *Via Negativa*, and in general, the media (audiovisual, computer, telephone) are all the more close to our lives that they are insidious and penetrate them without shouting about it, changing our perception of the world without our noticing it: modified states of consciousness that change us for want of changing the world. The media that really do become one body with us are narcoleptics or drugs, since, in their effects, they give up their status as exterior objects, foreign bodies, to assimilate themselves into our bodies. But this literal metaphor of assimilation is also valid for the relation of the 'real' media with dramatic texts. The media actually come into contact with dramatic texts through the intermediary of the body, as much the body of the feeling and writing author as the suffering and enjoying bodies of the characters with which the reader or spectator identifies. In this way the influence of the media on the text necessarily goes via an intermediary that must be discovered each time.

- *Dans la solitude des champs de coton*: the body looks for itself in the body of the other, similar and different, bent toward conflict, hitting itself while thinking that it is hitting the other.
- *Inventaires*: the humiliated body, suffering but irrepressible, is that of the mother, soiled by the radioactive speech, finally washed and revenged by filial writing.
- *Vous qui habitez le temps*: the body is not only material, it is inhabited by language hence the difficulty in making it materialise and there is a tendency to forget it in favour of language: '*c'est pas le corps qui est le tombeau des mots: seule la parole est la prison du moi*' (p. 27).
- *Allegria*: the excessive body of the artist projects itself into this work, persists in the interpretation of the pupil, reviving the pangs of creation.
- *Via Negativa*: the body subjected to depression, as much as to antidepressants, is incapable of pleasure and thought. Body of the unthought rather than the unthinkable, it mourns all subversive thought.
- Is this an accident? We note in these five examples, from 1987 to 1996, a constant interiorisation and a miniaturisation of the media machine.

- Koltès and film noir call up the great textual (neo-classical) and filmic (Hollywood) rhetoric.
- Minyana tries to 'recuperate' (as we used to say in 1968), in a literary and critical way, the radio media: a mass media that is effective, but not evolved.
- Novarina gives the anti-humanist version, challenges the computer and its printouts, but allows himself to be fascinated by them.
- Jouanneau still believes in liberation through art: his hymn to creativity is an attempt to bring about a voice of instruments, bodies and instruments as bodies, in the image of the feminine form of a cello.
- Durif biologises the media and the political debate of alienation.
- In any case, the struggle rages between the audiovisual media: computers on the one side, literary and human media on the other.

Coming back to the example of *Zulu Time*, we notice the paradox of media confronted with the theatrical event and dramatic text. In theatrical performance, the media does not dissolve; it remains a foreign body. In the dramatic text, on the other hand, it dissolves, merges into the scenery, becomes hardly recognisable; it assimilates itself into the flesh and blood of the texts. Only writing, if it opens itself up to intertextuality and intermediality, has the power to absorb the media shocks, to make of them a textual material where the influences, the intermedia structures resolutely flaunt themselves, recast in a writing that is currently more about intermediality than intertextuality.

This recuperation of the media by writing does not however signify a 'rehumanisation', a 'reincarnation', i.e. a return to humanistic concepts of identity, centring, subject, expressiveness, contextualisation, property. We notice in the five texts the same reflex of cultural humanism, a protest movement against alienation, the theft of individual speech and mechanisation. These five authors are on the defensive: writing helps them cut themselves from the hold of the media, it unifies what was dispersed: places, moments, actions – it homogenises scattered impressions.

However, the contemporary dramatic texts, whether they like it or not, consciously or unconsciously, are strongly disrupted by, and sometimes even made up of, the media. They are a product of our times, particularly of our media era. Nevertheless, these texts do not chase after the media: they have their pride!

Despite their attempts (their desire?) to cut themselves off from the media world, the dramatic texts are touched in their composition and their very presence by the media. As a result, there are several types of reaction given by the texts in the face of the media, which also constitute methods for getting the better of the media and the machines.

1] *The nervous outbidding attitude* of writing faced with the media, a defiant response in the face of the quest for authenticity: Novarina also adopts the process of printing-out or of system transformation, which are current and computerised, but which, applied to poetic language show themselves to be radical and exhausting.

2] *The slightly ironic treatment*, a mockery that counters the efficacy of the electronic message: the dealer and the client in *Dans la solitude* use extraordinarily complicated rhetoric to say to each other that they have nothing to exchange, save the taste of speech.

3] *A problematising of the contradiction* between the media (or the technique) judged repetitive, and vocal and physical inspiration, as a guarantee of authenticity. *Allegria* celebrates the art of interpretation as a means of escaping routine.

4] *An attempt to accept challenges and struggle* with the real world, but with a mistrust of dialogue and binary logic: Koltès and Durif no longer believe in dialectic except in the negative form.

The irruption of the media into dramatic text, the texts' refusal of it and then their taking of it on board accelerates and accentuates the crisis of representation in the *mise en scène*. It is no longer so much visual, spectacular and optical as vocal, gestural and kinaesthetic. *Rhythmisation* of dramatic text profoundly alters its texture and meaning. The *mise en scène*, like a solid monument (a monument to the dead) is cracking and crumbling: it finally takes refuge in voice, rhythm, vocal gesture and in the evanescent and vital presence of the actor.

The result is an urgent need, a burning desire for a new alliance between text and body, and, as a consequence, another kind of *mise en scène* and theatrical practice. Writing too should not fear to expose itself to the fury of the world and the media.

Mediatisation should not be seen absolutely as the devil, but as one of the mediating elements between texts and humans, along with structure, form, rhetoric, play on words, skilful seduction (much more effective besides). The dramatic text is the point of departure for another theatricality, a subtler theatrisation, and a more mobile *mise en scène*. Textuality opens itself up to intermediality and makes of the *mise en scène* the origin and purpose of the virtual and aesthetic meaning of plays.

NOTES ON CONTRIBUTORS

JOEL ANDERSON studied French and Drama at Queen Mary College, University of London and trained at the Ecole Jacques Lecoq. He is currently based in Paris, where he is jointly responsible for a project in Burundi, organised by the Theatre de l'Opprime, which has resulted in the establishment of a Theatre of the Oppressed centre in Bujumbura. He works as an actor, translator, teacher and director.

LISA D'AMOUR is a playwright and performer currently living in Minneapolis, Minnesota. She is the recipient of a McKnight Fellowship, and a MacDowell Colony residency. She is a member of New Dramatists.

MARIA DELGADO is Reader in Drama and Theatre Arts at Queen Mary, University of London. She is editor of *Valle-Inclan Plays: One* (Methuen, 1993 and 1997); co-editor of *In Contact with the Gods? Directors Talk Theatre* (Manchester University Press, 1996), and *Conducting a Life: Reflections on the Theatre of Maria Irene Fornes* (Smith and Kraus, 1999). A fellow of the Royal Society of Arts, she is currently working on a study of twentieth-century Spanish theatre for Manchester University Press.

JOSE ESTEBAN MUÑOZ is Associate Professor of Performance Studies at Tisch School of the Arts, New York University. He is the author of *Disidentifications: Queers of Color and The Performance of Politics* (University of Minnesota Press, 1999).

PATRICE PAVIS is the author of numerous articles and books on theatre including *Theatre at the Crossroads of Culture*, and *The Intercultural Performance Reader*, both published by Routledge.

CARIDAD SVICH is a playwright, songwriter and translator. She is the recipient of a Bunting fellowship from Harvard University's Radcliffe Institute for Advanced Study. She held a TCG/Pew residency at Intar Theatre in New York, and an NEA/TCG residency at the Mark Taper Forum Theatre in Los Angeles. She has been a guest artist at the Traverse Theatre (Edinburgh), the Royal Court Theatre, Actors Touring Company, Paines Plough, and has taught playwriting at Yale School of Drama, Denison University, and the US-Cuba Writers' Conference in Havana. She is co-editor of *Out of the Fringe: Contemporary Latina/o Theatre & Performance* (TCG, 2000), and her translations are collected in *Federico Garcia Lorca: Impossible Theatre* (Smith & Kraus, 2000). She holds an MFA from the University of California-San Diego, is founder of the performance collective NoPassport, and is a member of New Dramatists.

LISA WOLFORD teaches performance studies and cultural studies at Bowling Green University in Ohio. She has collaborated with Guillermo Gomez-Peña and the artists of the Pocha Nostra recurrently since 1997, serving as dramaturg for *BORDERscape 2000*, and various installation projects.

ISABEL WRIGHT is a playwright based in Scotland. Her plays have been produced by the Frantic Assembly, Tron Theatre, Traverse Theatre and BBC Radio 4. She trained at the Royal Scottish Academy of Music and Drama.

Voice & Vision's workshop of *The Booth Variations* directed by Nick Philippou

SELECT BIBLIOGRAPHY

Artaud, Antonin, *The Theatre and its Double*, trans. Mary Caroline Richards, New York: Grove Press, 1958.

Auslander, Philip, *Presence and Resistance: Postmodernism and Cultural Politics in Contemporary Performance*, Ann Arbor: University of Michigan Press, 1992.

Auslander, Philip, *Liveness: Performance in a Mediatized Culture*, London and New York: Routledge, 1999.

Barker, Howard, *Arguments for a Theatre*, Manchester: Manchester University Press, 1993.

Birringer, Johannes, *Media and Performance*, Baltimore and London: PAJ Books/John Hopkins University Press, 1998.

Bogart, Anne, *A Director Prepares: Seven Essays on Art and Theatre*, London and New York: Routledge, 2001.

Carlson, Marvin (ed.), *Performance: A Critical Introduction*, London and New York: Routledge, 1996.

Chaudhuri, Una, *Staging Place: The Geography of Modern Drama*, Ann Arbor: University of Michigan Press, 1995.

Delgado, Maria M. and Paul Heritage (eds), *In Contact with the Gods? Directors Talk Theatre*, Manchester: Manchester University Press, 1996.

Diamond, Elin (ed.), *Performance and Cultural Politics*, London and New York: Routledge, 1996.

Dolan, Jill, *Presence and Desire: Essays on Gender, Sexuality and Performance*, Ann Arbor: University of Michigan Press, 1993.

Eagleton, Terry, *The Illusions of Postmodernism*, Oxford and Cambridge: Blackwell Publishers, 1996.

Eagleton, Terry, *Sweet Violence: A Study of the Tragic*, Oxford and Cambridge: Blackwell Publishers, 2002.

Etchells, Tim, *Certain Fragments: Texts and Writings on Performance*, London and New York: Routledge, 1999.

Featherstone, Mike, *Consumer Culture and Postmodernism*, London and Newbury Park: Sage Publications, 1991.

Featherstone, Mike, *Undoing Culture: globalization, postmodernism and identity*, London and Newbury Park: Sage Publications, 1995.

Frow, John, *Time and Commodity Culture*, Oxford and New York: Oxford University Press, 1997.

Fusco, Coco, *The Bodies That Were Not Ours*, London and New York: Routledge, 2001.

Gomez-Peña, Guillermo, *Dangerous Border Crossings: The Artist Talks Back*, London and New York: Routledge, 2000.

Gottlieb, Vera and Colin Chambers (eds), *Theatre in a Cool Climate*, Charlbury: Amber Lane Press, 1999.

Goulish, Matthew, *39 Microlectures: In Proximity of Performance*, London and New York: Routledge, 2000.

Holmberg, Arthur, *The Theatre of Robert Wilson*, Cambridge and New York: Cambridge University Press, 1996.

Hunter, Lynette, *Critiques of Knowing: Situated Textualities in Science, Computing and the Arts*, London and New York: Routledge, 1999.

Iyer, Pico, *The Global Soul: Jet Lag, Shopping Malls, and the Search for Home*, New York: Vintage, 2001.

Jameson, Fredric, *Postmodernism of The Cultural Logic of Late Capitalism*, Durham: Duke University Press, 1991.

Kane, Sarah, *Complete Plays*, London: Methuen, 2001.

Kershaw, Baz, *The Radical in Performance: Between Brecht and Baudrillard*, London and New York: Routledge, 1999.

Kustow, Michael, *Theatre @ Risk*, London: Methuen, 2000.

Marranca, Bonnie and Gautam Dasgupta (eds), *Conversations on Art and Performance*, Baltimore and London: PAJ Books/John Hopkins University Press, 1999.

McGrath, John, *The Bone Won't Break: On Theatre and Hope in Hard Times*, London: Methuen, 1990.

Pavis, Patrice, *Theatre at the Crossroads of Culture*, trans. Loren Kruger. London and New York: Routledge, 1992.

Phelan, Peggy and Jill Lane (eds), *The Ends of Performance*, London and New York: New York University Press, 1998.

Ravenhill, Mark, *Plays: One*, London: Methuen, 2001.

Rogoff, Gordon, *Vanishing Acts*, New Haven: Yale University Press, 2000.

Rush, Michael, *New Media in Late 20th-Century Art*, New York: Thames & Hudson, 1999.

Samuel, Raphael, *Theatres of Memory*, London and New York: Verso, 1994.

Sierz, Aleks, *In yer Face*, London: Faber & Faber, 2001.

Svich, Caridad and Maria Teresa Marrero (eds), *Out of the Fringe: Contemporary Latina/o Theatre and Performance*, New York: Theatre Communications Group, 2000.

Taylor, Diana and Juan Villegas (eds), *Negotiating Performance*, Durham: Duke University Press, 1994.

Watson, Ian, *Towards a Third Theatre: Eugenio Barba and the Odin Teatret*, London and New York: Routledge, 1995.

INDEX